# Testing Handicapped People

**Warren W. Willingham**
**Marjorie Ragosta**
**Randy Elliot Bennett**
**Henry Braun**
**Donald A. Rock**
**Donald E. Powers**

Sponsored by
The College Board
Educational Testing Service
Graduate Record Examinations Board

**Allyn and Bacon, Inc.**
Boston    London    Sydney    Toronto

*Series Editor:* Mylan Jaixen
*Production Administrator:* Annette Joseph
*Production Coordinator:* Susan Freese
*Editorial-Production Service:* Editorial Services of New England
*Copyeditor:* Laura Bueno
*Manufacturing Buyer:* Bill Alberti
*Cover Administrator:* Linda K. Dickinson
*Cover Designer:* Susan C. Hamant

**Library of Congress Cataloging-in-Publication Data**

Testing handicapped people / Warren W. Willingham . . .[et al.].
   p.  cm.
   Sponsored by College Board, Educational Testing Service, Graduate Record Examinations Board.
   Bibliography: p. 207
   Includes index.
   ISBN 0-205-11388-5
   1. Universities and colleges—United States—Entrance examinations.   2. Handicapped—Education (Higher)—United States—Ability testing.   3. Scholastic aptitude test.   4. Graduate record examination.   5. Examinations—United States—Validity.
I. Willingham, Warren W.
LB2353.42.T47   1988                                87-29009
378'.1664—dc19                                      CIP

Printed in the United States of America

10  9  8  7  6  5  4  3  2  1      92  91  90  89  88

# Contents

# Preface

The research findings reported in this volume concern that group of disabled people who take special administrations of college and graduate school admissions tests. In concentrating our attention on this work over the past several years, we are impressed again with the complex nature of test validity and fairness in a national testing program. All admissions tests must meet a variety of standards of technical quality and sound use, but those standards must apply as well to many subgroups—small populations whose diverse characteristics and background may raise a seemingly endless variety of questions concerning a test's fairness and validity.

It is often not easy to resolve such questions, partly because these are not just technical issues. Standards of good practice engage other values, such as what constitutes a reasonable balance between attention to the characteristics and concerns of a particular subgroup and attention to the total group of examinees. By emphasizing different values, one can easily reach disparate conclusions on questions such as the use of separate test norms for handicapped individuals or the practice of identifying for users those scores that are based on nonstandard administrations. There are significant differences of opinion regarding such questions, even within particular groups of disabled individuals.

Our task is to address the technical aspects of test validity and test use for handicapped people. We have tried to draw conclusions that we feel are justified by the data, giving proper weight to scientific caution but also recognizing the practical need for whatever insights research might reasonably offer. People connected with the testing programs must make day-to-day decisions that can affect handicapped examinees; they include test developers who make up the exams, users who interpret the scores, and especially committees of the College Board and the Graduate Record Examinations Board, who have the final responsibility to address and resolve issues of test program policy.

We hope this work will prove useful, but it is important to bear its limitations in mind. We have focused on the validity and use of admissions tests because that is the area of primary responsibility for the three organizations sponsoring this inquiry. Fair treatment in admissions is important, but needless to say, it is only one aspect of the much larger problem of providing equal opportunity and effective education for disabled people. In addition, we recognize that making a valid, fair assessment of an applicant's preparation and capacity for college or graduate work is not the same as determining a sound admissions policy. Institutions must balance academic interests and institutional goals with the important social benefits that can accrue from an affirmative policy regarding the admission of disabled students. Also, those who carry out admissions policies must be objective and evenhanded, but flexible enough to recognize unusual character and merit in individual applicants.

## Acknowledgments

☐ In addressing the more limited questions of test validity and use for handicapped people, we are indebted to many individuals for their help. The Panel on Testing of Handicapped People, working under the auspices of the National Academy of Sciences, produced an especially useful analysis of issues in admissions testing. Their work made ours much easier, and we are grateful for their ideas and their leadership.

A number of our colleagues here at the Educational Testing Service (ETS) made important contributions to this report, in early dialogues, in their contributions to particular studies, or through technical reviews of various aspects of the work. We want to thank especially William Angoff, John Centra, Faye Frieson, Tom Jirele, Linda Johnson, Bruce Kaplan, Craig Mills, Catherine Nelson, Lawrence Stricker, Spencer Swinton, Susan Vitella, and John Winterbottom. We also appreciate the help of Linda Cook, Neil Dorans, Garlie Forehand, Gordon Hale, Harriet Johnson, Neal Kingston, Barbara Kirsh, Gary Marco, Robert Mislevy, Len Ramist, Puff Rice, Alfred Rogers, Paul Rosenbaum, Pat Taylor, Linda Wightman, Kenneth Wilson, and Michael Zieky.

In addition, the original technical reports on which this volume is based were reviewed extensively by knowledgeable individuals outside ETS. We are indebted to the following people for valuable help and sound counsel: Thomas Allen, Joan Chase, Jeannette Fleischner, Chris Kiler, Cindy Kolb, Robert Linn, June Morris, June Mullins, Kim Reid, William Scales, Lorrie Shepard, Michael Stinson, David Taggert, Susan Tillett, Joseph Torgesen, Raymond Trybus, Bernice Wong, and Naomi Zigmond.

When the draft of the final report was completed, another group of prominent experts was invited to ETS to discuss the document and its findings. The response was quite gratifying: virtually all of those invited were able to attend, and the discussion was very helpful in enabling us to amplify important points and to include additional suggestions for improving current practices and for further study. Attendees included disabled individuals, researchers, and educators: Paul Appleby, Emil del Busto, Hollie Hanes, Ira Hirsh, Roy Koenigsknecht, Cindy Kolb, Joan Laing, Frank Maglione, Daryl Mellard, Jack Merwin, June Morris, Mary Ann Nestor, Gary Olson, Susan Robinson, David Snyder, Michael Stinson, Gertrude Webb, and Maureen Welsh. We are especially grateful to these individuals for sharing their knowledge of this complex problem and for their willingness to make a special trip for that purpose.

In the course of this work, other staff at ETS made important contributions: Ka-Ling Chan, Linda DeLauro, Hazel Klein, Margaret Morris, Ingeborg Novatkoski, Shirley Perry, Nancy Robertson, Elsa Rosenthal, Colleen Scratchard, Peter Smith, and Nancy Wright. Debra Smolinski is due special recognition for her help in coordinating and producing the final report.

We want to express our personal thanks and appreciation to each of these colleagues. We thank also the three sponsoring organizations: the College Board, the Educational Testing Service, and the Graduate Record Examinations Board. Their support and interest made the project possible, though the opinions expressed here are those of the authors and do not necessarily reflect the views of the sponsoring organizations.

*W. W. W.*
*M. R.*
*R. E. B.*
*H. B.*
*D. A. R.*
*D. E. P.*

# Executive Summary

In 1977 the Department of Education issued regulations implementing Section 504 of the Rehabilitation Act of 1973. The regulations mandated that admissions tests for handicapped people must be validated and must reflect the applicant's aptitude and achievement rather than any disabilities extraneous to what is being measured. Another key provision was a prohibition against prior inquiry into an applicant's handicapped status. These mandates created a dilemma because they were widely perceived to be beyond the current technical capability of measurement specialists and inconsistent with professional standards that called for "flagging" (identifying) scores that may not be comparable to those on standard tests because they were earned under nonstandard conditions.

Because of these problems, the Office of Civil Rights held the implementation provisions of the 504 regulations in abeyance and requested the National Academy of Sciences to appoint a Panel on Testing of Handicapped People to study the issues. Its report, submitted in 1982, called for a four-year research effort by testing agencies to determine the validity and comparability of admissions tests administered to handicapped examinees.

This volume reports the findings of a project initiated by the College Board, the Educational Testing Service, and the Graduate Record Examinations Board in response to the panel's report. The project, carried out from 1982 to 1986 by a team of ETS researchers, involved an integrated series of studies on two major admissions tests: the Scholastic Aptitude Test (SAT) and the Graduate Record Examinations (GRE) General Test. Chapter 1 includes a discussion of the legal background, research issues, and recent trends in the participation of handicapped people in higher education and in these testing programs.

The individual studies are reported in Chapters 2 through 10. Chapters 2, 3, and 4 summarize previous research and data concerning the four principal groups involved: hearing-impaired, learning-disabled, physically handicapped, and visually impaired students. They discuss problems of definition and diagnosis, summarize data on the test performance of handicapped people, and provide a profile of the characteristics of students who take nonstandard tests. Chapters 5 and 6 report two studies of admissions: a survey of the experience and attitudes of handicapped students and an analysis of factors influencing actual admissions decisions for handicapped and nonhandicapped applicants. Chapters 7, 8, 9, and 10 present the results of a series of studies concerning the comparability of nonstandard and standard test scores with respect to reliability, speed, performance on particular types of items, abilities measured by the test, and the accuracy with which SAT and GRE scores forecast academic performance.

Chapter 11 integrates the findings of the various studies carried out during the four-year period, centering on the comparability of admissions tests administered to handicapped people to those administered to other students. Since disabilities often impair sensory-motor or encoding processes that are required to recognize and work with test material, admissions tests can not be comparable in the sense of posing identical tasks for handicapped and nonhandicapped examinees, nor can the average score levels of the two groups be assumed to be identical, because there is no way to know whether they are representative or have had comparable learning experiences. The goal in testing handicapped people is to remove extraneous sources of difficulty so that higher-order cognitive abilities (for example, verbal comprehension, quantitative reasoning) are assessed accurately. Eight indicators of comparability were evaluated:

1. *Reliability.* Nonstandard tests were comparable to standard tests with respect to reliability; that is, the precision of measurement was equally good for handicapped and nonhandicapped examinees.

2. *Factor structure.* With minor exceptions, the factor structure of the SAT and GRE was quite similar for handicapped and nonhandicapped examinees. This result supports the assumption that the cognitive abilities assessed by nonstandard tests are comparable to those tested by standard measures.

3. *Differential item functioning.* There was little evidence of differential item difficulty, indicating that the SAT and GRE are largely free of aberrant types of items that are unusually difficult for handicapped students compared with other test items measuring the same ability.

4. *Prediction of academic performance.* When academic performance was predicted on the basis of both test scores and prior grades, there was little consistent over- or underprediction for the major categories of handicapped students. This result supports the assumption that, overall, the nonstandard tests are comparable to the standard ones as to level of cognitive ability. However, the academic performance of students with disabilities tended to be somewhat less

accurately predictable, on the basis of either test scores or prior grades, than that of others. Handicapped students who had low test scores and prior grades tended to do somewhat better in college or graduate school than predicted, while those with high test scores and grades tended not to do as well as predicted.

5. *Admissions decisions.* In general, admissions decisions were related to test scores and prior grades in much the same manner for handicapped and nonhandicapped applicants. There were some small but statistically significant discrepancies, both positive and negative, between the actual and expected rates of admissions for handicapped students. There was no evidence, however, to connect those discrepancies with test-score flags per se.

6. *Test content.* Overall, the internal statistical analyses indicated that test content is generally comparable for both groups of examinees in the sense that the tests provide a fair assessment of the cognitive abilities they are intended to measure. Students' impressions concerning especially difficult test material were only sometimes confirmed by actual performance.

7. *Testing accommodations.* The great majority of examinees expressed satisfaction with testing accommodations.

8. *Test timing.* Three types of evidence indicated that nonstandard versions of the SAT and GRE are not comparable to the standard test with respect to timing: handicapped examinees were more likely than others to finish the tests; some items near the end of the tests were relatively easier for some groups of handicapped students; and in some instances, college performance was overpredicted by those test scores based on considerably extended testing time.

With the exception of test timing, these results indicate that the nonstandard versions of the SAT and GRE administered to handicapped examinees are generally comparable to the standard tests in most important respects. Some findings emerged of special interest in the analysis of particular groups of handicapped students:

## Hearing-impaired examinees

☐ Test scores underpredicted the college performance of students with hearing impairments, but only those in special programs for deaf students; predictions based on test scores plus high school average did not misrepresent performance in mainstream college programs. Admissions tests in standard English may not be useful for deaf students who are taught with a manual language throughout the school and college years.

## Learning-disabled examinees

☐ Equitable testing for learning-disabled students poses difficult problems. This group is very large and quite heterogeneous. There is much controversy as to which and how many students are appropriately identified as learning-disabled (LD) and how often the disability is specific as opposed to reflecting a more general cognitive or academic deficit. This is the group for which the findings most clearly suggested that college performance tends to be overpredicted for students who had considerably extended testing time. For these reasons it is not clear that all LD students should have extended testing time, especially unlimited time. This conclusion is conditioned by the recognition that there may be other reasons why some LD students do not perform up to expectations in the first year of college, and that these results should be checked against four-year performance data.

## Physically handicapped examinees

☐ Since most physical disabilities do not involve any sensory or cognitive component, testing accommodations for this group normally concern physical arrangements and timing. These data indicate that admissions tests are generally quite comparable for examinees with and without physical disabilities. There was some evidence of excessive time being allowed, a problem that may prove difficult to adjust because of the wide variety of physical disabilities.

## Visually impaired examinees

☐ Overall, admissions tests seem to be generally comparable for examinees with and without visual impairments. This group reported difficulty with reading, but it did not perform relatively less well on reading tasks than on other parts of the test. These examinees also reported problems with visually related material such as graphs and figures, and results on the mathematics tests in braille format supported their impression. Further research is needed to determine why some such items were differentially difficult while others were not.

What are the implications of these findings for the flagging problem? Should testing programs continue to identify nonstandard scores, modify that practice, or abandon it altogether? The principal reason for flagging nonstandard test scores is to warn users that they may not be comparable to standard scores. It is true that academic performance is somewhat less predictable from the test scores of students with disabilities than from the scores of those without, but variation in predictability has never been advanced as grounds for flagging individual test scores. Furthermore, the same pattern of lower predictability was observed when a student's previous grade average was used as a predictor. Thus, lower predictability does not necessarily represent a miscalibration of the test scores, nor does rescaling of scores appear to be a technically feasible solution. This lower predictability does suggest strongly, however, that test scores and previous grade average should be used jointly, never individually, in reaching admissions decisions, and that other relevant information should be examined carefully and given additional weight as appropriate.

The primary source of noncomparability of test scores is the amount of time available in test administrations. In principle, the problem can be corrected by setting time limits in nonstandard administrations so that examinees with and without disabilities are equally likely to finish the task. A principal conclusion of this report is that such empirically based timing should be attempted. However, this attempt may prove difficult from a practical standpoint because of problems in differentiating among types and severity of handicap.

Assuming success in establishing time limits that take appropriate account of disabling conditions, admissions tests would then be largely comparable from a technical perspective. In that event, it is recommended that testing programs reevaluate flagging policies, taking into account what is fair both to handicapped and nonhandicapped students, the interests of higher institutions, and other considerations that may be important.

These studies resulted in a number of additional suggestions for improving the comparability of admissions tests administered to handicapped examinees. In particular, tests should routinely be checked for differentially difficult items whenever sample sizes permit. A special effort is warranted to reproduce, in a format appropriate for handicapped examinees, the various ancillary materials and information available to nonhandicapped examinees. Similarly, admissions officers and other test users should have available a handbook or other materials to aid their understanding of types of disability, nonstandard testing conditions, and principles of good practice in interpreting scores of handicapped applicants. Finally, testing programs should encourage and assist colleges and graduate schools in carrying out studies of the performance of handicapped students over the course of their academic program. Such studies could be helpful in insuring that these students' potential for academic work is fully appreciated.

# 1

# Introduction

## ☐ *Warren W. Willingham*

Like everyone else, disabled people take admissions tests when applying to college, graduate school, or professional school. But, their ability to do well on that important test can be seriously hampered by a handicap that may be quite irrelevant to the skills and knowledge that the test is intended to measure. For some years most national testing programs have offered special testing arrangements and extended testing times to disabled examinees in order to minimize such effects. These special arrangements raise a variety of questions.

Is the content of the tests appropriate for people with particular types of disabilities? Are the special accommodations adequate or perhaps too lenient? Does unlimited time inflate test scores? Are the tests valid for these groups of students? How do disabled students perform academically in college or graduate school? Are predictions based on test scores reasonably accurate, or do they tend to be consistently too high or too low? Do colleges use the tests appropriately in making admissions decisions? Is it fair to require handicapped students to take the tests and then flag the scores as having uncertain meaning? It is important to get better answers to these questions, particularly on behalf of those who are most directly affected.

Interest in these issues has been greatly heightened since the Rehabilitation Act was passed in 1973 and federal regulations designed to protect the rights of handicapped people were promulgated under Section 504 of the act. Considerable confusion ensued as to the implications of the regulations for admissions testing, and in 1982 a panel appointed by the National Academy of Sciences (NAS) issued a report calling for research to clarify whether tests modified for examinees with disabilities are comparable to the standard tests and whether they give valid estimates of the academic abilities of these people.

The purpose of this report is to summarize the findings of a series of studies on the Scholastic Aptitude Test (SAT) and the Graduate Record Examinations (GRE) General Test that were undertaken jointly in response to that panel report by the College Board, the Educational Testing Service, and the Graduate Record Examinations Board. Appendix C lists the 10 technical reports that resulted from those studies and other directly related research reports produced by ETS staff since the NAS panel report in 1982. This research does not provide definitive answers, but it does represent progress on a difficult set of issues and a basis for determining next steps.

The issues addressed here are complex; they engage difficult technical questions, competing social values, and complicated policy issues for the testing programs and for education generally. The research centers on factual questions in order to illuminate policy issues, and it focuses on tests because their sponsors have a special responsibility to examine their validity and fairness in selective admissions. This focus does not reflect any assumption that admissions tests should be a dominant factor in admitting handicapped students to selective undergraduate or graduate institutions. Indeed, it is especially important to examine carefully the full record of such a student, to assess all strengths and talents, to evaluate the student's background and response to disability, and to consider the intended program and the institutional support available. Finally, in carrying out sound admissions policies concerning disabled applicants, it is essential to weigh the importance of educational opportunity and the social contribution that opportunity may allow a particular individual to make.

Handicapped individuals—like all other people—are unique, and to be fair, one must respect that uniqueness. At the same time institutions must have policy guidelines as a basis for fair practice and reasoned exception. It is in that spirit and with those important qualifications that we undertake the statistical analyses that will, we hope, help to inform the discussion and development of fair policy. The remainder of this chapter is devoted to several important aspects of the background to this topic and to an analysis of the research issues addressed here.

## Background

□  □  Federal regulations define a handicapped individual as any person who "(1) has a physical or mental impairment which substantially limits one or more major life activities, (2) has a record of such an impairment, or (3) is regarded as having such an impairment" (Dept. of Health, Education, and Welfare, 1977a, p. 22678, Sect. 843). Throughout this report the term *handicap* is used frequently, primarily because that term has been prominent in federal regulations as well as in programmatic and research literature. It should be noted, however, that some prefer the terms *impaired* or *disabled.* The three terms are analogous but not necessarily synonymous. For example, as Susser (1973) distinguishes them, *impairment* implies a physical defect and *disability* suggests a physical dysfunction, whereas *handicap* may imply a social dysfunction (often a judgment others make of disabled people). For ease of communication, we have used these terms somewhat interchangeably and do not mean to imply any such distinctions. In order to be consistent with the language of the legislation, the NAS panel report, and the testing programs, we have used *handicapped* in the title of the volume and elsewhere when convention makes it seem appropriate.

There is a wide variety of sensory, motor, and cognitive disabilities. In the literature pertinent to this report, they are typically categorized into four types:

1. *hearing impairment,* which includes deafness or difficulty in hearing;
2. *learning disability,* defined as a specific perceptual, neurological, or cognitive deficit but, as we shall see, identified mainly on the basis of school achievement;
3. *physical handicap,* which includes a variety of neurological and orthopedic disabilities; and
4. *visual impairment,* which may range from a serious visual deficit to blindness.

These four types of disability are quite different with respect to cognitive functioning and implications for testing—so different, in fact, that it would be a serious error to think of handicapped people as one group of examinees. It is also important to remember that even within a category there can be wide variation in the nature of the impairment, the degree of disability, and its possible impact on test taking.

For many years ETS has provided formal procedures on behalf of the College Board and the Graduate Record Examinations Board that allow handicapped examinees to take tests in a manner that attempts to accommodate their particular impairments. The objective is to provide a test that eliminates, insofar as possible, sources of difficulty that are irrelevant to the skills and knowledge being measured. For example, special administrations of the SAT are offered in four test formats or combinations thereof: regular, large type, braille, and audio cassette. Special administrations are individually arranged and supervised on flexible dates and in convenient locations. Accommodations may include extra space, extra rest periods, separate testing locations, a reader, an amanuensis or recorder, a sign language interpreter for test instructions, or other arrangements that may be needed to satisfy the requirements of the handicapped test taker. Such accommodations normally involve extended time—up to 12 hours total in the case of the SAT. Testing accommodations for the GRE are generally similar, though testing time is limited to six hours and tests are normally administered on national test dates at the regular test centers.

In 1985 the College Board added an option permitting learning-disabled students to take the regular version of the SAT in national administrations, but with 90 minutes' extra time. This option allows LD students to take advantage of the Board's question-and-answer service (i.e., after taking the test, they may obtain a copy of the questions, the correct answers, and their own answers). Nonstandard testing arrangements are described in student bulletins (College Entrance Examination Board, 1985; Graduate Record Examinations Board, 1986, see Appendix A).

## Section 504

☐ Titles I through IV of the Rehabilitation Act of 1973 (Public Law 93–112) follow in the federal tradition of rehabilitation and social welfare services for handicapped people. With the passage of Section 504 under Title V, however, Congress took a major step in extending civil rights protection to people with disabling conditions. The act marked the first time that federal law formally established that such people are entitled to the protection against discrimination enjoyed by other citizens. The language parallels that of the Civil Rights Act of 1964. Section 504 states in its entirety:

> No otherwise qualified handicapped individual in the United States as defined in Section 7(6), shall, solely by reason of his handicap, be excluded from the participation in, be denied the benefits of, or be subjected to discrimination under any program or activity receiving federal financial assistance.

The regulations implementing Section 504 contain three key mandates affecting college admissions tests (Dept. of Health, Education, and Welfare, 1977a). An institution receiving federal funds (b)(2) May not make use of any test or criterion for admission that has a disproportionate, adverse effect on handicapped persons or any class of handicapped persons unless the test or criterion, as used by the recipient, has been validated as a predictor of success in the education program or activity in question. . . .

(b)(3) Shall assure itself that admissions tests are selected and administered so as best to insure that, when a test is administered to an applicant who has a handicap that impairs sensory, manual, or speaking skills, the test results accurately reflect the applicant's aptitude or achievement level or whatever other factor the test purports to measure, rather than reflecting the applicant's impaired sensory, manual, or speaking skills (except where those skills are the factors that the test purports to measure) . . . .

(b)(4) May not make preadmission inquiry as to whether an applicant for admission is a handicapped person. (p. 22683, Sect. 84.42)

Testimony concerning the draft regulations soon revealed a critical inconsistency. Test publishers offer nonstandard tests in the spirit of (b)(3) above, but because they are unable to guarantee comparability of the modified test or conditions of administration, they commonly flag the scores in order to caution users and to protect the integrity of standardized test procedures generally. This step is seen as a probable violation of (b)(4) above because flagging the score reveals that the student has a handicap. Thus it was not clear how the mandate could be carried out. Faced with this dilemma, the Office of Civil Rights took two steps. One was to endorse, on a temporary basis, interim guidelines permitting flagging and the use of scores for which the stipulations of the regulations have not been fully met (Redden, Levering, & DiQuinzio, 1978).

The second step was to impanel a committee under the auspices of the National Academy of Sciences to reconcile the testing requirements of the 504 regulations with available testing technology and practice. In its report (Sherman & Robinson, 1982) the NAS panel concluded that "current psychometric theory and practice do not allow full compliance with the regulations as currently drafted" (p. 1). It was skeptical of the regulations' implication that abilities could be measured independent of handicapping condition. The panel recommended a four-year period of research directed particularly to validating tests that are modified for examinees with disabilities and to making those tests as comparable as possible to standardized tests. The research recommendations placed special emphasis on the use of advanced statistical methods to compare predicted and actual performance of handicapped students. One suggestion was the rescaling of test scores through the grade point average criterion so that predictions would be comparable and there would be no need to flag the test scores of handicapped examinees.

Since the announcement of the 504 regulations, there have been several legal decisions that bear upon the interpretation and scope of the mandate. Driscoll's (1985) review of legal challenges of minimum competency testing of handicapped students includes two points related to admissions testing. In a New York State decision (*Board of Education of Northport* v. *Ambach,* 1981), the court held that students who fail a competency test because of a mental impairment cannot be judged otherwise qualified for the diploma. In *Brookhart* v. *Illinois State Board of Education* (1982), an Illinois court concurred, noting that inability to learn cannot be overlooked in determining qualifications for a diploma.

In a related case, the Supreme Court (*Southeastern Community College* v. *Davis,* 1979) considered whether under Section 504 an educational institution can take a person's handicap into consideration when evaluating an applicant for admission and whether it must modify its program to accommodate the disability. The case involved a woman applying to a nursing program. The court ruled that Section 504 imposes no requirement on an institution to lower its standards or make substantial modifications in its program in order to accommodate a handicapped person.

In *Grove City College* v. *Bell* (1984), which has been called one of the most important civil rights cases of the decade (Di Donato, 1986), the Supreme Court ruled that only a specific program or activity receiving federal funds is covered by the stipulations of Title IX of the Educational Amendments of 1972. The language of Title IX, which concerns sex discrimination, is essentially the same as that of Section 504. Considering the realities of federal funding and the practical difficulty of determining whether such monies actually have a direct effect on such other areas as admissions, some observers fear that the effect will be to severely limit the scope of Section 504 and other civil rights legislation. For the past two years there has been a congressional effort, as yet unsuccessful, to enact legislation that would insure the broad applicability of Section 504 (e.g., the Civil Rights Restoration Act of 1985; H.R. 700/S.431).

## Recent trends

☐ A national survey (Harris, 1986) recently reported that "an overwhelming majority of disabled Americans believe that life has improved for disabled people in the past decade." Nonetheless, more than half of the respondents thought that their disabilities had prevented them from reaching their full potential. Two-thirds were unemployed, and there was a strong association between education and employment. The President's Committee on the Employment of the Handicapped (undated) reported that disabled people were seriously underrepresented in higher education—they constituted 2.6 percent of college freshmen in 1978 but made up 8.1 percent of the adult population. Has access to higher education improved for this group in recent years?

National statistics on the higher education of handicapped students are quite limited. A government report of statistics on disability (Department of Education, 1982) cites only the study mentioned above and another federal survey taken in the same year that gave a much lower estimate (.5 percent) for disabled college freshmen. The best source of data on the characteristics of enrolled freshmen is the Cooperative Institutional Research Program (CIRP) (Astin, Green, Korn, & Schalit, 1985 and earlier years). That survey indicates an increase in the percentage of college freshmen who report being disabled, from 2.6 percent in 1978 to 7.7 percent in 1985. It is not at all clear how much of that increase is real, because 88 percent of it occurred in two years when the wording of the survey question was changed. For example, an early version asked whether students *considered* themselves handicapped. That choice of wording may tend to elicit a negative reply, since half of the respondents with disabilities in the Harris poll said they did not consider themselves handicapped. There was almost no increase in the proportion of disabled freshmen over the five annual periods when the CIRP survey question remained unchanged (see Willingham, 1986, for details).

The Graduate Record Examinations Board has posed the same question each year to its test candidates: "What permanently disabling condition do you have, if any?" As Figure 1.1 indicates, there has been no substantial change overall in the number of graduate applicants identifying themselves as having such a condition. Data from the American College Testing Program show the stability from 1978–79 through 1982–83 (Laing & Farmer, 1984).

The Student Descriptive Questionnaire (SDQ) that is filled out by students taking the SAT did not contain a question on disability until fall 1985, so comparable trend data for those examinees are not available. But there are of course data on the number of SAT candidates who took a nonstandard test, and they are quite striking. As Figure 1.2 shows, there was a fourfold increase in the number of nonstandard SATs administered to learning-disabled students and only modest increases in the other three categories.

Table 1.1 shows the proportion of SAT and GRE examinees who identified themselves as disabled or who took a nonstandard test. Several interesting observations can be made here. The two columns on the left show that similar proportions of all candidates reported

**Figure 1.1   Number of GRE examinees in standard national administration who identified themselves as handicapped—by year and type of handicap**

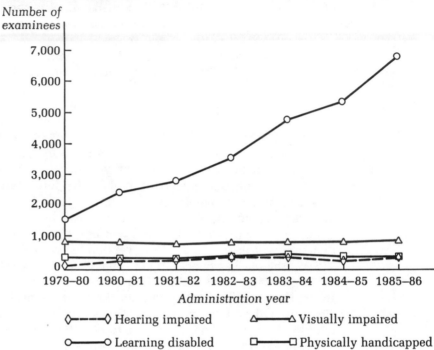

having each of the four types of disability, but for some unaccountable reason undergraduate applicants were much more likely to mark "Other."

Comparison of column A with column B shows that the great majority of examinees identifying themselves as having a disability— 9 out of 10 in three of the groups—took the standard test in a national administration. The learning-disabled group is the big exception. SAT data in column A are based upon part of a year and are not entirely reliable, but the major difference between the LD students and the other groups seems clear enough. More LD students took a nonstandard test than identified themselves as learning disabled in the standard SAT administration. This difference may be due partly to a reluctance on the part of these students to identify themselves and partly to their being more prone to take the nonstandard test. Identification of LD students is an important issue to which we will return.

**Figure 1.2   Number of examinees taking special administrations of the SAT—by year and type of handicap**

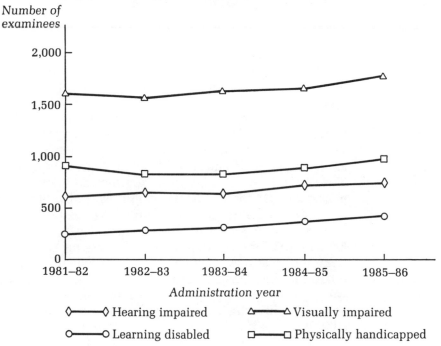

◇———◇ Hearing impaired      △———△ Visually impaired

○———○ Learning disabled      □———□ Physically handicapped

**Table 1.1   Number of examinees per thousand who (a) identify themselves as disabled and (b) take a nonstandard SAT or GRE**

|  | (a) Self-identified as disabled | | (b) Took nonstandard test | |
|---|---|---|---|---|
|  | *SAT* | *GRE* | *SAT* | *GRE* |
| Hearing impaired | 2.8 | 2.5 | .2 | .0 |
| Learning disabled | 2.5 | 1.3 | 3.3 | .4 |
| Physically handicapped | 2.9 | 3.3 | .2 | .4 |
| Visually impaired | 5.3 | 6.2 | .6 | .9 |
| Other | 8.7 | 3.7 | — | — |
| Total | 22.1 | 17.0 | 4.3 | 1.8 |

Note: All entries are based on the five-year period 1981–86 except column 1, which is based on 275,000 examinees in fall 1985, when the pertinent question was first added to the SDQ.

## Research issues

### Defining the validity problem

The Section 504 regulations *require* recipient institutions to demonstrate a selection measure's predictive validity if there is evidence of
adverse differential effects for handicapped applicants. The regulations also indicate that institutions should select tests so as best to
insure that modified tests accurately reflect the applicants' aptitudes
rather than their disabilities. This requirement, being far more problematic, is wisely couched in less strict language. The NAS panel
urged research to meet this broader requirement but characterized it
as a long-term scientific goal rather than a basis for enforcement.
Nonetheless, the panel emphasized the importance of validating admissions tests for handicapped groups and establishing their comparability so that flagging would not be necessary.

*Standards for Educational and Psychological Testing* (American
Educational Research Association, American Psychological Association, and National Council on Measurement in Education, 1985)
follows in that spirit. Standard 14.6 stipulates that, when feasible, the
validity and reliability of tests administered to handicapped people
should be investigated, as should the effects of test modifications.
Although this is a "conditional" (discretionary) standard, the drafting
committee wrote that the validation of modified tests was "urgently
needed." The standard is silent as to what constitutes adequate validation, leaving that question to professional judgment based on current theory and practice with respect to other subgroups of
examinees.

In selective admissions, it is common to think of test validity for
a group when that group represents applicants to a particular educational program or a job. In that case, validity is much associated with
utility: Does an admissions test, for example, make a useful contribution to enrolling more able students in the institution? But, in
considering the validity of a test for demographic subgroups of
examinees within applicant pools (for instance, people with disabilities, minority students, or women), institutions' major concern
has been test bias. Thus the issues here may have more to do with
accuracy of inferences that affect individuals and groups than with
the utility of the test to programs and institutions.

It is important to connect this problem with construct validity,
the more fundamental theoretical basis for evaluating the validity of a
test. As Cronbach (1971) made clear, "one validates, not a test, but an
interpretation of data arising from a specified procedure" (p. 447). In

other words, does the score mean what we take it to mean? An important mark of accurate and consistent meaning in a construct is, as Messick (1975) noted, "the extent to which a measure displays the same properties and patterns of relationships *in different population groups* and under different circumstances" (p. 956; emphasis added).

Population validity links test bias directly to construct validity (Willingham, 1976). Test bias represents various possible discrepancies across subgroups—discrepancies that have no intrinsic connection with the knowledge and skill being measured. Thus test bias or population invalidity reduces construct validity by introducing systematic error, as would undue speededness or an unfair advantage or disadvantage given to some examinees. These various considerations point in the same direction: In evaluating the validity of a test for a subgroup such as handicapped people, the primary concern is test fairness, and the measure of fairness is comparability.

## Principal questions

☐ To summarize the foregoing discussion, it seems clear that the overriding issue is the comparability of tests administered to people with disabilities to those administered to others. The 504 regulations call for tests that are as comparable as possible in the sense of not being distorted by the examinee's disability. The NAS panel suggests a variety of research avenues, all directed to better documentation and improvement of the comparability of tests used in educational or employment selection. The recently adopted *Standards for Educational and Psychological Testing* (American Psychological Association, 1985) characterizes flagging as the issue that "has created the most heated debate" and goes on to say, "Until test scores can be demonstrated to be comparable in some widely accepted sense, there is little hope of happily resolving from all perspectives the issue of reporting scores with or without special identification" (p. 78). For the purposes of this report, we summarize the problem by focusing on these three questions:

1. When admissions tests are modified for handicapped people, to what extent are the nonstandard tests and the resulting scores comparable to those of the regular national program?
2. Might the comparability of such tests be improved? If so, how?
3. What implications might be drawn for possible resolutions of the flagging problem?

These broad questions describe the purpose of this work collectively, and they serve as a framework for the discussion in chapter 11. The individual empirical studies reported in chapters 4 through 10 focus on more specific questions concerning particular aspects of comparability. As additional background, it is useful to clarify briefly what is implied by comparability.

## Marks of comparability

☐ Much research has been done over the past 20 years on the comparability of tests for special subgroups of examinees—minority students, women, older examinees, and so on—with tests for the population at large. Typically conducting their evaluations under the rubric of test bias or population validity, measurement specialists have examined extensively various aspects of test performance in order to determine the fairness of different types of tests for different subgroups. For example, there have been useful analyses and reviews of research on particular ethnic groups (Duran, 1983), sex differences (Clark & Grandy, 1984), intelligence tests (Jensen, 1980), admissions tests (Breland, 1979), statistical methodology (Berk, 1982), and so on. Such analyses have focused on both the comparative accuracy of tests in forecasting later performance and the degree of similarity in the internal structure of tests for various groups.

In the case of tests modified for handicapped students, there is an additional dimension to the question of comparability because tests and/or testing conditions are necessarily different to some degree. An important characteristic of standardized examinations is that conditions of administration and scoring and the tests themselves are the same for all examinees. (For useful discussions of the role of standardization in insuring fair and objective assessment, see Angoff & Anderson [1963], American Psychological Association [1985], and Schmeiser, Kane, & Brennan [1983].) In the case of disabled students, some aspects of standardization are breached in the interest of reducing sources of irrelevant difficulty that might otherwise lower scores artificially. Thus, one must also ask to what extent the nature of the test and its administration are comparable in light of the disability.

For these reasons, the NAS panel did not restrict itself to research recommendations concerning ways to achieve scientific or psychometric comparability of modified tests. It also discussed in some detail the problem of establishing comparable test content, conditions of administration, and so on (Sherman & Robinson, 1982, chapter 5). These two orientations to the topic can be distinguished as score comparability and task comparability.

*Score comparability* implies comparable meaning and interpretation of test performance, not necessarily the same distribution of scores for different groups. To expect the same average score for students with and without disabilities requires the assumption that handicapped groups are representative of examinees generally and have a comparable history of learning experiences. There are five important respects in which scores should be generally comparable. These can be examined empirically on the basis of the testing outcome.

1. *Reliability.* Ordinarily, reliability is not seen as an aspect of validity, though it does place a limit on validity. It is an indicator of the comparability of a measure across subgroups, telling us whether scores are likely to fluctuate more in the case of modified tests. Findings regarding the reliability of modified tests appear in chapter 7.

2. *Factor structure.* If sensory or cognitive dysfunction occasions a student's taking a modified test, it is certainly plausible that that test may not measure the same construct as the standard examination; that is, the score may not have quite the same meaning. The differences in construct could cause misinterpretation of the score in educational advising or instructional placement, even if it is comparable for admissions purposes. Studies involving confirmatory factor analysis of both the SAT and GRE are reported in chapter 8.

3. *Item functioning.* Even if modified tests measure quite similar constructs, it is certainly possible that particular types of items may be unfair because they are differentially difficult for reasons connected with particular disabilities. Furthermore, for the specific purpose of avoiding unfair difficulty, there may have been modifications in the selection of items, their wording, or the way they are presented. Studies of item functioning for different groups of handicapped examinees are a useful empirical check on that process, and they are reported in chapter 7.

4. *Predicted performance.* A major factor in judging the validity of an admissions test for a subgroup is how accurately it predicts the group's performance. Accuracy of prediction engages two critical questions: Does the test discriminate between successful and unsuccessful students as well for this subgroup as for applicants generally? And does the test systematically over- or underpredict the academic performance of the group, taking into account its previous grade records as well as its test scores? The findings regarding predictive validity are summarized in chapter 9.

5. *Admissions decisions.* Additional grounds for questioning the comparability of tests modified to accommodate examinees with disabilities arise from the fact that their scores carry flags signifying something unusual about them. Does a flag actually inspire invalid inferences? There is no very satisfactory way of determining whether and how often this occurs, though evidence of comparable admissions decisions does bear on the question. If disabled applicants are less likely to be admitted than nondisabled applicants with comparable credentials, it can be argued that a flag is harmful because it may facilitate a prejudicial practice by making it easier to identify handicapped individuals. If that were so, the score would lose comparability through its appearance alone by inviting different inferences than those that might otherwise be drawn. A study of admissions decisions is summarized in chapter 6.

The NAS panel considered the comparability of predictions to be particularly important. In the panel's view, if it could be demonstrated that the scores of handicapped examinees—as presently reported or adjusted in some appropriate manner—do yield predictions that are reasonably comparable to those of other examinees, that would be sufficient reason to remove the flags from nonstandard scores. Accordingly, the panel gave close attention to the possibility of adjusting scores, and it suggested that test producers undertake research to evaluate the feasibility of rescaling scores of handicapped students through the grade criterion. Thus a score of, say, 500 would imply the same college performance for all groups of examinees (Sherman & Robinson, 1982, pp. 114–122). Chapter 10 presents an analysis of this possibility, leaning particularly on the findings from the predictive studies reported in chapter 9.

In evaluating the comparability of the *task* that an admissions test poses for handicapped and nonhandicapped examinees, it is important to remember that the goal is equivalence in the cognitive demands placed on the individual, not necessarily in the superficial characteristics of the test situation. There are several critical features to consider:

□ Is the content comparable, especially in excluding items or item types that lie outside the normal experience of someone with a disabling condition (e.g., material that is not essential to the test but that requires hearing experience of a deaf person)? Do modified forms (braille, audio cassettes, etc.) present comparable tasks?

□ Are the accommodations appropriate (e.g., information about

the test, physical arrangements in the test center, instructions
etc.)?

□ Is the timing comparable to that imposed on nonhandicapped
examinees (taking into account that a disabled person may
take longer to read a question and record the answer even
though he or she takes the same time as a nonhandicapped
person to come up with the correct answer)?

These various forms of task comparability are evaluated partly
on the basis of advice from handicapped individuals and professionals
who work with them (chapters 2 and 5). The matter often comes
down, in the last analysis, to a judgment about what is reasonable and
fair in testing people with a particular disabling condition. Several
types of data are useful in making such judgments more informed and
objective: the performance of handicapped students on different types
of test materials or formats (chapters 7 and 8), the subsequent academic performance of examinees who have used a different test
format or taken varying amounts of time to complete a test (chapter
9), evidence of the speed with which handicapped students complete
tests (chapter 7), and the comparability of the accommodations in
admissions testing to the accommodations ordinarily found in college
testing (chapter 5).

# 2

# Handicapped People

## ☐ *Randy Elliot Bennett and Marjorie Ragosta*

In the admissions testing context, accurate definitions of handicapping conditions are important for both scientific and operational reasons. Precise description allows other scientists to determine exactly what population was studied so that they can confirm research results with different samples drawn from that population and then generalize to it as a whole. Operationally, definition is also important: Without clear definitions, it becomes difficult to reliably direct examinees to appropriate test modifications, and the extent to which modified tests benefit handicapped students begins to diminish. This chapter explores some of the problems encountered in defining handicapping conditions and discusses the characteristics of these conditions as they are relevant to educational testing.

## Defining handicapping conditions

☐ ☐ Precisely defining different handicapping conditions has generally proved a difficult task. Problems in description have arisen from several sources, including the definitions themselves, the structure and implementation of diagnostic assessment, and the conduct of special education research.

## Definitions

☐ As indicated in chapter 1, Section 504 defines handicap in terms of a limitation in one or more major life activities such as seeing, hearing, walking, speaking, and learning, among other things.

Who are the people with impairments that substantially limit the major life activity of, for example, hearing? The answer is complicated by considerable variety in definitions of deafness. The Conference of Executives of American Schools for the Deaf defines the deaf person as one whose hearing ability precludes successful processing of linguistic information through audition, with or without a hearing aid (*Report of the Ad Hoc Committee to Define Deaf and Hard of Hearing*, 1975). Davis (1970), by contrast, considers the disorder to manifest itself in those with hearing loss greater than 93 decibels. A third definition is offered by the National Research Council Panel on Testing of Handicapped People, which uses a 70-decibel threshold as indicative of deafness (Sherman & Robinson, 1982, p. 10). Finally, Hallahan and Kauffman (1978, p. 282) note that the impairment can be defined as a hearing loss suffered in the first two or three years of life that precludes the natural acquisition of language.

A second illustration of the problems of definition concerns people with impairments that substantially limit the major life activity of learning. What individuals make up this group? The largest single population in this category taking admissions tests is those with learning disabilities (Ragosta & Nemceff, 1982). The most widely accepted definition of this disorder is contained in Public Law 94–142, the Education for All Handicapped Children Act of 1975 (Dept. of Health, Education, and Welfare, 1977b, Sect. 121.5b9), which defines *learning disability* as

> a disorder in one or more of the basic psychological processes involved in understanding or in using language, spoken or written, which may manifest itself in an imperfect ability to listen, think, speak, read, write, spell, or to do mathematical calculations. The term includes such conditions as perceptual handicaps, brain injury, minimal brain dysfunction [sic], dyslexia, and developmental aphasia. The term does not include children who have learning problems which are primarily the result of visual, hearing, or motor handicaps, of mental retardation, or of environmental, cultural, or economic disadvantage.

Through its regulations, PL 94–142 offers an operational definition of the disorder (Dept. of Health, Education, and Welfare, 1977c,

Sect. 121a.541), characterizing it as an ability-achievement discrepancy, existing in spite of the provision of age-appropriate instruction, that is not caused primarily by other conditions. Both the constitutive and operational definitions offered by the act serve as bases for education code and administrative procedure in the states.

The federal definitions of *learning disability* have been the subjects of considerable controversy. For example, it has been noted that the disorders that comprise learning disability are at least as poorly conceptualized as the parent term. *Minimal brain dysfunction, perceptual handicap,* and *dyslexia* all refer to conditions whose etiology, symptoms, prevalence, and treatment are uncertain (Reid & Hresko, 1981, pp. 229–230).

A second element of concern is the definitional requirement that the ability-achievement discrepancy not be the result of other factors such as mental retardation, emotional disturbance, economic disadvantage, or sensory or physical impairment. This requirement presumes that the causes of learning failure can be differentiated reliably. Though promising advances in testing have been made (e.g., Ahn et al., 1980), the fact remains that no technology can dependably unwind the myriad causes of school failure (Bennett, 1981a; Reid & Hresko, 1981, p. 9).

Finally, the operational definition of *learning disability* is squarely built upon the construct of underachievement, as indicated by the requirement of ability-achievement discrepancy. This concept is seductively simple, but it is in fact problematic (Thorndike, 1963). For example, it assumes that potential can be measured accurately, but in reality, tests can only *predict* future achievement, from which potential is *inferred.* When predicted and actual achievement differ, it often makes as much sense to call tested performance an overprediction as it does to label the student an underachiever.

Underachievement also does not appear to be a phenomenon peculiar to learning disability. Discrepancies can indicate a lack of motivation, absence from school, or simply normal variation (Shepard, 1982). In fact, intraindividual discrepancies appear to exist as frequently among children classified as sensory impaired and behavior disordered as among those with learning disability (O'Donnell, 1980).

Because current federal definitions of *learning disability* give little practical guidance as to what it is, some 40 competing definitions have been suggested (Ysseldyke, 1983). The breadth of characteristics encompassed by these definitions is so great that a study of 17 of them found 85 percent of a normal student sample classifiable as learning disabled (Ysseldyke, Algozzine, & Epps, 1983).

## Structure and implementation
## of assessment

☐  The structure and implementation of the special education classification and placement process has also hampered accurate description
of students with handicapping conditions, particularly those with
learning disabilities. Typically, students enter the process as a result
of referral by their classroom teachers. Research has shown that such
referrals are sometimes based on such extraneous factors as race, sex,
physical appearance, and socioeconomic status, rather than on the
pupil's need for special services (Ross & Salvia, 1975; Stevens, 1981;
Tobias, Cole, Zibrin, & Bodlakova, 1982). The result of this biasing
effect is to introduce children having no readily identifiable handicapping condition into the pool of students being considered for
special education placement.

By federal law, those entered into the referral pool are assessed
by a team of professionals. The information gathered by this team is
meant to form the basis for subsequent classification and placement
decisions. Research on the assessment process has suggested,
however, that child-study professionals sometimes lack critical
evaluation competencies, including skill in selecting, administering,
and interpreting instruments and in recognizing normal variability in
children (Bennett, 1981b; Bennett & Shepherd, 1982; Davis & Shepard, in press; Keogh, Kukic, Becker, McLoughlin, & Kukic, 1975;
Miller & Chansky, 1972; Miller, Chansky, & Gredler, 1970; Shepard,
1983; Thurlow & Ysseldyke, 1979; Warren & Brown, 1973; Ysseldyke, Algozzine, Regan, & Potter, 1980).

Assessment is followed by a classification meeting at which a
diagnosis is made. Investigations of this aspect of the process report
little consistency in diagnostic statements among professionals
assigned to the same case, only a slight relationship between assessment data and team judgments, and the influence of irrelevant pupil
characteristics on classification decisions (Epps, McGue, & Ysseldyke, 1982; Mercer, 1973; Vinsonhaler, Weinshank, Wagner, &
Polin, 1983; Ysseldyke, Algozzine, Richey, & Graden, 1982; Ysseldyke, Algozzine, & Thurlow, 1980). As a result, studies suggest that
over half of the classification decisions made by child-study teams are
erroneous (Algozzine & Ysseldyke, 1981; Craig, Myers, & Wujek,
1982; Shepard, Smith, & Vojir, 1983). One effect of these placement
errors is to confuse attempts to characterize the true nature of handicapping conditions even further.

### Research results

☐ The intent of educational and psychological research is usually to clarify the nature of some phenomenon. Unfortunately, a good deal of the research on handicapping conditions has had the opposite effect. One reason for this unintended consequence is the poor quality that sometimes characterizes special education research (Applebee, 1971; Cohen, 1976; Torgesen & Dice, 1980). Perhaps the best illustration of the confounding effect of poor research on the understanding of handicapping conditions is the problem of sample selection. Researchers interested in learning disability have often selected study samples on the basis of placement in school district LD programs, for example. But because many of the students in these programs are known to be misdiagnosed, results derived from studying them offer a distorted picture of the basic nature of learning disability (Keogh, 1983; Shepard, 1982; Shepard, Smith, & Vojir, 1983), compounding the problem of diagnosis.

In summary, several factors have hindered attempts to describe the basic nature of handicapping conditions. Among them are unclear definitions, an often inaccurate diagnostic assessment process, and the limitations of past research. In combination, these factors have led to confusion and disagreement about the defining characteristics of handicapping conditions. Recognizing these difficulties, we next discuss what is known about the characteristics of handicapped individuals to understand better how they are affected by the testing process.

## Characteristics of handicapped people

☐ ☐ Because of significant differences among subgroups of people with handicapping conditions, they are not typically treated as a single entity. We therefore discuss the characteristics of each of the four major disability groups taking admissions tests separately.

### Learning disability

☐ Over 1.8 million pupils were classified as learning disabled by the nation's elementary and secondary schools in the 1983–84 academic year (Dept. of Education, 1985). Perhaps the most assured generalization that can be made about this group is that it is heterogeneous. In one of the most extensive epidemiological studies of the disorder made to date, Shepard, Smith, and Vojir (1983) detected four major groups, composed of 18 distinct subgroups, within the population of students served as learning disabled by school districts in Colorado. The major groupings were children with

1. other handicaps such as mental retardation, emotional disturbance, and hearing disorder;
2. learning problems such as native-language interference and slow learning;
3. no dependable assessment data or no detectable learning problem; and
4. learning disabilities.

The learning-disabled group identified by Shepard, Smith, and Vojir (1983) included children falling into eight different empirically determined subgroups. Assignment to each subgroup was based on an analysis of test and other data contained in pupil records. The resulting subgroups were children with: significant ability-achievement discrepancy (48.1 percent); medium-quality processing deficit and verbal-performance discrepancy (15.5 percent); high-quality processing deficit (11 percent); weak significant ability-achievement discrepancy and verbal-performance discrepancy (8.5 percent); medium-quality processing deficit only (8.2 percent); hyperactivity (4.7 percent); weak significant ability-achievement discrepancy and medium-quality processing deficit (2.5 percent); and brain injury (1.4 percent).

Although Shepard, Smith, and Vojir (1983) took a significant step toward understanding the composition of the LD population, their classification scheme more accurately describes current decision-making practices than the true nature of learning disability. To be sure, with the possible exception of children with hyperactivity, none of the groups they detected has been studied extensively. In addition, several other subtype classifications have been posited (see, for example, Boder, 1971; Mattis, French, & Rapin, 1975; McKinney, 1984; Sattler, 1982, pp. 396–397). Finally, no identified subgroup can be said to be based on either sound theoretical underpinnings or a unique set of diagnostic characteristics.

Even though the precise nature and number of subgroups composing the LD population is open to question, the heterogeneity of the population is not. It is therefore surprising to discover that the research literature supports several important generalizations about the learning-disabled population. Those most relevant to testing relate primarily to cognitive-academic and motor characteristics. Generalizations about the cognitive-academic characteristics of learning-disabled students are derived primarily from research conducted with school-age pupils and relate to their intelligence and ability structure, cognitive processing, perception, and specific academic difficulties.

Most conceptualizations of learning disability posit average to above-average intelligence as a defining criterion (see Bryan & Bryan, 1975, p. 89; Johnson & Myklebust, 1967, p. 9; Reid & Hresko, 1981, p. 4). Research, however, shows the average performance of LD pupils on cognitive ability tests to be somewhat below that of the general population (Bennett, Ragosta, & Stricker, 1984; Kirk & Elkins, 1975; Norman & Zigmond, 1980; Stanovich, 1986).

The ability structure of the learning-disabled student is by definition uneven; that is, the pattern of cognitive abilities these individuals evidence is thought to be composed of highs representing skilled performance in some areas and lows denoting deficits in other (e.g., see McCarthy & McCarthy, 1969, p. 7). In fact, the degree of variability show by LD students in cognitive test subscale and subtest scores, while substantial, differs little from that evidence by nondisabled children (Bennett, Rock, & Chan, 1987; Kaufman, 1976a, 1976b, 1981).

Much research has recently been published on the cognitive processing characteristics of the LD population. Among the findings of these studies has been a general failure to use strategic behavior in performing cognitive tasks. LD students may fail to use mnemonic strategies such as rehearsal and category clustering spontaneously when trying to memorize, even though these strategies are available to them (Bauer, 1977; Freston & Drew, 1974; Parker, Freston, & Drew, 1975; Tarver, Hallahan, Kaufman, & Ball, 1976). They also lack self-checking behaviors and tend not to be thorough or exhaustive in attacking tasks (Wong, 1982). As a result, some investigators now view the LD student as an inactive learner who lacks a general awareness of the demands of the task, the motivation for seeking a solution, and the cognitive strategies that can be brought to bear upon the task (Torgeson, 1977).

In addition to strategic behavior, the perceptual processing capabilities of LD students have been a target of frequent study. Research on this topic is of particular interest because of the widely held belief that perceptual handicaps underlie the academic deficits associated with learning disability (e.g., see Frostig, 1972). Results indicate that LD students do perform more poorly than the general population on a wide variety of auditory and visual perceptual tasks (Kavale, 1981, 1982; Reid & Hresko, 1981, p. 81). Whether such performance causes, is caused by, or is simply a correlate of academic deficits is open to question (Reid & Hresko, 1981, pp. 79–83; Vellutino, Steger, Moyer, Harding, & Niles, 1977).

One of the most obvious cognitive characteristics of LD students is their poor academic performance. Most of those identified as learning disabled have reading difficulties (Reid & Hresko, 1981, p. 232), which tend to be accompanied by problems in spelling, writing, and spoken language (Anderson, 1982; Andolina, 1980; Carpenter & Miller, 1982; Menyuk & Flood, 1981; Poplin, Gray, Larsen, Banikowski, & Mehring, 1980; Semel & Wiig, 1975; Vogel, 1974). These difficulties appear to be persistent, following learning-disabled individuals into adulthood (Frauenheim, 1978; Horn, O'Donnell, & Vitulano, 1983; Wiig & Fleischmann, 1980).

Among the physical characteristics of learning-disabled students most widely reported in the clinical literature is a tendency toward motor anomalies (e.g., see Clements, 1966, pp. 11–13, cited by Bryan & Bryan, 1975; Johnson & Myklebust, 1967, p. 14). Reported anomalies include clumsiness, lack of body awareness, poor directionality, lack of gross and fine motor coordination, and generally disorganized motor behavior (Reid & Hresko, 1981, p. 83). Although research evidence supports these clinical observations, motor difficulties do not appear to be strongly associated with academic success (Reid & Hresko, 1981, p. 83).

Relatively little is known about the LD student in higher education. However, because learning disability is primarily an academic disability (unlike physical or visual impairment), it is reasonable to expect the demands of higher education to cause special problems for this group. Consistent with this presumption are the results of a study of students entering college in 1978 (Lawrence, Kent, & Henson, 1981), which found that those with learning disabilities distinguished themselves from other handicapped college students by a lack of confidence in their ability to perform at the college level and by less adequate academic preparation (as indicated by poorer high school records).

Perhaps related to the academic problems of this group is the finding that learning-disabled students constitute only 3 percent of the total population of freshmen with disabilities (Lawrence, Kent, & Henson, 1981), though they presently represent just under half of the school-aged handicapped population. In addition, of those LD students who did enroll in college in 1978, over half attended public two-year colleges.

What causes learning disability? Reid and Hresko (1981, pp. 9–13) suggest two general classes of etiology. Organic etiologies include problems related to brain injury (genetic, prenatal, perinatal, postnatal) and biochemical disorders. Among environmentally based causes are poor nutrition, lack of early stimulation, and emotional disturbance. As has been noted, no practical, dependable means exists for differentiating among these etiologies (Bennett, 1981a; Reid & Hresko, 1981, p. 9).

Most authorities posit some subtle neurologically based anomaly as the probable cause of learning disability (e.g., see McLoughlin & Netick, 1983). Evidence is beginning to emerge that suggests abnormalities in brain physiology and anatomy and other neurological factors in this population (e.g., see Galaburda & Geschwind, 1982). As yet, however, the causal link between neurological integrity and LD is by no means clear, and the root causes of the disorder remain controversial (Coles, 1978; Sattler, 1982).

The characteristics of learning-disabled students pose important challenges to admissions testing programs. One such challenge is the poor basic skills that often typify the LD student, which make the accurate assessment of higher-level abilities exceedingly difficult. For instance, underdeveloped reading skills may prevent some LD students from demonstrating superior mathematics reasoning ability when problems are presented in text form. Reading difficulty may additionally hamper the understanding of written test directions, which may in turn result in incorrect performance on groups of items or entire sections of the test.

The obvious solution to the problems in assessing the abilities of the LD student is to modify the conditions of testing. While modifications to standard administrative procedure may help, they by no means solve the dilemma. For example, one alternative approach to assessing mathematics reasoning ability is to present problems on cassette tape. Some students with learning disabilities, however, are believed to have auditory-perceptual problems, so if this approach were used with them, the resulting scores might represent perceptual skills more than math reasoning ability.

Perceptual skills may hamper the accuracy of assessment in still another way. The LD student may solve problems accurately, yet, mark the wrong boxes on the machine-scorable answer sheet because of visual perceptual deficits. The result, again, is an invalid assessment of problem-solving ability.

## Hearing disability

☐ Hearing disabilities cover a range of conditions, from total deafness to mild defects correctable by hearing aids. According to Meadow (1980), the assessment of hearing is based on two qualities of sound:

loudness and pitch. Loudness, or intensity, is measured in decibels (dB), from 0 for the softest audible sound to 120 for sound that is extremely loud and possibly painful. Whispered speech is about 20 to 30 dB; conversational speech is 60 to 70 dB. Pitch, or the frequency of sound waves, is measured in hertz (Hz), or cycles per second. The frequencies that are most important for understanding speech are in the range of 500, 1,000, and 2,000 Hz.

Hearing loss may be defined as a condition in which the unaided, average pure-tone threshold in the better ear is at 500, 1,000, and 2,000 Hz (Karchmer, Milone, & Wolk, 1979). As noted, disagreement exists on the classification of hearing loss, with different threshold levels used to define loss. Various definitions understandably encompass different numbers of individuals with diverse distributions of characteristics (Schein & Delk, 1974).

One classification developed by Karchmer, Milone, and Wolk (1979) organizes hearing loss into three groups:

1. less than severe, in which the person can hear sounds of less than 70 dB;
2. severe, in which the softest audible sounds are in the range of 70 to 90 dB; and
3. profound, in which the person can hear only sounds of more than 91 dB.

Another categorization of hearing loss in current use is that based on definitions of deaf and hard of hearing:

A deaf person is one whose hearing disability precludes successful processing of linguistic information through audition, with or without a hearing aid.
A hard-of-hearing person is one who, generally with the use of a hearing aid, has residual hearing sufficient to enable successful processing of linguistic information through audition. (*Report of the Ad Hoc Committee to Define Deaf and Hard of Hearing*, 1975, p. 509, cited in Hallahan & Kauffman, 1978, p. 283)

Several characteristics of hearing-impaired individuals are associated with the degree of their hearing loss. Karchmer, Milone, and Wolk (1979) noted that students with less than severe loss relied primarily on speech when communicating with parents and teachers. More than 85 percent were rated as having intelligible speech, and almost two-thirds were in mainstreamed, integrated school programs. In contrast, profoundly deaf students relied heavily on manual communication, 80 percent of them using signs either alone or in combination with speech. Fewer than one-quarter of them were rated as having intelligible speech, and almost two-thirds were in residential schools for deaf students. Severely impaired pupils characteristically fell between those who were profoundly deaf and those with less than severe impairments on these communication and educational placement characteristics.

Poor language development is the outstanding characteristic of hearing-impaired children. There is considerable agreement that the greater the hearing loss, the greater the communication problem, in both reception and production of language (Meadow, 1980; Quigley, 1979; Stark, 1979). Without hearing and imitating the sounds of human language, deaf children are slow to acquire communication skills. It is not surprising, then, that those who are prelingually deaf have greater linguistic difficulty than those whose deafness was acquired after some language experience (Meadow, 1980).

Methods of communicating with deaf children have been the subject of continuing controversy among educators (Hallahan & Kauffman, 1978). The two dominant methods have been oralism and a combined manual-oral approach. Oralism focuses on lip reading and training, while the combined approach also incorporates such techniques as sign language and finger spelling. The use of manual and oral methods in combination is termed *total communication.*

Even with a combined approach to communication, problems remain. There are many systems of sign from which to choose, each having its own advantages and limitations (Bornstein, 1979). American Sign Language (ASL)—once considered a reduced, imprecise, ungrammatical version of English—has recently emerged as a sophisticated linguistic system (Stokoe, 1980) and is the primary mode of communication in the deaf community. Since ASL does not parallel English, speech training and reading must be taught using another system. Finger spelling—the manual alphabet—parallels English but can be used at no better than 40 percent of the rate of speech. There is a variety of other sign systems that parallel English, a continuum consisting of dialects of ASL (e.g., Ameslan) at one end and contrived systems (e.g., Signed English) at the other. A major difficulty with all such systems is that they must be learned by hearing parents, educators, and others if the ability to communicate generally is to result.

Given that poor language development is the major characteristic of hearing-impaired students, what can be said about their cognitive skills? These have usually been measured by performance tests because for this group, the use of language would confound the measurement of mental ability with that of language deficiency. With the use of performance measures and nonverbal instructions, deaf children usually score within the normal range on cognitive ability tests, although their mean scores are somewhat lower than those of hearing children (Anderson & Sisco, 1977; Meadow, 1980; Mindel & Vernon, 1971).

Educational achievement, however, stands in sharp contrast to the findings on intellectual ability. A standardization sample of seven thousand hearing-impaired children between 8 and 19 years of age was used to develop norms for the 1974 Hearing-Impaired version of the Stanford Achievement Test (Trybus & Karchmer, 1977). The median performance of hearing-impaired 18-year-olds on reading comprehension ranged from third- to fourth-grade level on the standard test norms. For mathematics computation, their median performance was close to seventh-grade level. While the performance of less than severely deaf pupils on reading comprehension consistently averaged between one-half and one grade level higher than that of their profoundly or severely deaf peers, much less difference was observed among the three groups on mathematics computation (Karchmer, Milone, & Wolk, 1979).

The incidence of hearing disabilities in the United States is relatively low: Less than 1 percent of school children are deaf or hearing impaired (Meadow, 1980). According to the 1977–78 Annual Survey of Hearing-Impaired Children and Youth conducted by the Office of Demographic Studies at Gallaudet College, an estimated 67,500 hearing-impaired students were enrolled in special education programs in the nation's schools (Karchmer, Milone, & Wolk, 1979). Of the more than fifty-four thousand for whom complete audiological data were available, 44 percent were classified as profoundly deaf, 25 percent as severely deaf, and 31 percent as less than severely deaf. The etiology of deafness was related to the extent of hearing loss, with maternal rubella, hereditary factors, and meningitis accounting for more than half the cases of profound loss. Mumps, infections, trauma after birth, and otitis media tended to be associated with severe or less than severe hearing losses.

The number of severely hearing-impaired students enrolled in higher-education programs in the United States has steadily grown, from fewer than four hundred in 1955 to between six and ten thousand in the 1980s (Armstrong, Schneidmiller, White, & Karchmer, 1983). Increased enrollments in college occurred in the early 1980s as children deafened during the rubella epidemic of 1963–65 graduated from high school.

The language deficiencies of deaf individuals pose important dilemmas for traditional college and graduate assessment programs. Such individuals appear to have difficulty with such constructions as negation (e.g., *not*), conditionals (e.g., *if, when*), comparatives (e.g., *greater than*), inferentials (e.g., *should, because*), and low-information pronouns (e.g., *it, something*) (Rudner, 1978). In addition, they may encounter difficulty with lengthy passages, unfamiliar vocabulary, or modes of communication different from their native one (Trybus & Karchmer, 1977).

Clearly, the language deficiencies of deaf students may substantially impede the accuracy of college and graduate admissions testing. Potential problems occur in communicating directions and in measuring nonlinguistic skills, such as spatial ability, through the medium of language. For those whose native language is sign, the problem might appear to be solved by presenting test instructions and content in that mode. To prevent differences in the skills of signers and in the extent to which they successfully translate content from affecting scores, the test might be presented on videotape. However, here as in any major test modification, the extent to which the abilities being measured are changed by the modification must be considered.

The language deficits of deaf examinees may not always impair the accuracy of assessment because success in college and graduate programs is frequently dependent upon language skills. To some degree, then, the measurement of the deaf student's linguistic competence may prove a useful predictor of accomplishment in higher education.

## Visual disability

☐   Visual disability connotes a variety of handicapping conditions. On the one end of the continuum are individuals with no visual perception whatsoever, while for those at the other end, corrective glasses may provide 20/20 vision (the ability to see at 20 feet what the average person would). Between the two extremes of visual disability are partially sighted and legally blind people. The former are those individuals whose visual acuity in the better eye with corrective lenses falls between 20/70 and 20/200. Legal blindness is defined as central visual acuity of 20/200 or less in the better eye with corrective lenses, or visual acuity greater than 20/200 if there is a restricted visual field subtending an angle no greater than 20° (National Society for the Prevention of Blindness, 1966, cited in Reynolds & Birch, 1977, p. 605).

Although legal definitions of blindness and partial sightedness are useful for determining who is to get social security payments, income tax benefits, and other categorical provisions, they are of little value in describing the functional abilities of visually handicapped individuals for educational purposes. Between 70 and 80 percent of legally blind individuals have some measurable vision (Smith, 1982; Vander Kolk, 1981). Most partially sighted and many legally blind people differ from their totally blind peers in that they can use vision for learning; they can read print using large-type materials, holding a page very close to their eyes or using a device for magnification. In contrast, totally blind persons must use their tactual or auditory senses as their primary means of receiving information.

The distinction between the ability to use vision and the need to employ alternative sensory modalities gives rise to one educational definition of *blindness* as the inability to read print (Hallahan & Kauffman, 1978). The adaptive characteristics blind college students have developed for coping with visual material are described by Smith (1982):

> By the time blind students reach college (unless newly blinded), they have probably developed various methods for dealing with the volume of visual materials. Most blind students use a combination of methods including readers, brailled books, and audio-tape-recorded books and lectures. . . .
>
> Students may use raised line drawings of diagrams, charts, and illustrations; relief maps; and three-dimensional models of physical organs, shapes, microscopic organisms, etc. Modern technology has made available other aids for blind people including talking calculators, and speech time compressors. Paperless braille machines, braille computer terminals and reading machines are more recent devices. . . .
>
> Most blind students who use braille prefer to take their own notes in class using a slate and stylus or a Perkins Brailler. Some students have a classmate make a copy of his or her notes using carbon paper or a copy machine. The blind student's reader later reads the notes onto tape for future use. Some blind students audio record lectures and later transcribe notes from them into braille. (p. 4)

Partially sighted students use many of the same coping strategies as blind pupils and in addition employ large-print materials, magnification devices, and large-print typewriters (Smith, 1982).

Much research has been done on the cognitive characteristics of blind and partially sighted students. Researchers have studied the verbal ability of visually impaired individuals over many years, under many conditions, using a variety of tests. The accumulated evidence suggests that blind and partially sighted students possess verbal abilities equivalent to those of their sighted peers (Smits & Mommers, 1976; Tillman, 1967; Vander Kolk, 1977).

Blind people have, however, been found to differ from sighted people on some cognitive dimensions, in particular abstract reasoning (Tillman, 1967; Hallahan & Kauffman, 1978) and cognitive style

(Witkin, Birnbaum, Lomonaco, Lehr, & Herman, 1968). Some blind individuals learn words and concepts in a superficial manner, without understanding the underlying meaning, a phenomenon termed *verbalism* (Cutsforth, 1951). Such learning may be the result of the limited potential of the tactile sense for concept formation (Lowenfeld, 1971; Hallahan & Kauffman, 1978). Perhaps as a result, researchers have found that visually impaired children often do poorly on tasks requiring abstract thinking and are likely to deal with their environment in concrete terms (Hallahan & Kauffman, 1978; Nolan & Ashcroft; 1969, Suppes, 1974).

Others attribute conceptual deficits in visually impaired students to a lack of appropriate learning experience. Supporting this view is the work of Friedman and Pasnak (1973), which suggests that targeted training can increase blind children's conceptual ability to the level demonstrated by their sighted peers. Many authorities now feel that the cognitive development of blind people can equal that of the general population if adequate early stimulation opportunities are provided (Schlesinger & Lee, 1980).

Relatively little research has been done on the academic achievement of visually impaired students relative to that of sighted pupils. Available studies suggest that both blind and partially sighted children perform below the level of their chronological age peers when matched for mental age (Hallahan & Kauffman, 1978), but when time limits are extended and differentially difficult items removed, their performance may equal that of the nondisabled population (Trismen, 1967).

About one-tenth of 1 percent of children in the United States are severely visually disabled (Hallahan & Kauffman, 1978). Of the total visually impaired population, two-thirds are elderly; only 9 percent are below age 45 (Vander Kolk, 1981).

The causes of visual impairment are varied. Blindness tends to occur with aging; the young may be congenitally blind or become blind adventitiously. Congenital blindness may be genetically determined, may be caused by diseases affecting the mother during embryonic development, or may result from birth complications. Adventitious blindness may result from accident, injury, diabetes, cataracts, glaucoma, or infection. Currently, visual disabilities coincident with other impairments are increasing; fully half of the children with impaired vision are considered multiply handicapped (Reynolds & Birch, 1977).

The major challenges the characteristics of visually impaired people pose for admissions testing relate to the presentation of test items and the recording of responses. Clearly, the standard paper-and-pencil format is inappropriate for many of these students. Alternative presentation modes such as braille, large type, amanuensis, and cassette must be employed.

Selected item formats may prove problematic for visually impaired examinees. Complex graphical representations of data, for example, must be depicted as raised-line drawings. By virtue of their complexity, such drawings may be confusing unless successively complex drawings are used or test items include greater detail about the type and content of the drawing.

Finally, some items included in standard versions of a test may introduce difficulties for visually impaired examinees because the content area being measured requires visual capability. Tasks designed to assess the spatial skills needed to function in a graduate program in architecture might fall into this class. These items may be considered appropriate to the extent that similar task performance is required by the college or graduate program to which the candidate aspires.

Like other test modifications, the changes in presentation mode and item format often needed to accommodate the visually impaired examinee do not necessarily result in accurate assessment. Translation to braille along with removal or modification of items requiring visual capabilities may produce a test so different from the original as to prevent meaningful comparison of the scores obtained on it with those obtained on the standard version.


## Physical handicap

☐ The term *physical handicap* is sometimes used to cover the vast majority of impairments, including those already discussed. The phrase is here employed in a more restricted sense, excluding visual, hearing, and learning disabilities. Still, the remaining group of physically handicapped people is large and varied. It includes individuals with disabilities resulting from neuromuscular diseases, physical injuries, chronic health problems, and other conditions.

Neuromuscular diseases such as cerebral palsy, epilepsy, poliomyelitis, muscular dystrophy, and multiple sclerosis may generally be characterized by weakness, clumsiness in voluntary motion, or troublesome involuntary movements. Mobility may be impaired and, in severe cases, a wheelchair may be necessary. In addition, there may be such symptoms of brain injury as impairments of learning ability, verbal skills, form and space perception, or motor coordination (Corcoran, 1981).

Cerebral palsy (CP) is a disability of the motor centers of the brain occurring before or during birth and manifesting itself in muscular uncoordination and speech disturbances. Its most common forms are ataxic, manifesting in marked inability to coordinate bodily movements; athetoid, appearing as slow, repeated movements of the limbs; and spastic, characterized by abrupt contractions of muscles producing interference with and distortion of movement (Reynolds & Birch, 1977). Some individuals with CP walk well, others use braces or crutches, and some require wheelchairs. Sometimes the speech and mouth muscles are affected so that words sound garbled and verbal communication is impaired. Additional complications can include visual or auditory impairment, seizures, degenerative joint disease, respiratory infections, and fatigue (Easton & Halpern, 1981).

The mean IQ of cerebral palsied children is well below the average for the general population (Cruickshank, Hallahan, & Bice, 1976). However, some individuals with CP have normal intellectual ability, and a few test within the gifted range (Hallahan & Kauffman, 1978). Cruickshank (1976) estimates the childhood prevalence of cerebral palsy at .15 percent of the population.

Epilepsy is a convulsive disorder in which recurrent seizures are caused by abnormal discharges of electrical energy in the brain. Hallahan and Kauffman (1978) describe the traditional classifications of epilepsy as grand mal, focal, Jacksonian, and petit mal. The usual grand mal seizure involves a diffuse, quickly spreading electrical discharge that may manifest itself by a cry, loss of consciousness, a short period of muscle rigidity, or a period of involuntary muscle contractions of the extremities, trunk, and head. Focal seizures involve a fairly circumscribed part of the brain and may have sensory or psychomotor manifestations. Jacksonian seizures produce rhythmic twitching in one area that may spread to the whole body. Petit mal seizures are characterized by brief lapses of consciousness, lasting from 1 to 30 seconds. Although such seizures are less severe than other types, they may occur more frequently, in some cases as often as a hundred times a day.

Most people with epilepsy function normally between seizures, and many have average or above-average intelligence (Dikman, Matthews, & Harley, 1975). Epilepsy can generally be controlled with medication, but the medication itself, if required in large amounts, may affect coordination, vision, attention, and memory (Ward, Fraser, & Troupin, 1981). Estimates of the prevalence of epilepsy range from .5 to 1 percent of the population (Hallahan & Kauffman, 1978).

Multiple sclerosis (MS) is a common neurological disease affecting as many as five hundred thousand persons in the United States. Kraft (1981) describes it as a disease that attacks the myelin sheaths of the nerve fibers in the brain and spinal cord. Where myelin is destroyed, plaques of hardened tissue (sclerosis) occur in many places. The lesions of MS can therefore cause almost any type of central nervous system symptom: impaired sensation, lack of coordination, double vision, slurred speech, memory loss, spasticity, or paralysis of the extremities. The disease is progressive but unpredictable: some individuals with MS are never severely incapacitated, others suffer exacerbations and remissions, while in perhaps 10 percent of cases there is severe and rapid deterioration. The combination of weakness, spasticity, ataxia, and tremor may interfere with walking and necessitate a wheelchair for mobility.

Poliomyelitis is an infectious disease that attacks nerve tissue in the spinal cord and/or brain, sometimes leaving its victims with severe muscular weakness, spasticity, paralysis, or skeletal deformities (Hallahan & Kauffman, 1978). Since the Salk vaccine was perfected in the mid-1950s, poliomyelitis has been virtually eliminated in the United States, but those disabled by polio are still encountered at the college level (Ragosta, 1980) and in vocational rehabilitation settings (Stolov & Clowers, 1981). Although polio does not affect intelligence directly (Hallahan & Kauffman, 1978), cognitive development may be slowed by illness-induced reductions in opportunities to learn.

Hallahan and Kauffman (1978) describe muscular dystrophy (MD) as a hereditary disease characterized by progressive weakness resulting from degeneration of muscle fibers. There are two major types, Duchenne and Landouzy-Dejerine. In the former, the muscles become replaced by fatty tissue. It affects only boys, and they seldom live into adulthood. The latter form of the disease affects both males and females, some of whom become totally disabled, while others live a relatively normal life. The major effects of muscular dystrophy are impaired physical mobility and the prospect of early total disability or death. The disease itself does not affect intellectual functioning directly, though it may limit learning opportunities.

The second major category of physical disability is injury. Orthopedic impairments may result from the amputation of limbs or injury to the spinal cord. In cases where amputation has resulted in the loss of arms or legs, prostheses may be prescribed or alternative methods of accommodation found.

Injury to the spinal cord frequently results in paralysis. Paralysis restricted to the lower half of the body is called *paraplegia*, while that involving both arms and both legs is termed *quadriplegia*. Capabilities of spinal cord–injured individuals vary widely according to the precise location of the lesion. Overall functional ability depends upon the level of lesion and the residual muscle function, the extent and success of adaptation and rehabilitation, psychological adjustment, and general health and ability level (Donovan, 1981). Impairment in mobility is characteristic of spinal cord injuries, and modifications such as braces and wheelchairs provide the primary means of adaptation. Since spinal cord injury or loss of limbs does not affect the cognitive processes directly, cognitive development is hampered only by restrictions in the chance to learn.

The proportion of orthopedically disabled students in the population of college freshmen with disabilities is reported by Lawrence, Kent, and Henson (1982) to be 22 percent. When surveyed, these students indicated to a greater degree than those with other handicaps that their disability did not affect their general college functioning. Orthopedically disabled pupils were underrepresented in public and private four-year colleges and were somewhat more likely than average to have entered public two-year colleges in 1978.

Chronic health problems, the third major category of physical disability, includes cardiac conditions, severe allergies, cancer, and other difficulties that impair physical well-being. In a recent study of 41 disabled student service programs, Scales (1983) found those with chronic health problems to constitute 17 percent of the nine thousand students served. Lawrence, Kent, and Henson (1982), in a followup survey of handicapped freshmen, found those with health-related disabilities almost twice as likely as the average handicapped student to have dropped out and reenrolled in college during the three-year study period. Their health-related disabilities tended to be diagnosed either at birth or after they reached 18 years of age and to be hidden.

This brief summary of diagnostic categories makes clear the wide range of conditions that fall under the rubric of physical disability. The physical characteristics of this group vary widely according to the specific disability, its onset, its course (whether it is permanent or temporary, chronic or acute, cyclical or degenerative, etc.), its severity, and the individual's adaptation to it.

The cognitive development of people with disabilities varies significantly both across and within diagnostic categories. It may be slowed by a reduction in opportunities for normal interaction and development or by neurological involvement. Medication may also affect academic performance negatively. In many cases (e.g., for orthopedic disabilities), the impairment will not directly affect cognitive processes.

The incidence of physical handicaps in postsecondary students appears high relative to that of visual or learning disabilities. In a recent study of service programs for disabled students, Scales (1983) found paraplegic, quadriplegic, semiambulatory, and chronically health-impaired students to constitute over half of the known handicapped student population.

The challenges physically handicapped students present to college and graduate admissions testing programs are generally less severe than those posed by other disability groups. Some of the problems these examinees encounter relate to the recording of responses and to fatigue. To assist those lacking the physical ability to complete a machine-scorable answer sheet, an amanuensis (a person who records responses) is typically provided. The problem of fatigue is addressed by allowing extra time to complete sections of the test and by providing longer or additional rest periods between sections.

## SUMMARY

This chapter reviewed some of the problems encountered in defining handicapping conditions and discussed the characteristics of these conditions relevant to educational testing. Problems affecting the precise description of disabling conditions were found to include conflicting definitions for the same condition, an imprecise educational classification and placement process, and the uneven quality of research on the characteristics of special populations. Four general handicapped groups—learning disability, hearing impairment, visual disability, and physical handicap—were described, and their implications for admissions testing were discussed.

# 3

# Test Results

□ *Randy Elliot Bennett,*
*Marjorie Ragosta, and*
*Lawrence J. Stricker*

In addition to the description of characteristics of handicapped people provided in the previous chapter, information on their typical test performance may be helpful in clarifying the context in which our research was carried out and may be interpreted. Accordingly, this chapter selectively documents existing research on the test performance of handicapped people. Because the following chapters present evidence on admissions tests and handicapped people, we concentrate here on their performance on other scholastic tests.

Studies cited here were selected on the basis of several criteria. First, tests needed to be similar in content or format to college and graduate admissions examinations; school ability tests and academic achievement measures were included for this reason. (There has been a long history of test research at the U.S. Office of Personnel Management (e.g., Nester, 1984), but the agency's work is focused on employment testing and hence is not included in this chapter.) Second, examinees needed to be similar to college and graduate school applicants. Studies of high school and college-age students were particularly sought, though research on younger subjects is sometimes cited when little other pertinent work could be located. A final criterion was the quality of research. Where feasible, consideration was given to only those studies with samples large enough to offer dependable results (more than 40 subjects) and to those that offered comparable data for nonhandicapped subjects.

Authors' names are listed alphabetically.

The review is organized by handicapping condition, covering students with learning disabilities, hearing impairments, visual impairments, and physical handicaps. For each group, research on level of performance, reliability, and validity are discussed.

# Learning-disabled students

## Level of performance

☐ Studies have been made of the performance of learning-disabled (LD) students on college admissions tests, school ability tests, and school achievement measures. The most comprehensive study of the SAT performance of LD students was conducted by Ragosta and Nemceff (1982), who looked at all such students taking special administrations between 1979 and 1981. These investigators found LD students to perform substantially below (by at least .5 standard deviation) nonhandicapped students taking the test during the same period. Using a subset of the Ragosta and Nemceff sample, Centra (1986) studied LD students who took both special and timed administrations. For this self-selected group, scores from the standard administration were well below (by more than .5 standard deviation), while those from the untimed administration were only somewhat below the national average (by less than .3 standard deviation).

Data on the performance of LD students on school ability tests have been reported for the Wechsler Adult Intelligence Scale (WAIS) (Wechsler, 1955) and the Wechsler Intelligence Scale for Children (WISC) (Wechsler, 1949). In an investigation of students enrolled in a large university (Cordoni, O'Donnell, Raminiah, Kurtz, & Rosenshein, 1981), learning-disabled and nonhandicapped students differed appreciably (by about .5 standard deviation) on their mean Full-Scale WAIS IQ: the means were 108 for the former and 115 for the latter. (Verbal and Performance IQ data were not reported.) The two groups also differed significantly and substantially in their means on 5 of the 11 WAIS subtests—Information, Similarities, Vocabulary, Digit Span, and Digit Symbol—the means for the learning-disabled students being consistently lower.

A study of 14-year-old males (Ackerman, Dykman, & Peters, 1977) found that the mean Full-Scale and Verbal IQs on the WISC were significantly and appreciably lower (by at least .6 standard deviation) for learning-disabled than for nonhandicapped pupils: 103 versus 112 for Full-Scale IQ and 101 versus 112 for Verbal IQ. The mean Performance IQ was not significantly different for the two groups.

In addition to overall performance, the subscale and subtest performance of learning-disabled students on cognitive ability tests have been investigated. An extensive review of WISC–R research (Kaufman, 1981) found that both the Verbal IQ–Performance IQ discrepancy and subtest scatter were slightly larger for children with learning disabilities than for nonhandicapped children. However, differences in the amount of scatter and subscale discrepancy were too small to be of diagnostic value.

With respect to subtest performance, a review of a large number of WISC investigations (Rugel, 1974) found that learning-disabled children with reading disabilities typically had their highest mean scores on the Block Design, Object Assembly, and Picture Completion subtests and their lowest on the Digit Span and Coding subtests; the subtest means for nonhandicapped children followed no consistent pattern. In the Ackerman, Dykman, and Peters study, the means on 4 of the 11 WISC subtests—Arithmetic, Coding, Information, and Digit Span—were also significantly and appreciably lower for the learning-disabled boys. (Two of these subtests, Information and Digit Span, and the WAIS counterpart [Digit Symbol] of a third, Coding, also differentiated learning-disabled from other college students in the previously described study by Cordoni, O'Donnell, Ramaniah, Kurtz, & Rosenschein). These same four WISC subtests make up the "ACID" cluster (an acronym composed of the first letter of each subtest name) reported to be associated clinically with learning disability in children (Sattler, 1982).

Pertinent data on the level of learning-disabled examinees' performance on achievement tests are sparse. In the Ackerman, Dykman, and Peters (1977) study of 14-year-old males, the means for all three scales on the Wide Range Achievement Test (WRAT) (Jastak & Jastak, 1965)—Reading, Spelling, and Arithmetic—were appreciably lower for the learning-disabled than for the other students.

## Reliability

☐ Relatively few data on the reliability of cognitive tests for LD students are available. McCullough and Zaremba (1979) reported findings about the internal-consistency reliability of the Woodcock Reading Mastery Test (Woodcock, 1973) and the KeyMath Diagnostic Arithmetic Test (Connolly, Nachtman, & Pritchett, 1971) for a sample of 12- to 17-year-old males. The Coefficient Alpha reliabilities of the total scores on these tests were similar for the learning-disabled and the other pupils in the sample: .88 for the learning disabled and .92 for the others on the Woodcock; and .94 and .97, respectively, on the KeyMath.

## Validity

☐ Validity research has been reported for admissions, school ability, and school achievement tests. Jones and Ragosta (1982) studied the predictive validity of SAT scores for freshmen attending a small Massachusetts college. The Verbal (SAT–V) and Mathematical (SAT–M) tests had similar correlations with first-semester average for 55 LD and 111 other students attending the school. However, a regression equation based on the SAT data for nonhandicapped students systematically *overpredicted* the grades for LD students.

Factor analyses of the WISC–R (Wechsler, 1974) for children of elementary school age provide further insight into the validity of cognitive tests for learning-disabled pupils. Several investigations of these examinees (Blaha & Vance, 1979; Naglieri, 1981; Petersen & Hart, 1979; Schooler, Beebe, & Koepke, 1978; Wallbrown & Blaha, 1979) generally found the factor structure that had been identified in the WISC–R standardization sample (Gutkin & Reynolds, 1981; Kaufman, 1975; Raminiah, O'Donnell, & Ribich, 1976; Reynolds & Gutkin, 1980; Silverstein, 1977; Wallbrown, Blaha, Wallbrown, & Engin, 1975). This structure consisted of a large verbal comprehension factor (mainly defined by the Information, Similarities, Vocabulary, and Comprehension subtests); a large perceptual organization factor (primarily defined by the Picture Completion, Picture Arrangement, Block Design, Object Assembly, and Mazes subtests); and often a smaller, less stable, freedom-from-distractibility factor (usually defined by the Arithmetic, Digit Span, and Coding subtests).

Factor analyses of the Woodcock Reading Mastery Test (Woodcock, 1973) and the KeyMath Diagnostic Arithmetic Test (Connolly, Nachtman, & Pritchett, 1971) were conducted by McCullough and Zaremba (1979). In their study of 12- to 17-year-old males, they found that the factor structure of the Woodcock was the same for the learning-disabled and the other students: one factor, defined by all the subtests, emerged. However, the factor structure of the KeyMath differed for the two groups. Two factors were identified for learning-disabled pupils, an operations factor (defined by the Addition, Subtraction, Multiplication, and Division subtests) and a content and application factor (defined by most of the other subtests: Numeration, Fractions, Geometry and Symbols, Word Problems, Missing Elements,

Money, Measurement, and Time). Only one factor (defined by all the subtests) emerged for the other subjects.

# Hearing-impaired students

## Level of performance

☐ Performance data for deaf students come from studies of the SAT, school ability, and school achievement measures. The most comprehensive data on the SAT performance of hearing-impaired students are those reported by Ragosta and Nemceff (1982), who found the mean scores of such students taking nonstandard administrations between 1979 and 1981 to be well below the means (between .5 and 1.2 standard deviations) of nondisabled students, with Verbal scale performance more discrepant from national norms than Mathematical scores.

Information on the school ability test performance of deaf and hearing-impaired students comes from studies using individually administered nonverbal tests such as the Performance scales of the WISC (Wechsler, 1949), WISC–R (Wechsler, 1974), and WAIS (Wechsler, 1955). Schildroth (1976) reported the nonverbal IQ scores from a national study of students enrolled in programs for the hearing impaired in the 1970–71 school year. The mean nonverbal IQ for all hearing-impaired students was 95.6, slightly below the normative mean of 100. However, for hearing-impaired children with no additional handicapping condition, the mean nonverbal IQ was 100.1, whereas students with at least one additional handicapping condition registered a mean score of 86.5.

Scores on the WAIS Performance and Verbal scales were reported by Ross (1970) for deaf students aged 16 to 21. Testing was accomplished using simultaneous manual and verbal communication, with responses in either mode accepted. The mean Performance IQ was 106, and the mean Verbal IQ was 72.

Data on the achievement test performance of deaf students come from the 1974 national standardization of the Special Edition of the 1973 Stanford Achievement Test for Hearing Impaired Students (SAT–HI) (Trybus & Karchmer, 1977). Trybus and Karchmer reported the median reading comprehension score at the test's highest age level (20+ years) to be at grade level 4.5, with only 10 percent of hearing-impaired 18-year-olds scoring at an eighth-grade level. In mathematics computation, the median score at age 20+ was just below eighth-grade level, with only the top 10 percent of hearing-impaired students scoring at the level of hearing students.

## Reliability

☐ Internal consistency coefficients for the SAT–HI subtests have been found to range from a low of .64 to a high of .96, with most estimates in the .80 range (Jensema, 1978). These estimates are roughly comparable to reliabilities typically found for nondisabled students on the Stanford Achievement Test. Subtest reliabilities for Intermediate Form E of that test range from .42 to .84, with most values falling in the .60s and .70s for fifth-grade students (Gardner, Rudman, Karlsen, & Merwin, 1982).

## Validity

☐ Research on the validity of tests for deaf students is limited to one study of the SAT and one of the Gallaudet Entrance Exam. Jones and Ragosta (1982) investigated the validity of the SAT for predicting the first-year grades of deaf students attending a California state university. Coefficients were .14 and .41 for SAT–V and SAT–M, respectively, for deaf students, and .38 and .32 for SAT–V and SAT–M for hearing examinees. While the coefficients for deaf and non-handicapped students did not differ significantly, the difference between the SAT–V coefficients did approach statistical significance ($P = .06$), suggesting the need for further study with larger samples. In addition, in some score ranges SAT scores alone were found to underpredict the college performance of deaf students, while high school grades overpredicted it. In combination, however, grades and SAT scores predicted freshmen performance in the hearing and deaf populations equally well.

The Gallaudet Entrance Examination (Greenberg & Greenberg, 1971) consisted of 13 tests, including some published measures and some developed especially for deaf students. The tests were selected or designed to measure subject-matter knowledge such as algebra and vocabulary, special skills such as writing and paragraph arrangement, and academic potential, for example by concept formation. The best predictors of college performance in the Gallaudet class of 1965 were two verbal tests, vocabulary and writing. Each measure correlated .44 with college grade-point average, correlations similar in magnitude to those typically found in the general population between the verbal scales of admissions tests and first-year grades (Educational Testing Service, 1980).

# Visually impaired students

## Level of performance

☐ Data on the performance of visually impaired students are available for admissions tests (both the SAT and American College Testing Program's ACT Assessment), school ability tests, and school achievement measures. On the SAT, Ragosta and Nemceff (1982) found visually impaired students taking special administrations from 1979 to 1981 to score only slightly differently (within .3 standard deviation) from others. For the subset of this population that took both timed and untimed tests, Centra (1986) reported that performance marginally exceeded national norms for untimed administrations and fell below them for timed ones (.3 to .5 standard deviation).

Finally, for the ACT Assessment, the mean composite score of visually impaired candidates taking special test administrations in the 1979–1980 academic year (Maxey & Levitz, 1980) was 17.7, comparing favorably with a composite of 18.5 for the nonhandicapped (a difference of less than .2 standard deviation).

The performance of visually impaired people on the Verbal scales of the WISC (Wechsler, 1949) and WAIS (Wechsler, 1955) has also been investigated. In general, their scores appear equivalent to those of the sighted population (Jordan & Felty, 1968; Smits & Mommers, 1976; Tillman, 1967; Vander Kolk, 1977). Similar results have been found using the Hayes-Binet and Interim Hayes-Binet intelligence scales (Hayes, 1941). These studies have also found higher than average Digit Span scores and lower than average Comprehension scores for visually impaired examinees. Finally, no differences between the performance of blind and partially sighted examinees are evident on the Wechsler tests (Vander Kolk, 1977).

Although the performance of visually impaired people appears roughly equivalent to that of the general population on academic ability tests, their achievement test performance does not. For example, Ozias (1975) reported that three separate investigations found blind children well below the mathematics achievement level of their sighted peers. Hallahan and Kauffman (1978), in a review of the characteristics of visually impaired children, concluded that both partially sighted and blind children achieve more poorly than their sighted peers when matched for mental age. Finally, the Special Assessment of Visually Impaired Students of the Florida Statewide Assessment Program (Florida Department of Education, 1981) reported that the achievement of visually disabled students tested in 1979 and 1980 was well below that of regular students.

The cause of the reported discrepancies between the ability and achievement test performances of visually impaired students is not immediately clear. Such discrepancies may be due to differences in the segments of the visually impaired population that take ability and achievement tests (e.g., a more select segment may take ability tests), the use of achievement tests with content or administrative procedures that are less appropriate for visually impaired students (e.g., group versus individually administered measures), or a real difference between general cognitive ability and accumulated academic knowledge.

Limited evidence that modifications in achievement test content and procedure affect the performance of visually impaired students was provided by Trismen (1967). In a study designed to produce an equivalent form of the Sequential Tests of Educational Progress for blind students, this investigator found their performance to be roughly comparable to national norms when time limits were relaxed and unsuitable items removed.

## Reliability

☐ Reliability data are available for school ability and achievement tests. Tillman (1973) summarized several studies of blind students' performance on the WISC Verbal scale. Internal consistency reliabilities on the WISC subtests ranged from .71 to .83. For the Verbal scale, the split-half reliability was estimated to be .89 and the test-retest reliability to be .91, results that are generally comparable to those reported for the WISC standardization sample. Split-half reliabilities for that sample range from .50 to .91 for the Verbal subtests and .88 to .96 for the Verbal IQ (Wechsler, 1949).

The test-retest reliability of the Interim Hayes-Binet used with visually handicapped students was reported by Hayes (1950) to be .90. Preliminary estimates of the split-half reliabilities for the Perkins-Binet Intelligence Test for Blind Children (Davis, 1970) were reported by Coveny (1972) to be .96 for braille readers on Form N and .94 for print readers on Form U. These estimates are generally comparable to those found in uses of the Stanford-Binet with nondisabled students, for which alternate-form reliabilities range from .83 to .98 (Terman & Merrill, 1973).

Reliability coefficients for modified achievement tests standardized on students at the Perkins School for the Blind are reported by Bauman and Hayes (1951). Retests with Forms D–H of the Stanford Achievement Tests yielded reliability coefficients from .87 to .95. These reliabilities are roughly comparable to those typically found for the general population. For the nondisabled population, retest reliabilities range from .87 to .93 on Intermediate 1 Forms E and F (Gardner, Rudman, Karlsen, & Merwin, 1982).

## Validity

□  Very few data exist on the validity of cognitive tests for blind or partially sighted students. Lewis (1957) found correlations of .45, .46, and .53, respectively, between their scores on the Interim Hayes-Binet and their grade averages in elementary, junior high, and high school. These results are generally similar to those typically found in studies comparing academic ability test scores with grades for older nonhandicapped students (Educational Testing Service, 1980).

## Physically handicapped students

□ □  Only two studies of the performance of physically handicapped students on cognitive tests were identified, both of which concern the SAT. Ragosta and Nemceff (1982) found such students taking the SAT in special administrations between 1979 and 1981 to score only slightly below nonhandicapped students (within .3 standard deviation). Centra (1986), again using the subset of students who took both timed and untimed exams, found this group to fall somewhat below national norms on the timed exams (within .4 standard deviation) and to score up to .2 standard deviation above the national average on special administrations.

### Reliability

□  No data relevant to the reliability of cognitive tests for this group were located.

### Validity

□  No data relevant to the validity of cognitive tests for this group were located.

## SUMMARY

This chapter has documented the available data on the performance of handicapped people on scholastic tests. The most obvious conclusion to be drawn from this review relates to the paucity of relevant, dependable data. The investigations reviewed here were located through extensive searches of the ERIC and *Psychological Abstracts* databases, journals such as the *Journal of Learning Disabilities* and *American Annals of the Deaf,* and standard texts such as Sattler's (1982) *Assessment of Children's Intelligence and Special Abilities.* Because of the considerable amount of special education testing done in the nation's schools, reports were also obtained from several large school districts. Despite this search, few useful data on the cognitive test performance of handicapped students and the psychometric characteristics of tests used with these individuals were found.

The major implication of this lack of data is that any conclusions must necessarily be tentative. With this caveat in mind, we offer some tentative judgments about the test performance of handicapped people. First, students with visual and physical impairments generally appear to perform similarly to nonhandicapped students on cognitive tests. The major exception to this generalization concerns achievement tests, on which visually impaired students appear to perform less well. Learning-disabled and hearing-impaired students, in contrast, seem more frequently to perform below national norms on a variety of cognitive tests, with the hearing-impaired group having most difficulty on verbal measures.

The limited data on reliability and validity indicate few important differences in these psychometric characteristics between handicapped and nonhandicapped groups. Of note, however, are suggestions of overprediction of future academic performance for learning-disabled students and underprediction for hearing-impaired students taking admissions tests.

# 4

# Examinees who Took Nonstandard SATs

## ☐ *Marjorie Ragosta*

Every year since 1972, the College Board has issued a national report about the Admissions Testing Program (ATP) test scores and responses from the Student Descriptive Questionnaire (SDQ). In 1984 the board published *College-Bound Seniors: Eleven Years of National Data from the College Board's Admissions Testing Program 1973–1983.* This chapter describes highlights of a detailed comparison of analogous information for 1980–83 for college candidates who took special administrations of the SAT through ATP Services for Handicapped Students (Ragosta, 1986).

Readers will undoubtedly find here interesting information in addition to the highlights. In interpreting this information, however, remember that the data from *College-Bound Seniors* are based on voluntary, self-reported responses by approximately one-third of the nation's high school graduates and two-thirds of its college entrants. Hence they do not reflect the total high school or college-bound population. Data from students taking special test administrations of the SAT ought also to be interpreted with caution. They reflect the SAT performance and, for those who completed the SDQ, the questionnaire responses of those disabled candidates who requested special testing accommodations. The percentage of disabled students responding to the SDQ is lower than that of college-bound students in

This chapter is based upon a study funded separately by the College Board.

general. Those disabled candidates who do complete the SDQ earn, on
the average, slightly higher SAT scores than those who do not. In
addition, many more candidates with disabilities are able to take
*standard* administrations of the SAT on national test dates; their data
are not reflected in this report because they are not identified as
having disabilities.

# Findings

☐ ☐     ☐ The number of students registering to take the SAT under ATP
Services for Handicapped Students increased by more than 80 percent
from 1980 to 1983. Most of the change was due to a rapid increase in
the number of learning-disabled test takers, from 57 to 71 percent of
the total. Almost fifteen thousand disabled students were tested over
the four-year period (see line 3 of Table 4.1).

☐ Males used ATP Services for Handicapped Students more
frequently than did females. Over the four years there were 27 percent
more visually impaired males, 40 percent more physically handicapped males, and 170 percent more learning-disabled males than
females. Only hearing-impaired test takers were predominantly
female, with 10 percent more females than males—a ratio consistent
with that in the general population of college-bound seniors (see lines
1 and 2 of the table).

☐ Consistently across the four years of the study, test takers
using ATP Services for Handicapped Students earned mean SAT
Verbal scores lower than the norms for college-bound seniors. Visually impaired and physically handicapped examinees earned higher
mean scores than learning-disabled test takers, who in turn did better
than those with hearing impairments. The SAT Verbal scores of
learning-disabled students averaged almost three-quarters of a standard
deviation below those of college-bound seniors in general, and those
of hearing-impaired students were more than a full standard deviation
lower. About 60 percent of hearing-impaired test takers earned scores
in the lowest range, 200 to 299 (see lines 4 and 5 of the table).

☐ The pattern of SAT mathematical scores was similar to that of
SAT Verbal scores but not quite as extreme. Again, the scores of
visually impaired and physically handicapped students were higher
than those of learning-disabled students, who again earned higher
mean scores than did hearing-impaired students. The SAT Mathematical means of disabled students ranged between about one- and

three-quarters of a standard deviation below those of college-bound seniors (see lines 6 and 7 of the table).

□ The estimated high school grade-point averages of students with disabilities follow a slightly different pattern than that for SAT scores. Although as a group they earn slightly lower GPAs than do college-bound seniors in general—from about a quarter to nine-tenths of a standard deviation unit—hearing-impaired students earn grades only slightly lower than do students with physical or visual disabilities. Learning-disabled students, on the average, earn much lower grades (see lines 8 and 9 of the table).

□ The average number of years of study of English, mathematics, foreign languages, biological sciences, physical sciences, and social studies is remarkably consistent across all groups. Only in the study of foreign languages are mean differences very great. College-bound seniors in general and visually impaired students on the average report more than two years of study, physically handicapped students slightly less than two years, learning-disabled students more than one year, and hearing-impaired students less than one year. Moreover, although 14 percent of all college-bound seniors report taking no foreign language, the percentages are much larger for students with disabilities, comprising about 19 percent of the visually impaired, 24 percent of the physically handicapped, 42 percent of the learning-disabled, and 58 percent of the hearing-impaired students (see odd-numbered lines 13–23 of the table).

□ The self-reported grades of college-bound seniors in general are higher in all subject areas than those of students who request special test administrations. Learning-disabled students report the lowest grades, while hearing-impaired students usually report grades only slightly below those of students with physical or visual disabilities (see even-numbered lines 12–22 of the table).

□ Self-reported class rank follows the pattern reported for grades: visually impaired and physically handicapped students report slightly higher ranks than hearing-impaired students, and learning-disabled students report much lower ranks. For example, the percentages of students reporting that they are in the top tenth of their classes are 22 for college-bound seniors in general, 18 for visually impaired students, 17 for physically handicapped candidates, 15 for hearing-impaired individuals, and 4 for those with learning disabilities. Except for a slight inconsistency among hearing-impaired students, the SAT scores of disabled students taking special test administrations show the same direct relationship to class rank as do the data for college-bound seniors in general. Higher rank is associated with higher SAT scores (see lines 24–35 of the table).

□ Although minority students represented 18 percent of college-bound seniors, they were present in lesser proportions in the subgroups of disabled test takers. About 10 percent of students with a hearing impairment, 8 percent of those with a learning disability, 12 percent of those with a physical handicap, and 13 percent of those with a visual impairment were classified as minority (see lines 36–40 of the table).

□ Learning-disabled candidates came from families with relatively high incomes. More than 63 percent of learning-disabled students in 1980–83 came from families with incomes above $30,000, compared to 39 percent of all college-bound seniors, 44 percent of the visually and hearing impaired, and 39 percent of the physically handicapped students. Similarly, the median family income of learning-disabled students is more than $10,000 higher than that of college-bound seniors in general (see lines 41–47 of the table).

□ Compared to college-bound seniors in general, a slightly larger percentage of disabled candidates reported goals associated with two years of postsecondary education and a slightly smaller percentage reported a goal of graduate study. For example, 43 percent of all college-bound seniors report goals of graduate study, while 41 percent of visually impaired students, 37 percent of physically handicapped students, 31 percent of hearing-impaired students, and 26 percent of learning-disabled students do so (see lines 48–50 of the table).

□ Fifty-two percent of college-bound seniors plan on advanced placement in at least one curriculum. The percentages for disabled students ranged from a low of 30 for the learning disabled to a high of 38 for the visually impaired. Whereas a quarter of all college-bound seniors ask for advanced placement in English, 10 percent or fewer of hearing-impaired and learning-disabled students and 17 percent of physically handicapped and visually impaired students make such requests. In general, fewer handicapped than nonhandicapped students apply for advanced placement or course credit in any subject area except art and music, where learning-disabled and visually impaired candidates apply in approximately equal percentages with all college-bound seniors (see lines 51–58 of the table).

□ Similar proportions of nonhandicapped and handicapped students planned to ask the college for special assistance, but students with disabilities intended to ask for help in more areas. One-quarter or more of the handicapped students planned to apply for aid in reading, writing, and mathematical skills. Hearing-impaired and learning-disabled students planned to request such aid more frequently than did students with physical or visual disabilities. For example, special assistance for reading skills was planned by 11 percent of all college-bound seniors, 21 and 23 percent respectively of physically handi-capped and visually impaired students, and 32 and 39 percent respec-tively of hearing-impaired and learning-disabled students (see lines 59–67 of the table).

□ The field of business and commerce was the most popular with handicapped males (favored by 16–25 percent), followed by computer sciences (5–17 percent), engineering (7–12 percent), and social sciences (6–12 percent). Those four fields were also popular with male college-bound seniors in general, who selected engineering (22 percent) business and commerce (18 percent), computer science (8 percent), health and medicine (9 percent), and social sciences (7 percent) as their top choices (see lines 68–76 of the table).

□ Education (13–21 percent), business and commerce (13–15 percent), and health and medicine (12–19 percent) were the preferred choices of disabled females as well as college-bound females in general, though relatively more disabled females preferred education. About 17 percent of hearing-impaired females chose computer sciences, and 13 percent of learning-disabled females intended to major in art (see lines 77–84 of the table).

□ Overall, half of the hearing-impaired students clustered in four intended fields: computer science, business and commerce, educa-tion, and health and medical. Five categories accounted for the choices of half of the learning-disabled students: business and com-merce, engineering, education, art, and undecided. Physically han-dicapped students preferred business and commerce, computer sciences, social sciences, or health and medical fields, while half of all visually impaired students listed their choices as business and com-merce, education, computer sciences, social sciences, or health and medical fields (see lines 85–93 of the table).

□ For all college-bound seniors, and for disabled students as well, the higher mean SAT scores were associated with the fields of social sciences and engineering and the lower mean SAT scores with education and art (see lines 94 to 102 of the table).

□ Physically handicapped students report a preference for living at home rather than in a dormitory, fraternity, or apartment. Students with other disabilities as well as college-bound seniors in general report a preference for living in a dormitory open to both men and women (see lines 103–108 of the table).

□ Fewer physically handicapped and visually impaired students were active in athletics in high school or planned to be active in college than college-bound seniors in general or students with hearing and learning disabilities. However, visually impaired students more often reported being active in high school and planning to be active in college in some extracurricular activities, including art, music, and dance; journalism, debating, and dramatics; and departmental or pre-professional clubs. With those exceptions, handicapped students in this study tended to be less involved in extracurricular activities than college-bound seniors generally (see lines 109–124 of the table).

□ Compared to all college-bound seniors, smaller percentages of hearing-, learning-, or visually disabled candidates had attended public schools (see lines 125–126 of the table).

□ Among the students who rated themselves in the top 10 percent of their classes in various skills and abilities, there were proportionately fewer disabled students. Differences of 10 percent or more occurred for the following categories:

*Athletics*: Fewer physically handicapped or visually impaired students.

*Creative writing*: Fewer hearing-impaired or learning-disabled students.

*Leadership*: Fewer hearing-impaired students.

*Mathematics*: Fewer learning-disabled students.

*Music*: Fewer hearing-impaired students.

*Organizing*: Fewer learning-disabled students.

*Science*: Fewer learning-disabled students.

*Spoken expression*: Fewer hearing-impaired students.

*Written expression*: Fewer hearing-impaired and learning-disabled students.

(See lines 127–140 of the table.)

□ Even more differences of 10 percent or more existed, especially for physically handicapped students, when the skills and abilities of people who rated themselves above average were compared (see lines 141 to 154 of the table).

**Table 4.1 Comparison of college-bound seniors in general and disabled candidates who took nonstandard tests: 1979–80 to 1982–83**

| | All college-bound seniors | Hearing-impaired students | Learning-disabled students | Physically handicapped students | Visually impaired students |
|---|---|---|---|---|---|
| *Number (test takers)* | | | | | |
| (1) Male | 1,898,000 | 357 | 7,294 | 658 | 1,683 |
| (2) Female | 2,038,000 | 395 | 2,707 | 467 | 1,325 |
| (3) Total | 3,936,000 | 752 | 10,001 | 1,125 | 3,008 |
| *SAT scores* | | | | | |
| (4) SAT-V: $\overline{X}$ (SD) | 425(110) | 291(90) | 350(91) | 402(111) | 404(110) |
| (5) Relative Standing[1] | — | -1.22 | -0.68 | -0.21 | -0.19 |
| (6) SAT-M: $\overline{X}$ (SD) | 467(117) | 375(109) | 389(108) | 421(121) | 434(128) |
| (7) Relative standing[1] | — | -0.79 | -0.67 | -0.39 | -0.28 |
| *High school grades* | | | | | |
| (8) Estimated HSGPA[2] | 3.06 | 2.83 | 2.52 | 2.89 | 2.86 |
| (9) Relative standing[1] | — | -0.38 | -0.90 | -0.28 | -0.33 |
| (10) Number with data | 3,651,000 | 537 | 6,246 | 809 | 2,035 |
| (11) Percent of total | 93 | 71 | 62 | 72 | 68 |
| *Academic grades* | | | | | |
| *Years of study (% none)* | | | | | |
| (12) English grade | 3.12 | 2.84 | 2.54 | 3.00 | 2.89 |
| (13) Yrs/study (% none) | 4.0(0) | 4.0(0) | 3.9(0) | 3.9(0) | 4.0(.5) |
| (14) Mathematics grade | 2.85 | 2.73 | 2.43 | 2.69 | 2.71 |
| (15) Yrs/study (% none) | 3.6(0) | 3.6(0) | 3.4(0) | 3.4(0) | 3.4(0) |
| (16) Foreign language grade | 3.02 | 2.80 | 2.19 | 2.85 | 2.81 |
| (17) Yrs/study (% none) | 2.2(14) | 0.9(58) | 1.3(42) | 1.9(24) | 2.1(19) |
| (18) Biological science grade | 3.04 | 2.68 | 2.49 | 2.83 | 2.85 |
| (19) Yrs/study (% none) | 1.4(5) | 1.3(6) | 1.4(7) | 1.3(6) | 1.3(6) |
| (20) Physical science grade | 2.94 | 2.73 | 2.49 | 2.73 | 2.79 |
| (21) Yrs/study (% none) | 1.8(9) | 1.6(12) | 1.5(13) | 1.5(13) | 1.6(12) |
| (22) Social studies grade | 3.20 | 2.88 | 2.66 | 3.05 | 3.01 |
| (23) Yrs/study (% none) | 3.2(1) | 3.2(1) | 3.2(1) | 3.3(0) | 3.3(1) |

[1] In standard deviation units from the mean of college-bound seniors.

[2] HSGPA = High school grade-point average.

# Table 4.1 (continued)

| | All college-bound seniors | Hearing-impaired students | Learning-disabled students | Physically handicapped students | Visually impaired students |
|---|---|---|---|---|---|
| **Class rank (self-report, %)** | | | | | |
| (24) Top tenth | 22 | 15 | 4 | 17 | 18 |
| (25) Second tenth | 22 | 14 | 8 | 16 | 17 |
| (26) Second fifth | 27 | 26 | 20 | 26 | 25 |
| (27) Third fifth | 26 | 35 | 49 | 32 | 32 |
| (28) Fourth fifth | 3 | 9 | 15 | 7 | 6 |
| (29) Lowest fifth | 1 | 1 | 4 | 2 | 2 |
| **SATs/class rank** | V[3]  M[3] | V  M | V  M | V  M | V  M |
| (30) Top tenth | 510  568 | 325  439 | 408  452 | 480  497 | 518  562 |
| (31) Second tenth | 447  496 | 297  405 | 385  439 | 439  462 | 443  480 |
| (32) Second fifth | 413  453 | 306  414 | 375  424 | 404  425 | 410  450 |
| (33) Third fifth | 372  402 | 292  362 | 342  381 | 374  384 | 377  407 |
| (34) Fourth fifth | 348  374 | 273  337 | 323  361 | 331  351 | 338  363 |
| (35) Lowest fifth | 341  368 | 234  329 | 304  335 | 268  314 | 328  358 |
| **Percent minority** | | | | | |
| (36) 1980 | 17.9 | 9.9 | 7.0 | 16.8 | 14.6 |
| (37) 1981 | 18.1 | 7.9 | 8.5 | 11.1 | 12.3 |
| (38) 1982 | 18.3 | 10.1 | 8.6 | 9.2 | 14.0 |
| (39) 1983 | 18.9 | 11.0 | 8.1 | 10.6 | 12.8 |
| (40) 1980–83 | 18.3 | 9.7 | 8.1 | 11.9 | 13.4 |
| **Parental income (%)** | | | | | |
| (41) Below $12,000 | 15.2 | 16.7 | 7.6 | 16.2 | 15.3 |
| (42) $12,000–23,999 | 31.4 | 26.7 | 19.5 | 33.6 | 29.3 |
| (43) $24,000–29,999 | 14.3 | 12.6 | 9.3 | 11.1 | 11.9 |
| (44) Above $30,000 | 39.0 | 44.0 | 63.6 | 39.1 | 43.5 |
| **Median parental income** | | | | | |
| (45) All students | 25,525[4] | 26,900 | 37,736 | 24,085 | 26,603 |
| (46) Black | 13,175[4] | 14,100 | 17,117 | 12,250 | 13,968 |
| (47) White | 27,500[4] | 28,575 | 38,759 | 26,080 | 27,970 |

[3]V = Verbal; M = Math.

[4]The mean of four medians for 1980–83.

*Degree goals (%)*

| | | | | | |
|---|---|---|---|---|---|
| (48) Two-year program | 6 | 8 | 9 | 9 | 6 |
| (49) BA or BS | 38 | 34 | 43 | 41 | 32 |
| (50) Graduate study | 41 | 37 | 26 | 31 | 43 |

*Planning advanced placement in:*

| | | | | | |
|---|---|---|---|---|---|
| (51) English | 17 | 17 | 8 | 10 | 25 |
| (52) Mathematics | 13 | 12 | 9 | 15 | 22 |
| (53) Foreign language | 9 | 7 | 3 | 2 | 11 |
| (54) Biological sciences | 6 | 5 | 5 | 6 | 9 |
| (55) Physical sciences | 6 | 6 | 5 | 5 | 10 |
| (56) Social studies | 11 | 9 | 8 | 8 | 13 |
| (57) Art and music | 7 | 4 | 7 | 4 | 6 |
| (58) Any subject | 38 | 34 | 30 | 32 | 52 |

*Percent who will request special assistance in:*

| | | | | | |
|---|---|---|---|---|---|
| (59) Educational counseling | 44 | 46 | 29 | 40 | 34 |
| (60) Vocational counseling | 37 | 41 | 24 | 35 | 26 |
| (61) Math skills | 25 | 25 | 27 | 26 | 17 |
| (62) Reading skills | 23 | 21 | 39 | 32 | 11 |
| (63) Writing skills | 24 | 25 | 36 | 35 | 14 |
| (64) Study skills | 28 | 27 | 37 | 26 | 23 |
| (65) Part-time work | 37 | 29 | 23 | 30 | 40 |
| (66) Personal counseling | 10 | 13 | 5 | 11 | 4 |
| (67) Totals | 82 | 84 | 82 | 85 | 81 |

*First-choice fields of study (%)*
*Most popular: males[5]*

| | | | | | |
|---|---|---|---|---|---|
| (68) Engineering | 12 | 7 | 12 | 12 | 22 |
| (69) Business/commerce | 17 | 20 | 25 | 16 | 18 |
| (70) Health/medicine | (5) | (6) | (3) | (3) | 9 |
| (71) Computer sciences | 13 | 17 | 5 | 15 | 8 |
| (72) Social sciences | 7 | 12 | 6 | 8 | 7 |
| (73) Undecided | (5) | (6) | (3) | (6) | (5) |
| (74) Architecture | (1) | (-) | 7 | 7 | (3) |
| (75) Education | (4) | (2) | 5 | (5) | (3) |
| (76) Communications | 9 | 10 | (4) | (2) | (3) |

---

[5]Top five choices for each group are listed without parentheses.

# Table 4.1 (continued)

**Most popular: females[6]**

| | All college-bound seniors | Hearing-impaired students | Learning-disabled students | Physically handicapped students | Visually impaired students |
|---|---|---|---|---|---|
| (77) Health/medicine | 20 | 19 | 14 | 14 | 12 |
| (78) Business/commerce | 19 | 13 | 14 | 15 | 13 |
| (79) Education | 8 | 21 | 18 | 13 | 17 |
| (80) Social sciences | 7 | (3) | (6) | 8 | 9 |
| (81) Computer sciences | 6 | 17 | (3) | (7) | (6) |
| (82) Undecided | (5) | 7 | 6 | (5) | (5) |
| (83) Art | (5) | (5) | 13 | (4) | (5) |
| (84) Psychology | (5) | (3) | (5) | 8 | 9 |

**Most popular: all[6]**

| | All college-bound seniors | Hearing-impaired students | Learning-disabled students | Physically handicapped students | Visually impaired students |
|---|---|---|---|---|---|
| (85) Business/commerce | 19 | 15 | 22 | 18 | 15 |
| (86) Health/medicine | 15 | 11 | (6) | 9 | 8 |
| (87) Engineering | 12 | (6) | 9 | (5) | (7) |
| (88) Computer sciences | 7 | 16 | (5) | 13 | 10 |
| (89) Social sciences | 7 | (5) | (6) | 10 | 8 |
| (90) Education | (5) | 13 | 9 | (7) | 10 |
| (91) Undecided | (5) | 6 | 7 | (5) | (5) |
| (92) Art | (4) | (6) | 7 | (3) | (3) |
| (93) Communications | (4) | (1) | (4) | 7 | (7) |

**$\overline{X}$ SAT scores by field of study**

| | All college-bound seniors | | Hearing-impaired students | | Learning-disabled students | | Physically handicapped students | | Visually impaired students | |
|---|---|---|---|---|---|---|---|---|---|---|
| | V[3] | M[3] | V | M | V | M | V | M | V | M |
| (94) Business/commerce | 400 | 446 | 292 | 377 | 339 | 385 | 383 | 422 | 394 | 439 |
| (95) Health/medicine | 428 | 468 | 306 | 376 | 339 | 380 | 404 | 407 | 387 | 435 |
| (96) Engineering | 447 | 536 | 321 | 442 | 374 | 448 | 437 | 535 | 430 | 534 |
| (97) Computer sciences | 416 | 490 | 272 | 373 | 348 | 422 | 392 | 437 | 426 | 482 |
| (98) Social sciences | 459 | 474 | 319 | 382 | 376 | 386 | 471 | 458 | 456 | 460 |
| (99) Education | 392 | 418 | 289 | 362 | 319 | 347 | 378 | 385 | 383 | 409 |
| (100) Undecided | 441 | 480 | 305 | 376 | 351 | 394 | 394 | 407 | 400 | 446 |
| (101) Art | 403 | 420 | 303 | 346 | 343 | 362 | 322 | 340 | 391 | 393 |
| (102) Communications | 445 | 446 | 326 | 344 | 354 | 361 | 412 | 371 | 444 | 432 |

[6]Top five choices for each group are listed without parentheses.

| | | (A) | (B) | (C) | (D) | (E) |
|---|---|---|---|---|---|---|
| *Housing preferences (%)* | | | | | | |
| (103) | At home | 24 | 18 | 17 | 33 | 18 |
| (104) | Single-sex dorm | 22 | 31 | 22 | 24 | 27 |
| (105) | Coed dorm | 35 | 38 | 43 | 28 | 40 |
| (106) | Fraternity/sorority | 4 | 3 | 5 | 2 | 2 |
| (107) | Apartment on campus | 8 | 8 | 8 | 7 | 7 |
| (108) | Apartment off campus | 6 | 2 | 5 | 6 | 6 |
| *Extra curricular activities in high school (%)* | | | | | | |
| (109) | Athletics | 69 | 62 | 68 | 35 | 49 |
| (110) | Ethnic organization | 7 | 7 | 5 | 6 | 6 |
| (111) | Journalism/dramatics/debating | 29 | 20 | 19 | 29 | 33 |
| (112) | Art/music/dance | 43 | 27 | 35 | 32 | 45 |
| (113) | Departmental/professional clubs | 13 | 8 | 8 | 10 | 14 |
| (114) | Religious organizations | 33 | 23 | 26 | 28 | 32 |
| (115) | Social/community clubs | 42 | 35 | 34 | 34 | 41 |
| (116) | Student government | 23 | 14 | 14 | 21 | 22 |
| *Will be active in college in (%):* | | | | | | |
| (117) | Athletics | 56 | 52 | 55 | 24 | 37 |
| (118) | Ethnic organizations | 6 | 5 | 4 | 5 | 6 |
| (119) | Journalism/dramatics/debating | 26 | 18 | 18 | 28 | 31 |
| (120) | Art/music/dance | 36 | 25 | 30 | 29 | 39 |
| (121) | Departmental/professional clubs | 18 | 14 | 13 | 17 | 23 |
| (122) | Religious organizations | 23 | 17 | 16 | 22 | 24 |
| (123) | Social/community clubs | 45 | 37 | 36 | 41 | 43 |
| (124) | Student government | 21 | 14 | 15 | 22 | 22 |
| *Type of high school (%)* | | | | | | |
| (125) | Public | 81 | 70 | 69 | 81 | 75 |
| (126) | Private | 19 | 30 | 31 | 19 | 25 |
| *Skills & abilities: % self-rating in top 10% of class* | | | | | | |
| (127) | Get along | 62 | 53 | 58 | 57 | 53 |
| (128) | Acting | 15 | 15 | 13 | 11 | 14 |
| (129) | Art | 16 | 22 | 18 | 13 | 14 |
| (130) | Athletics | 31 | 34 | 37 | 12 | 19 |
| (131) | Creative writing | 24 | 14 | 13 | 23 | 24 |
| (132) | Leadership | 41 | 25 | 37 | 33 | 34 |
| (133) | Mathematics | 31 | 27 | 14 | 23 | 25 |
| (134) | Mechanics | 17 | 14 | 22 | 13 | 14 |
| (135) | Music | 21 | 7 | 13 | 13 | 22 |

**Table 4.1 (continued)**

| | All college-bound seniors | Hearing-impaired students | Learning-disabled students | Physically handicapped students | Visually impaired students |
|---|---|---|---|---|---|
| (136) Organizing | 34 | 30 | 22 | 30 | 29 |
| (137) Sales | 23 | 14 | 24 | 21 | 23 |
| (138) Science | 23 | 15 | 13 | 17 | 20 |
| (139) Spoken expression | 30 | 15 | 25 | 31 | 33 |
| (140) Written expression | 31 | 15 | 13 | 29 | 28 |
| *Skills & abilities (%): self-rating as above average* | | | | | |
| (141) Get along | 90 | 83 | 86 | 85 | 82 |
| (142) Acting | 39 | 43 | 34 | 32 | 38 |
| (143) Art | 41 | 49 | 41 | 35 | 38 |
| (144) Athletics | 61 | 64 | 65 | 24 | 42 |
| (145) Creative writing | 58 | 40 | 38 | 56 | 57 |
| (146) Leadership | 71 | 51 | 66 | 53 | 62 |
| (147) Mathematics | 60 | 54 | 37 | 45 | 52 |
| (148) Mechanics | 41 | 37 | 48 | 27 | 35 |
| (149) Music | 43 | 17 | 30 | 32 | 47 |
| (150) Organizing | 71 | 65 | 53 | 60 | 63 |
| (151) Sales | 54 | 36 | 54 | 48 | 49 |
| (152) Science | 52 | 40 | 37 | 41 | 45 |
| (153) Spoken expression | 64 | 42 | 57 | 63 | 68 |
| (154) Written expression | 65 | 46 | 38 | 61 | 61 |

# 5

# Views of Disabled Students

☐ *Marjorie Ragosta and Bruce Kaplan*

A survey was conducted to obtain directly from disabled students information that could help in evaluating testing accommodations for them. It was designed to answer the following questions: How do disabled test takers become aware of special test administrations? How satisfactory are these administrations? How can they be improved? What kinds of SAT and GRE questions are most difficult for people with disabilities? How do the accommodations provided in SAT and GRE special administrations compare to those provided in college testing?

Two versions of the questionnaire were developed: one for SAT test takers and one for GRE test takers. The SAT questionnaire was sent to all candidates using special administrations of the SAT during the 1982–83 school year except that, because of the large number of LD students needing only extra time, only a random sample of those students was contacted. Forty percent of hearing-impaired, physically handicapped, and visually impaired students returned the SAT questionnaire, but only a quarter of LD contacts responded. Of 2,555 people contacted, 856 returned their SAT questionnaires.

The SAT respondents included a smaller percentage of males and a larger percentage of higher scoring students than had the sample contacted initially. Like those obtained in other studies in this series (Bennett, Ragosta, & Stricker, 1984; Bennett, Rock, & Kaplan, 1985), the data from the SAT sample in this study showed the test performance of visually and physically handicapped respondents to be generally better than that of LD respondents, with hearing-impaired respondents earning the lowest scores. Respondents with sensory disabilities (visual or hearing impairments) tended to have been diagnosed at birth or shortly afterwards, whereas the majority of LD respondents had been diagnosed in elementary school. Physically handicapped respondents had been diagnosed at all ages—about one-quarter at birth and another quarter in high school.

The GRE questionnaire was sent to all candidates who took special administrations of the exam in the 1983–84 school year. Of 368 people contacted, 268 completed the questionnaire, for a response rate of 73 percent.

The GRE sample contained many respondents with relatively new or newly diagnosed disabilities. Half of the physically handicapped and learning-disabled respondents and more than one-quarter of the visually handicapped respondents reported that their disabilities had not been diagnosed until after they had left high school. There were no GRE respondents who had classified themselves as hearing impaired at the time of the special test administration.

Overall, both SAT and GRE respondents tended to report that their disabilities had little or no effect on their academic performance, with some reporting a moderate effect and very few a severe effect. Respondents with learning disabilities tended to report a moderate effect more often than a slight effect. Hearing-impaired and LD respondents reported severe effects more often than did visually or physically handicapped respondents—a pattern reflected in their test scores.

In the remainder of this chapter, we will discuss the respondents' awareness of special test administrations of the SAT and GRE, their satisfaction with testing accommodations, and test questions that posed special problems for them. Finally, we will include a comparison of accommodations made for college testing and admissions testing.

## Testing accommodations

□ □ Respondents reported whether or not they had been aware of special accommodations for handicapped students at the time they first took the SAT or GRE. A follow-up question asked from what source(s) information was obtained. As might be expected, GRE respondents were more likely to be aware of special testing accommodations available for disabled people than were the high school students taking the SAT. Whereas 68 percent of SAT respondents were unaware of them, only 19 percent of GRE respondents were. Although all of the respondents to this questionnaire eventually took the SAT under special testing arrangements, some handicapped students who have taken a standard SAT administration have reported not knowing that special accommodations exist (Ragosta, 1980). The current data can give us no estimate of the percentage of disabled students who did *not* find out about special accommodations and who took regular test administrations or were afraid to take the tests because of their disabilities. The current surveys can, however, give us an estimate of the sources of information available to disabled test takers.

The source of knowledge about special testing accommodations for the SAT is relatively consistent across all disability groups, with 84 to 93 percent of respondents being made aware of special testing by either high school counselors or special education teachers. For 16 percent of the visually impaired test takers, an agency for the handicapped provided information, a much larger percentage than for any other group. The third largest source of information was "others," including parents, neighbors, friends, relatives, medical professionals, and school administrators.

The source of knowledge about special accommodations for the GRE looks quite different. Only 5 percent of high school students reported learning about special test accommodations through Educational Testing Service, but about two-thirds of GRE respondents reported that their information came from the GRE *Information Bulletin*. LD students were less likely than others to use that source, however, and were more likely than physically or visually impaired respondents to use "other" sources, such as their parents.

## Satisfaction with testing accommodations

**SAT survey**  Over all, 94 percent of respondents to the SAT survey reported that their special test arrangements were satisfactory. That satisfaction ranged from a high of 97 percent for physically disabled students to a low of 88 percent for students with hearing disabilities.

Although respondents were overwhelmingly positive, we will concentrate here on why some were dissatisfied. This knowledge will help us improve services to disabled students. Sources of dissatisfaction included: (1) the test itself; (2) time and space considerations; (3) problems with test administration; and (4) other difficulties.

1. The test itself was reported as hard to comprehend, too advanced, having vocabulary that was too difficult, unfair to hearing-impaired test takers, and different from the tests taken by non-handicapped people. Two respondents mentioned not being able to

take advantage of the test disclosure service available to non-handicapped test takers.

2. Some respondents reported they would have liked a different room, or a less noisy or busy room, in which to take the test. Other handicapped students felt that the test should not have been timed, that the test was given before the student was ready, that the students didn't have enough time, and that extra time was needed.

3. Other conditions with which handicapped respondents were unhappy included not having a reader, not having an interpreter, having a reader who was impatient, or having a reader who would not reread questions for the test taker. In other cases, respondents reported that some test booklets were incomplete, a large block answer sheet was missing, or the braille graphs were incorrect.

4. A fourth group of problems related to respondents' feelings in the testing situation. Students reported wanting to take the SAT with others despite the refusal of the school district and that they thought it was unfair to be treated differently.

**GRE survey**   Overall, 86 percent of GRE respondents were satisfied with the special testing accommodations provided them, and that level of satisfaction was almost uniform across disability groups.

GRE respondents reported similar kinds of difficulty in the same four categories as the SAT respondents had noted:

1. The recorded (cassette) math section was described as inadequate. Braille, cassette, and print versions of the test did not always match. For some of the math questions, there was no braille diagram to describe the concept. Several respondents had difficulty with separate answer sheets.

2. The largest number of complaints (13) had to do with the need for extra time. One braille test taker reported, "It is difficult to read over four pages of braille and answer four questions at the end. Braille does not permit skimming." Additional respondents reported fatigue or pain as the result of stress over the long period of testing. One respondent suggested that we give "half the test one day, the other half the next day. Fatigue affected my score." Some respondents were concerned about the space provided for them. A small hand desk was inconvenient for a test taker with a large-print test and large-block answer sheet. Another respondent needed space to write while standing. A third had requested a special desk but had not been able to get one. Finally, some respondents were unhappy with their location. "Too noisy," "distracting," "too hot," "too cold," and "too many

interruptions" were the comments received. One student wrote, "You can't concentrate when placed in a busy hallway at the entrance to the building."

3. There were frequent complaints about readers: the reader was hard to follow, was not literate, did not pace the test, was no good, was unsatisfactory, read too fast, would not reread questions, kept talking to the test taker, or made guttural sounds that were distracting. Two respondents reported receiving the wrong test or incorrect braille graphs. Other complaints about test administration included not enough resting time, not enough lighting, and the test location being too far from handicapped parking.

4. Several respondents felt dissatisfied because, despite special accommodations, they still received low scores. Another respondent had wanted to test under standard conditions but was not allowed to. One respondent wrote, "They sat me in the front of the room in my wheelchair where over two hundred students could see me. I felt like a performer on stage."

**Discussion**  Dissatisfaction arising from the tests themselves—especially complaints about the difficulty level—is inevitable among people taking tests like the SAT and GRE. Standardized tests are likely to be difficult for some nonhandicapped people as well as for handicapped people. However, one disability group, hearing-impaired students, has been shown to perform well below the general population on the SAT, especially on the verbal portion. That consistent finding is probably the result of the well-documented English-language deficiencies of deaf people. The college performance of hearing-impaired students, however, appears to be better, perhaps in part because college support services often include sign language interpreters. It may be that testing accommodations geared to the special needs of some deaf students could help compensate for their language deficiencies and bring their SAT scores more into line with their college performance. More research is needed on this issue.

The criticism that the tests are different from those taken by nonhandicapped people is partly true. The forms of SAT tests used for special test administrations have a history of use for the general population, but they are retired from that use for test security reasons when they are selected for use in special administrations of the SAT.

For some national administrations of the SAT and GRE, a test disclosure service enables test takers to pay for a copy of the test, a copy of their own answer sheet, and a scoring key. The disclosure service is available only on certain national test-administration dates because once the material has been made public, it cannot be used again. Since special administrations of the SAT are offered on any day throughout most of the year, a test-disclosure policy for those administrations would result in the need to retire thousands of tests each year. Clearly, that is not possible. In the 1985–86 school year, the College Board and ETS initiated a new, experimental service for learning-disabled college candidates taking the SAT. For those LD students requiring only extra time (up to one and a half hours), special test administrations will be offered on national test dates. Participants who elect this special testing option will be taking tests identical to those offered to nonhandicapped people. They will be able to take advantage of the question-and-answer service whenever that service is available to other candidates.

An alternate strategy for monitoring one's own test performance is the use of actual released forms of the tests for preparation prior to taking either the SAT or GRE. *Ten SAT's* (College Entrance Examination Board, 1983) contains 10 actual tests; *Practicing to Take the GRE General Test* (Educational Testing Service, 1984) contains three tests used in recent years. There is a small charge for each of the publications. These publications are not now available in braille, large-type, or cassette versions, but these may become available in the future.

The question of how much time to allow in special test administrations is a serious one on which there is considerable disagreement. On the one hand, unlimited time allows disabled test takers an opportunity to complete the test—but that opportunity is not given to people in standard testing situations. On the other hand, time limits—wherever they were set—would continue to penalize the most severely handicapped test takers.

Test space is a much less controversial issue. Testing accommodations should be comfortable, the noise and distraction levels should be minimal, and space enough for large-type or braille testing materials should be available. The 1984–85 *Guide to Administering ETS Tests* (Educational Testing Service, 1984) deals with just such issues. Increased monitoring and subsequent improvement of special test administrations could result from a process by which disabled students could inform ETS of the adequacy of their testing accommodations. One method would be the use of an evaluation form sent to the disabled student along with other testing information; a second might be the establishment of a hot line for disabled students encountering problems.

Additional complaints of respondents concern readers and, occasionally, incorrect testing materials. On the second point, we know that errors do occur. They occur very, very infrequently, and every effort will be made to see they happen even less frequently in the future. Complaints about readers have led to discussions about a manual of guidelines for readers. The manual has already been started and will soon be in print.

Despite the aforementioned problems with special test administrations, the satisfaction of most students was gratifying.

## Difficult test questions

☐ Recipients of the survey questionnaires were asked what kinds of SAT and GRE test questions were most difficult *because of their disabilities*. Their replies are summarized in Table 5.1.

Overall, more than 25 percent of SAT and GRE respondents reported that no test questions were rendered more difficult by their disabilities. One physically handicapped individual explained his answer this way: "Of course there were areas of the SAT that were

**Table 5.1  Difficult test questions for disabled students overall and by disability**

|  | | *Disability* | | | |
|---|---|---|---|---|---|
|  | *Total* | *Hearing* | *Learning* | *Physical* | *Visual* |
| *SAT survey* | | | | | |
| N(respondents) | 857 | 123 | 276 | 131 | 307 |
| *Percent reporting  difficult test questions:* | | | | | |
| None | 29 | 24 | 11 | 66 | 33 |
| Lots of reading | 43 | 40 | 57 | 13 | 43 |
| Reading comprehension | 37 | 51 | 54 | 8 | 28 |
| Vocabulary | 27 | 59 | 44 | 8 | 9 |
| Mathematics | 20 | 18 | 27 | 24 | 14 |
| Graphics | 15 | 11 | 9 | 8 | 24 |
| *GRE survey* | | | | | |
| N (respondents) | 261 | — | 59 | 66 | 120 |
| *Percent reporting  difficult test questions:* | | | | | |
| None | 28 | — | 2 | 61 | 25 |
| Verbal ability | 13 | — | 31 | 9 | 7 |
| Quantitative ability | 23 | — | 34 | 23 | 18 |
| Analytic ability | 20 | — | 29 | 17 | 14 |
| Graphic material | 31 | — | 19 | 11 | 48 |
| Lots of reading | 44 | — | 66 | 18 | 44 |

*Note:* Percentages do not sum to 100 because respondents often identified more than one type of difficult question.

harder for me, just as they are for others, because they are not my best subjects. However, no particular difficulty with questions was related to my disability." When difficult test items were identified, the hardest items for one group might be the easiest for another. For example, 59 percent of SAT respondents with hearing disabilities reported most difficulty with vocabulary items, while only 8 or 9 percent of physically handicapped or visually impaired respondents agreed.

**Hearing-impaired respondents**    These respondents reported that vocabulary (59 percent), reading comprehension (51 percent), and lots of reading (40 percent) created problems on the SAT. Perhaps their language problems are serious enough to deter hearing-impaired people from graduate education: no takers of special GRE administrations in 1983–84 categorized themselves as hearing impaired.

**Learning-disabled respondents**    Lots of reading (57 percent), reading comprehension (54 percent), and vocabulary (44 percent) created difficulty, according to LD respondents at the SAT level; lots of reading was also a problem for 66 percent at the GRE level. Verbal, analytical, and quantitative questions on the GRE were perceived as almost equally difficult, about one-third of respondents checking each of these categories.

**Physically handicapped respondents**    Almost two-thirds of SAT and GRE respondents with these disabilities reported that no questions were made more difficult by their handicaps. Respondents at both levels reported mathematics or quantitative ability questions more difficult than other types of questions.

**Visually impaired respondents**    At the SAT level, lots of reading was perceived as difficult by 43 percent of these respondents and reading comprehension by 28 percent. In addition, 24 percent reported difficulty with questions containing graphic material. At the GRE level, graphic material was a problem for 48 percent and lots of reading for 44 percent.

The perceived difficulties reported by disabled test takers appear reasonable in light of their disabilities. Language development problems encountered by hearing-impaired people could account for their difficulty with vocabulary on the SAT. Problems in reading—a characteristic of most learning-disabled individuals—may be responsible for their perception that excessive reading causes the most difficulty on SAT and GRE tests. Large quantities of reading and graphic material create problems for people with visual impairments.

These data on perceived difficulties may provide guidance in interpreting the results of item-analysis studies.

# Comparison with college testing

☐ ☐ Only 472 of the more than eight hundred SAT respondents (57 percent) reported attending college the year after their special test administrations. A larger proportion of GRE respondents (74 percent) were attending college the year they took their special GRE administrations. As might be expected, SAT respondents who reported freshman grades were a less able group than those applying to graduate school. Overall, the modal response from the SAT survey indicated students earning grade-point averages from 2.5 to 2.9, while the GRE survey's modal response was in the highest category, above 3.5.

## SAT respondents

☐ College tests are offered less frequently than the SAT and GRE in special versions such as braille, cassette, or large type. For example, 31 percent of SAT special administrations in this sample were given with large-type tests, but only 8 percent of respondents reported ever using a large-type test in college. More use of the regular-type test is reported for college testing. Whereas 58 percent of respondents had used a regular-type SAT, 81 percent had used a regular-type college test. Ten percent of college-attending respondents reported sometimes taking a different final exam from that given to their classmates.

An overall pattern that generally held up across disability categories was the use of special testing conditions. Larger percentages of respondents reported having extra time and a separate room for SAT testing (84 and 72 percent, respectively) than for college testing (51 and 34 percent, respectively). Conversely, larger percentages of respondents reported using an amanuensis, a reader, an interpreter, or special equipment for college testing than for SAT testing. More specific results are discussed below by disability group.

1. *Hearing-impaired students.* Almost all such students took the regular-type version of the SAT, many with extra time or in a separate room. About one-fourth had an interpreter for instructions. In college, about 88 percent reported using regular-type tests, but 29 percent reported sometimes or often taking a different examination.

2. *Learning-disabled students.* Fewer LD respondents reported using cassette or large-type tests in college (7 and 5 percent, respectively) than for SAT testing (32 and 19 percent, respectively). A larger percentage (76 percent) reported using regular-type tests in college than in SAT testing (61 percent). Six percent of LD students reported sometimes or often taking a different examination in college. Whereas 90 percent of LD respondents reported using extra time for the SAT, only 45 percent reported having extra time for college testing. A similar reduction was reported in the use of a separate testing room.

3. *Physically handicapped students.* These respondents reported no use of braille, cassette, or large-type tests in college, yet a few had used these versions of the SAT. Although 79 percent of respondents had extra time for the SAT, only 61 percent reported having extra time in college. Eighty-five percent had separate accommodations for SAT testing, but only 45 percent reported separate accommodations for college testing. Sixteen percent reported the use of special equipment for college testing, though none was used for SAT testing.

4. *Visually impaired students.* More of these students (81 percent) used regular-type tests in college than elected to use regular-type SATs (22 percent). Whereas 64 percent of visually impaired respondents used large-type versions of the SAT, only 14 percent reported ever using large-type tests in college. Fewer were given extra time or a separate room in college (66 and 32 percent, respectively) than were given those accommodations for SAT testing (91 and 77 percent, respectively). In college testing, more use was made of readers and special equipment. For example, only 5 percent of visually impaired respondents reported the use of readers for the SAT, while 31 percent used them for college testing.

## GRE respondents

☐ Overall, respondents used braille and large-type tests more often for GRE testing (7 and 28 percent, respectively) than for college testing (1 and 8 percent, respectively). Cassette and regular-type tests were used more often in college testing (12 and 82 percent, respectively) than they were selected for GRE testing (6 and 61 percent, respectively). Twelve percent of GRE respondents reported taking different examinations in college. Specific results are reported by disability.

1. *Learning-disabled respondents.* The most evident differences in accommodations for GRE and college testing were in extra time and separate rooms. Whereas 98 percent of LD respondents used

extra time for the GRE, only 53 percent ever used it for college tests. A similar difference appeared for the use of a separate room. Also, 24 percent of LD respondents reported the use of a reader for the GRE, while only 11 percent reported that use in college. Fourteen percent of LD students reported sometimes taking different examinations from the rest of the class.

2. *Physically handicapped respondents.* Fewer physically handicapped students (84 percent) reported taking regular-type tests in college than selected them for the GRE (94 percent). In college, 8 percent reported some use of cassette tests and the same percentage reported sometimes taking different tests. Fewer reported having extra time and a separate room for college tests (47 and 46 percent, respectively) than for GRE testing (76 and 94 percent, respectively).

3. *Visually impaired respondents.* Fewer visually impaired respondents reported using braille or large-type tests in college (3 and 16 percent, respectively) than on the GRE (14 and 53 percent, respectively). More respondents reported using cassette or regular-type tests in college (20 and 77 percent, respectively) than on the GRE (9 and 28 percent, respectively). Fifteen percent reported sometimes taking different examinations. Fewer visually impaired students used extra time and a separate room in college (54 and 56 percent, respectively) than for the GRE (87 and 93 percent, respectively). Amanuenses, readers, and special equipment were reportedly used more frequently in college testing (45, 44, and 41 percent, respectively) than for the GRE (35, 28, and 19 percent, respectively).

## SUMMARY

For respondents to the SAT and GRE questionnaires, the special testing accommodations they received were largely satisfactory. The greatest sources of dissatisfaction reported by handicapped respondents were the difficulty of the tests and not having enough time to finish—problems that might well be reported by nonhandicapped people as well. Less frequent complaints concerned procedural errors and poor testing environments, two problems that should occur with less frequency if we increase our capabilities for monitoring special test administrations.

Respondents with hearing, learning, physical, and visual disabilities reported their areas of greatest difficulty in admissions tests. For hearing-impaired respondents (SAT only), vocabulary and reading comprehension were hardest. The amount of reading and problems of reading comprehension were difficulties reported by learning-disabled respondents. Almost two-thirds of physically handicapped respondents reported that no questions were made more difficult by their handicaps. Graphic material and large amounts of reading created difficulty for visually impaired respondents.

In a comparison of admissions and college testing, the College Board, the Graduate Record Examinations Board, and ETS appear to offer as much in the way of testing accommodations for disabled individuals as do colleges and universities, and often more. Multiple versions of admissions tests permit personal choice, and extra testing time may help to compensate for slower modes of testing or decreased speed of performance resulting from a disability.

# 6

# Admissions Decisions

## ☐ *Warren W. Willingham*

The various studies in this series provide useful information concerning the reliability and validity of admissions test scores of handicapped examinees, but ultimately, decisions regarding the testing of disabled applicants are not likely to be based upon measurement considerations alone. How tests are used and the consequences of their use must be considered as well, because the prohibition against flagging implied by the 504 regulations presents a problem of conflicting values.

On the one hand, it is important to protect the privacy of handicapped individuals and to guard against any possible bias in admissions decisions. On the other, a principal function of standardized admissions tests is to provide a common, objective standard against which to evaluate fairly the academic promise of all applicants. Not only can consequential exceptions to that standardization that are allowed to pass unnoticed be unfair to other students, they may also jeopardize the integrity of the tests and the admissions process. An important consideration in weighing these conflicting values is the degree of disadvantage handicapped persons may experience in admissions.

To what extent standards are applied equally to handicapped applicants is the central theme of a study of undergraduate admissions decisions reported in this chapter. The first step in answering this question is to establish, on the basis of school grades and test scores, the likelihood that a given applicant would be admitted to a

This chapter is based upon a study separately funded by the College Board.

particular college. The second is to determine whether handicapped applicants are admitted as frequently as would be expected. If they are not, that would suggest a possible bias in the selection process.

It may not be possible, of course, to distinguish the effect of a flag on a score from knowledge of a student's record. Without further information, it would be unwarranted to conclude that an apparent pattern of bias in admissions decisions affecting a particular group with flagged scores was due to the flags per se. A flag on a test score might have a negative influence if an admissions officer perceived the score as "too high" as a result of the test's nonstandard administration. But it is equally plausible to assume that it was the knowledge of a handicapping condition rather than the flag itself that influenced the decision. In any event, it is readily argued that flags can facilitate a bias by making it easier to identify an applicant as handicapped when that fact might not otherwise have been obvious. So one reason for this study was to examine the possibility of unintended consequences of flagging. This analysis focuses on several specific questions:

1. How do handicapped applicants stand on SAT scores and high school grades compared to other applicants at the same institution?
2. Are handicapped applicants more or less likely to be admitted to college than nonhandicapped applicants with comparable high school grades and SAT scores?
3. Does the pattern of expected versus actual admission rates vary for important subgroups of handicapped students—by type of disability, men and women, or students at different levels of admissibility?
4. Does the pattern of expected and actual admission rates vary by type of college—especially control (public-private), size, selectivity level, and availability of special programs for handicapped students?
5. In making admissions decisions regarding handicapped applicants, do institutions place greater or lesser weight on high school grades and SAT scores than is the case for nonhandicapped students?

## Related research

☐ Two areas of research have some relevance for the present study. One concerns the effect on decision making of the knowledge that someone is handicapped, the other bears on the admission of handicapped students to college. The NAS Panel on Testing of Handicapped People was especially concerned with the former issue, which might be called the *labeling effect.* It commissioned a review of research on that topic, a brief version of which appears as an appendix to its report (Guskin, 1982).

Three types of labeling studies are relevant even though they speak to possible effects in employment selection rather than college admissions. Some research has indicated that the more severe the handicap, the less employable the individual was perceived to be (Nickoloff, 1962; Rickard, Triandis, & Patterson, 1963). Such studies demonstrate the potential for prejudice in selection, but they are hard to interpret because they are so far removed from real situations.

In other studies (Krefting & Brief, 1977; Rose & Brief, 1979), students rated simulated job resumes in which applicants were labeled "handicapped" or "nonhandicapped," all other facts remaining constant. The results revealed no consistent negative effect of disability. In fact, among inexperienced applicants, those with disabilities were somewhat preferred.

There appears to be more evidence of selection bias in research involving personnel directors in natural situations (Farina & Felner, 1973; Johnson & Heal, 1976). The tactic used in these studies was to send confederates out on job interviews, in half of which they identified themselves as disabled but otherwise well qualified. Several lines of evidence suggested that "handicapped" applicants were treated in a biased fashion, receiving fewer offers of jobs, more discouragement by the interviewer, and so on.

After reviewing the entire body of research available on this topic, the NAS panel concluded:

> The research literature on the effects on decision making of knowing a person is handicapped shows varied results. Knowing that an individual is handicapped may, in different situations, have negative, positive, or negligible effects. In short, research does not support the common assumption that knowledge of a person's handicapping condition works to that person's disadvantage. Opinions expressed in the panel's open meeting were similarly varied. (Sherman & Robinson, 1982, p. 24)

A second body of research concerns the admissions process. One question of interest is to what extent handicapped individuals may be underrepresented in higher education and whether there is any evidence of improved access since the promulgation of the 504 regulations. The best source of information on the college enrollment of handicapped people is the annual survey of college freshmen carried out by the Cooperative Institutional Research Program (Astin, Green, Karn, & Shalit, 1985). Those surveys indicate that from 1978 to 1985, the percentage of handicapped freshmen increased from 2.6 to 7.7. Closer analysis suggests that the form in which the question was put to the freshmen affected their replies. In fact, 88 percent of the overall increase occurred in those two yearly intervals when there was a change in the wording of the question, whereas only 12 percent occurred over the five intervals when there was no change. Thus it is not clear whether there was any significant change from 1978 to 1985 in the access of handicapped persons to higher education. It is worth noting, however, that in 1978 the same proportion of handicapped and nonhandicapped college freshmen (about three out of four) reported that they were accepted by their first-choice institution (President's Committee on Employment of the Handicapped, undated).

One might also look to institutional admissions practices and policies for signs of possible changes affecting handicapped students. Two surveys separated by six years (American Association of Collegiate Registrars and Admissions Officers [AACRAO] and the College Board, 1980; Breland, Wilder, & Robertson, 1986) contained parallel questions concerning handicapped students. The later report indicated some increase in the recruiting of handicapped students, but typically that increase was not nearly as large as that reported for other subgroups such as minorities, adults, and students with special talents. Colleges said that they were making fewer exceptions to admissions standards for handicapped applicants in 1985 than in 1979, but the same trends were reported in the cases of minority students, alumni children, and athletes. This trend may not represent a real tightening of admissions standards; heightened recruiting efforts and the general enrollment picture suggest the opposite.

Neither of these two lines of research—college admissions nor the effects of labeling—seems to offer any very clear-cut conclusions as to how handicapped students fare in the admissions process. Part of the problem is that much of this work is based upon what respondents say they do or would do in a given situation. Such sentiments are significant as expressions of personal values or policy positions, but they are not an accounting of actions and can not necessarily be generalized to real situations. Some of the studies cited do clearly suggest that handicapped status can affect an observer's behavior and judgment. How often that occurs in college admissions and to what net effect is an open question. For that reason, the present study complements what we now know about this topic.

## Procedure

☐ ☐   The central question this study asked was whether colleges use comparable standards in reaching admissions decisions for handicapped and nonhandicapped applicants. Admissions officers report that high school performance and admissions test scores receive by far the most weight in admissions decisions (AACRAO and the College Board, 1980). Accordingly, the approach followed here was to determine for individual colleges the likelihood that an applicant would be admitted with given SAT scores and school grades and then to determine whether a handicapped applicant with the same scores and grades was equally likely to be admitted. Information on admissions decisions was available from the College Board's Summary Reporting Service (SRS). Information on handicapped applicants came from a separate ETS file of applications for special test administrations.

The analysis was based primarily upon 532,750 applicants to 121 institutions that participated in the Summary Reporting Service in 1983 and received 12 or more reports of scores on special test administrations. There were 1,539 handicapped applicants for whom data were complete. A preliminary analysis indicated that for predicting admissions decisions it made relatively little difference whether Verbal and Mathematical scores were kept separate or combined into one SAT total score, so the total score was used in order to simplify analysis and reporting. Self-reported information on school performance—the most recent grade in four subjects and a rough approximation of class rank—was available from the Student Descriptive Questionnaire. The two types of information were combined into a composite High School Grade (HSG).

Larger and smaller institutions were defined here, arbitrarily, as those having a freshman class above or below one thousand, respectively. An admission rate of .50 was considered the dividing line between colleges of higher and lower selectivity. Each of the 121 institutions was coded as to whether or not it reported a special program designed for each of the four types of handicaps (Liscio, 1986a, 1986b; Mangrum & Strichart, 1985; Rawlings, Karchmer, & DeCaro, 1983). The analysis followed a model described and used extensively in the Personal Qualities Project (Willingham, 1985; Willingham & Breland, 1982). It involves these steps: A group of applicants is identified for evaluation (for example, physically disabled students who applied to small colleges). An estimate is made of the likelihood that each individual in the group will be admitted, using a logistic function for the college in question. The summation of these estimates yields the proportion of the group that would be expected to be admitted purely on the basis of the academic measures. This figure is compared with the proportion of the group that was actually admitted; the result is a residual selection rate. For example, if one would expect to admit 46 percent of a group on the basis of academic credentials but 54 percent were actually admitted, the residual selection rate would be +.08.

# Results

## Descriptive data

☐    Overall, 62 percent of the applicants to these 121 institutions were admitted; the corresponding figure in a recent national survey was 75 percent (Breland, Wilder, & Robertson, 1986). Thus this sample of colleges leans to the more selective, but it includes a good representation of institutions at all levels of selectivity. As might be expected, this sample of handicapped students had somewhat higher SAT scores than the total population of handicapped students who take the SAT under special conditions of administration. The 504 regulations (Dept. of Health, Education, and Welfare, 1977a) stipulate that an institution "may not make use of any test or criterion for admission that has a disproportionate, adverse effect on handicapped persons unless the test has been validated" (Sect. 0, p. 22683).

Therefore, it is useful to examine the standing of these handicapped applicants relative to that of other applicants to the same college. Figure 6.1, which shows for each handicapped group a distribution of $z$ scores for SAT and HSG, is based upon the full group of applicants to the college to which the handicapped student applied. Visually impaired and physically handicapped applicants have approximately the same mean SAT scores as other applicants to the same colleges. The test scores of learning-disabled applicants were lower, and those of hearing-impaired applicants were substantially lower. On HSG, handicapped applicants ranked lower than other fairly consistently. Overall, about two handicapped applicants out of three ranked higher on SAT scores than on HSG relative to the nonhandicapped applicants.

In determining whether the same standards are employed in admitting handicapped applicants, it is useful to ask first, to what extent SAT scores and HSG are correlated with admissions decisions. The median correlations were essentially the same—.37 for SAT, .36 for HSG (multiple $R$ .45). The figure for HSG probably underestimates the true effect of high school record on admissions decisions because this index is based upon self-report information and so is certainly an incomplete representation of the student's work in secondary school.

In order to compare the predictability of admissions decisions for handicapped and nonhandicapped applicants, the predicted decisions

**Figure 6.1   Mean, standard deviation and range for SAT and HSG of handicapped applicants relative to those of all applicants at the college of application**

*z Score*

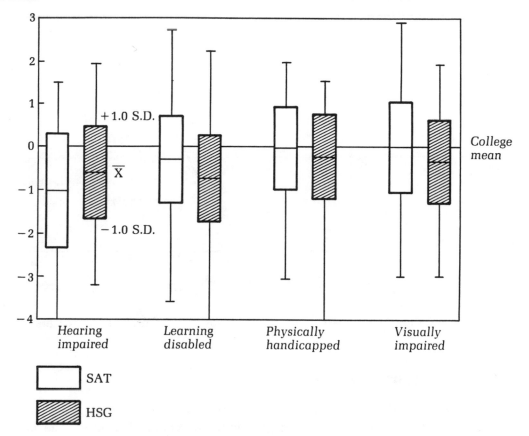

(based on the logistic functions for individual colleges) were correlated with the actual decisions. For all applicants, the correlations for SAT, HSG, and the two combined were .55, .55, and .61, respectively; corresponding correlations for handicapped applicants were .51, .51, and .57—lower to a marginal but statistically significant degree.

Figure 6.2 is a visual representation of the increasing probability of an applicant's being admitted as SAT and HSG increase. This figure confirms that for applicants with the same SAT and HSG, admissions decisions for handicapped students correspond quite closely to those for nonhandicapped applicants. The next step was to examine various subgroups of handicapped applicants in search of

**Figure 6.2   Logistic functions showing the probability of admission for handicapped and nonhandicapped applicants, based on best weighted composite of SAT and HSG within colleges**

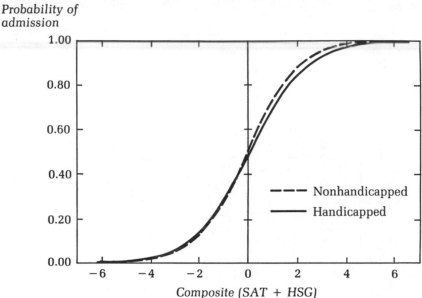

*Probability of admission*

significant positive or negative residual admission rates (the actual minus the predicted proportion admitted).

## Residual analysis

☐   Figure 6.3 shows predicted (white bars) and actual admission rates (cross-hatched bars) for the four handicapped groups. The dashed lines indicate the admission rate for all applicants at the institution to which the handicapped students applied, weighted according to the number of handicapped applicants that applied to each. The key comparison is between the predicted and actual rate. In two cases that difference was significant. The group of hearing-impaired applicants was small but had a large and significant positive residual (.20). The learning-disabled group was very large; its residual was small and negative (−.05), but also highly significant.

The data did not indicate any important sex differences, nor did there appear to be any significant difference in residual rates for public and private institutions or for institutions that are more or less selective. Physically handicapped and visually impaired applicants did show a significant negative residual in the smaller institutions.

**Figure 6.3    Predicted versus actual admission rates for handicapped applicants**

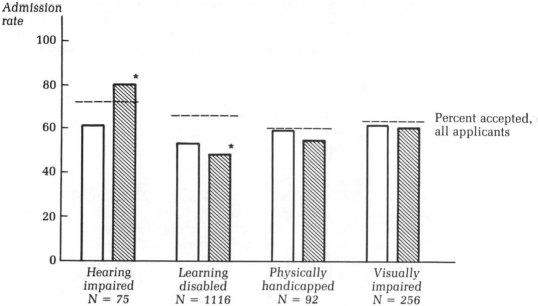

*Difference between predicted and actual significant at .05 level.

Predicted

Actual

This "size effect" suggests that students with disabilities that require special equipment or resources may be less likely to be admitted in smaller institutions that are perhaps less able to provide those resources.

Is a college more likely to accept a disabled student, other things being equal, if it has developed a program specifically to serve students with that disability? Hearing-impaired students who applied to institutions that have special programs for the deaf were far more likely to be admitted (97 percent) than would be predicted (66 percent) on the basis of their test scores and grades, but that result was based largely upon data from a single college. No significant program effects were found for the other three handicapped groups.

Another useful way to break down the handicapped groups is to analyze residual admission rates according to what test form the examinee took (braille, cassette, and so on). If residual admission rates are more negative for students who took those test forms that depart from the regular edition, that result might suggest discrimination in admissions against students who are more severely disabled. For the most part, test form was not associated with significant residuals. A small group of learning-disabled students who took the large-type edition of the SAT did show a significant negative residual (.53 predicted, .33 actually admitted). These applicants may have presented a picture of having unusual difficulty in academic work: their HSG was half a standard deviation lower than the normal pattern of underachievement for LD students.

Residual admission rates for the four handicapped groups were also examined within three ranges: where the probability of admission was low, uncertain, or high on the basis of SAT and HSG. The main finding of interest was the fact that the small negative residual for the learning-disabled group was observed only in the uncertain and high ranges. One possible explanation is that admissions officers may be somewhat skeptical of high academic credentials for this group on the basis of some factors visible in the student's background, academic record, references, and the like. Braun, Ragosta & Kaplan (1986b; see also chapter 9) found that learning-disabled students who ranked high on SAT and high school grades made substantially lower freshman grades than predicted.

Skepticism as to the academic potential of a learning-disabled applicant could be tied specifically to a relatively high test score if it is not quite believed. In order to test that hypothesis, residual admission rates were compared for LD students who had discordant score patterns (high SAT, low HSG as opposed to high HSG, low SAT). The analysis indicated that score pattern played no role in admissions decisions. This result makes the SAT discounting hypothesis seem implausible.

## SUMMARY

Analysis of actual admission decisions is relevant to several issues: the relative standing of handicapped applicants, the comparable use of test scores in selection decisions, the comparable outcome of decisions for handicapped and nonhandicapped applicants with similar qualifications, and the possibility of test-score flags facilitating any bias in admissions. The principal findings of the study were as follows:

1. Compared to other applicants to the same colleges, the physically handicapped and visually impaired groups were slightly below

average with respect to their academic qualifications, learning-disabled students were lower, and hearing-impaired applicants ranked lowest. In general, handicapped applicants tended to rank significantly lower on HSG than on SAT.

2. Overall, the selection process for handicapped applicants was comparable to that for the nonhandicapped in the sense that decisions followed quite closely what one would expect from HSG and SAT scores. Admissions decisions predicted on the basis of either SAT or HSG correlated slightly less with actual decisions in the case of handicapped applicants than for others. This result suggests that factors other than SAT and HSG play a slightly larger role in the case of handicapped applicants, though not necessarily to their advantage.

3. Within the total group of handicapped applicants, there were three pockets of students for whom the actual admissions rate was significantly different from that predicted on the basis of all-applicant logistic equations:

   a. hearing-impaired applicants were substantially more likely to be admitted (particularly those applying to special college programs);
   b. learning-disabled students who ranked in the mid- to upper range among applicants at the college to which they applied were slightly less likely to be admitted;
   c. admissions were lower than predicted for a relatively small number of visually impaired and physically handicapped students applying to the smaller institutions.

4. Discordant score patterns (high SAT, low HSG; high HSG, low SAT) were examined in order to evaluate the possibility that relatively high test scores of learning-disabled students might be discounted by admissions officers. Decisions were not found to differ according to score pattern.

The main finding of this study is that the handicapped applicants were admitted on much the same basis as the other applicants, though in some instances particular groups of handicapped applicants were somewhat more or somewhat less likely to be admitted than would be expected. To the extent that there were differences in admissions decisions between handicapped and nonhandicapped students, those different decisions seem to be based upon the full record of the student and her or his perceived likelihood of success rather than on a particular item of information. The findings are inconsistent with the assumption that admissions officers focus special attention on test scores.

# 7

# Psychometric Characteristics

☐ *Randy Elliot Bennett,*
*Donald A. Rock,*
*Bruce A. Kaplan, and*
*Thomas Jirele*

This chapter reports data on four psychometric characteristics relevant to establishing the comparability of scores for handicapped and nonhandicapped groups on the SAT and the GRE General Test. The first psychometric characteristic considered is level of test performance. Differences in performance are important for at least two reasons. First, they suggest the need to study more closely other psychometric characteristics. While performance differences do not necessarily affect comparability, they may be caused by test tasks that do not function in the same way for one group or another. Second, performance level often affects other psychometric characteristics, and knowledge of performance level permits data relevant to these characteristics to be more meaningfully interpreted.

The frequency with which different groups of students complete a test is also an important factor in comparability. The SAT and the GRE General Test are intended primarily to be power tests; that is, tests on which most examinees complete all items. Differences in completion rates across groups may imply a problem in the comparability of scores because examinees from one group may be less likely to reach items that they otherwise might answer correctly. Even for extended-time administrations, speed is a concern: the amount of extra time afforded may not be enough to permit the same proportion of disabled students to complete the test as their nondisabled peers do.

The third psychometric characteristic studied, *reliability*, refers to the precision or accuracy with which a test measures. Differences in the precision of measurement across groups can have negative effects for the group less accurately measured, thereby affecting score comparability. For example, if an admissions test measured less precisely for deaf than for hearing students, the admissions officer's decision to admit a deaf student would be subject to a greater likelihood of error than would decisions for nonhandicapped applicants.

The last psychometric characteristic considered is unexpected differential performance. This concept is derived from the notion that items on a test measuring a single attribute should measure that same attribute across groups (Shepard, 1982b). Items found to measure different attributes in different groups are biased in the sense that, for some groups, they may be assessing factors irrelevant to the purpose of assessment. Total scores based on a substantial number of such items would obviously not be comparable.

# Procedure

## Subjects

☐ Data for evaluating the psychometric characteristics of the SAT and the GRE General Test were derived from databases of handicapped students categorized by disability and test format. For the SAT, data were drawn from special administrations of Forms WSA3 and WSA5 occurring from March 1980 through June 1983. Nine disability-by-test-format groups constructed from this database contained sufficient numbers of students (roughly one hundred or more) to support dependable results and justify study. These were, for the *regular-type* edition of the test (with extra time and, in some instances, use of adaptive devices such as magnifiers), learning-disabled, visually impaired, hearing-impaired, and physically handicapped students; for *large type*, visually impaired and learning-disabled test takers; for *braille*, visually impaired examinees; and for *cassette* and *cassette and regular type*, learning-disabled students. Sample sizes averaged across test forms were about 100 for learning-disabled students using cassettes and for visually impaired students using braille; 160 for LD students using large type; 200 for visually impaired and hearing-impaired students using regular type and for LD students using cassette and regular-type editions; 290 for physically handicapped students; and 2,650 for LD students using the regular-type edition (see Table 7.1).

**Table 7.1  Sample sizes and acronyms used to denote SAT study groups**

| Acronym | Group | WSA3 sample size | WSA5 sample size |
|---------|-------|------------------|------------------|
| HIR | Hearing-impaired students using regular-type edition | 287 | 150 |
| LDC | Learning-disabled students using cassette edition | 107 | 113 |
| LDCR | Learning-disabled students using cassette and regular-type editions | 192 | 253 |
| LDL | Learning-disabled students using large-type edition | 185 | 136 |
| LDR | Learning-disabled students using regular-type edition | 2,983 | 2,316 |
| NH | High school students using regular-type edition in standard timed administrations | 35,424 | 33,161 |
| PHR | Physically handicapped students using regular-type edition | 346 | 230 |
| VIB | Visually impaired students using braille edition | 98 | 105 |
| VIL | Visually impaired students using large-type edition | 486 | 498 |
| VIR | Visually impaired students using regular-type edition | 223 | 175 |

**Table 7.2  Sample sizes and acronyms used to denote GRE study groups**

| Acronym | Group | N |
|---------|-------|---|
| NH | Nonhandicapped students using regular-type edition in timed national administrations | 20,499 |
| PHN | Physically handicapped students using regular-type edition in timed national administrations | 108 |
| VIL | Visually impaired students using large-type edition in special administrations | 151 |
| VIN | Visually impaired students using regular-type edition in timed national administrations | 188 |

For the GRE General Test, data were drawn from standard administrations of Form C–3DGR–3 in October 1981 and April 1982 and from special administrations occurring from October 1981 through June 1984. Sufficient data for study were available for three groups of handicapped students: visually impaired students taking the national administration, visually impaired students taking extended-time, large-type administrations, and physically handicapped examinees taking the national administration. Respective sample sizes for the three groups were 188, 151, and 108 (see Table 7.2).

To evaluate the psychometric characteristics of the SAT and the GRE General Test properly, some reference population was needed. Without such a population, the typical behavior of the tests would not be known, and any departures from this behavior by subpopulations could not be detected. For the SAT, two reference groups were used. The first consisted of the 5.1 million high school students taking all forms of the SAT offered between March 1980 and June 1983. The second group included 35,424 high school students in Texas and California who took Form WSA3 under typical testing conditions during October 1974 and 33,161 high school students who took WSA5 nationally in December of that same year. The high school students taking WSA3 performed better than those taking the SAT during the period 1980–83 on both the Verbal and Mathematical tests, whereas those taking WSA5 performed similarly to students taking the test during the period 1980–83.

For the General Test also, two reference groups were used. The first was composed of 441,654 students taking administrations of the test during the time period October 1981 to June 1984. The second standard group was a subset of this larger group consisting of 20,499 individuals who took Form C–3DGR3 under typical testing conditions in October 1981 and April 1982. These two reference samples differed only minimally in their General Test performances.

## Method

☐   For all analyses, values for each handicapped group in turn were contrasted with comparable values for the appropriate nonhandicapped reference group. For level of performance, values are reported as differences in standard deviation units from the mean for nonhandicapped examinees taking the test during the same time period. The statistical significance of these differences is not reported because the extremely large reference sample sizes insure that even trivial results will be significant. As suggested by Cohen (1969), however, a .2 standard deviation difference can be used as a minimum guideline for identifying practically meaningful differences.

For test completion, two indices, the percentage of students completing the section and the percentage finishing three-quarters of it, were computed and presented as ratios of handicapped to non-handicapped students, where both groups took the same test form. These two indices were computed for each of four separately timed SAT sections (two Verbal and two Mathematical) and six separately timed GRE sections (two Verbal, two Quantitative, and two Analytical). Because neither the percentage completing the test nor the percentage completing three-fourths of it is a fully satisfactory measure of speed, the two are considered jointly in the evaluation of test timing.

For the reliability analyses, comparisons are made with non-handicapped students taking the same test form. The standard error of measurement is reported instead of the reliability coefficient because the latter is affected by the amount of test-score dispersion in a group and, as such, is limited as a comparative measure of precision across groups. The standard error of measurement is relatively unaffected by score variance and, therefore, is better suited to the comparison of measurement accuracies.

The analysis of differential item operation was intended to detect broad, general classes of items that function differently across groups. Differential functioning was defined as a difference in performance between groups of equal developed ability. To detect the possible presence of such item types, a two-stage method was used. First, items were organized logically into clusters on the basis of item characteristics that might prove unusually troublesome for particular groups of handicapped examinees and of groupings typically used in the SAT and the General Test development processes. Cluster structures used for the SAT included one for the Verbal section based on item type and three for the Mathematical section based on the presence of graphical material, the type of mathematical content, and the degree of reading load. For the General Test, six structures were assessed: one Verbal structure based on item type; four Quantitative structures based on item type, content, graphics, and reading load; and one Analytical structure based on item type. For both tests, structures were composed of between three and seven item clusters. The several types of items included in the SAT and GRE are illustrated in Appendix B.

To examine the performance of clusters, we computed the regression of each item-type cluster score of the appropriate total test score for nonhandicapped students taking the same test form, and we used it to develop a prediction of performance for each handicapped group. If the difference between predicted and actual cluster means for a handicapped group was larger than .2 standard deviation (cf. Cohen, 1969), the cluster was tagged for item-level study.

Once the study of clusters was completed, we conducted the second stage of analysis, in which items belonging to deviantly operating clusters were studied to determine whether the cluster itself defined a potentially biased item type (that is, whether most members of the cluster showed differential effects consistent with the cluster result) or, alternatively, whether only a few aberrant items accounted for the unusual cluster performance. For each deviant item cluster, logistic regression was used to contrast the item performance of the handicapped group with a random sample of five hundred non-handicapped students taking the same test form to determine whether, after adjusting for differences in total test score, each group had an equal probability of passing the item. Differences in item performance were judged to exist when statistically significant discrepancies between the two groups occurred; these differences were considered to be of practical consequence when the groups' probabilities of passing differed by at least .1.

It is important to note that the sample sizes for the handicapped groups used to study these four psychometric characteristics are generally very small and that, as a result, the values for these groups may not be stable. To increase confidence in the dependability of results, departures from the nonhandicapped reference population were considered seriously for the SAT only if they occurred in both of two samples taking different forms of the test. Because of their co-occurrence, such findings are probably stable results that will manifest themselves in other samples from the same disability group and on other forms of the SAT. For the General Test, a second sample was not available, so differences observed on this test need to be viewed all the more cautiously.

# SAT results

□ □ Table 7.3 presents level of performance, test completion, and reliability statistics for handicapped students taking special administrations of the SAT. For the purposes of this chapter, values have been averaged across test forms. The original values for each form can be found in Bennett, Rock, and Kaplan (1985).

## Level of performance

□ Table 7.3 reports the Verbal and Mathematical performance of each of the nine disability groups as compared to that of nondisabled students taking the SAT during the same time period. The values in the table

**Table 7.3 Performance level, test completion, and reliability, averaged across forms for different groups of handicapped students taking the nonstandard SAT**

| | *Verbal* | | | |
| Group | *Performance, in SD units from nonhandicapped mean* | *Ratio of percent completing test* | *Ratio of percent completing 75% of test* | *Standard error of measurement, in items* |
| --- | --- | --- | --- | --- |
| HIR | −1.18 | 1.22 | 1.01 | 3.80 |
| LDC | −0.81 | 1.22 | 1.02 | 3.75 |
| LDCR | −0.69 | 1.13 | 1.02 | 3.81 |
| LDL | −0.64 | 1.13 | 1.01 | 3.82 |
| LDR | −0.48 | 1.11 | 1.01 | 3.79 |
| NH | 0.00 | 1.00 | 1.00 | 3.74 |
| PHR | 0.02 | 1.21 | 1.02 | 3.80 |
| VIB | −0.01 | 1.25 | 1.02 | 3.80 |
| VIL | −0.07 | 1.21 | 1.02 | 3.78 |
| VIR | −0.07 | 1.17 | 1.02 | 3.78 |
| | *Mathematical* | | | |
| HIR | −0.73 | 1.35 | 1.02 | 3.15 |
| LDC | −0.93 | 1.15 | 0.99 | 3.10 |
| LDCR | −0.81 | 1.15 | 1.00 | 3.12 |
| LDL | −0.74 | 1.18 | 1.02 | 3.12 |
| LDR | −0.50 | 1.22 | 1.01 | 3.12 |
| NH | 0.00 | 1.00 | 1.00 | 3.12 |
| PHR | −0.21 | 1.30 | 1.02 | 3.15 |
| VIB | −0.53 | 1.20 | 1.01 | 3.07 |
| VIL | −0.16 | 1.32 | 1.03 | 3.13 |
| VIR | 0.03 | 1.35 | 1.03 | 3.09 |

Note: All values are weighted averages taken across two samples of students, each taking a different form of the SAT. Ratios are of handicapped to nonhandicapped students.

See Table 7.1 for an explanation of acronyms. For level of performance, NH denotes all students taking forms of the SAT administered between March 1980 and June 1983. For standard errors of measurement and test completion statistics, nondisabled students are examinees taking the same test form.

indicate the difference between the handicapped and nondisabled students' means, expressed in units of the standard deviation of the nondisabled group. On the Verbal scale, the mean performance of the three visually impaired groups (VIB, VIR, VIL) and of the physically handicapped group (PHR) is little different from that of the non-handicapped reference group (NH). In contrast, the learning-disabled

(LDR, LDCR, LDC, LDL) and hearing-impaired (HIR) groups have substantially lower mean scores than the reference group did, usually by more than half a standard deviation. This pattern generally appears to hold for the Mathematical scale also, with the exception of visually impaired students taking the braille format (VIB). Though it is not discernible from the averaged value, these students score just beyond the .2 criterion on one test form and dramatically beyond it on the other. (Physically handicapped students, whose *averaged* scores also exceed the .2 criterion, performed differently from the reference group on one—but not both—test forms.)

## Test completion

☐ Two test completion statistics are presented in Table 7.3. The first is the ratio of the percentage of members in each disability group completing the test to the same value for nonhandicapped students taking the test form. The second is the ratio of the percentage of handicapped students completing 75 percent of the test to the reference group value. Each of these values is averaged across the two sections that compose each SAT scale (Verbal and Mathematical) and across forms of the test.

For both statistics, values of 1.00 indicate equal percentages completing the section (or three-fourths of it) for both groups, while those above 1.00 suggest greater completion rates for disabled students. When both indices of speed are considered, it is clear that, in comparison to the reference samples, no disability group is consistently disadvantaged by lack of time (that is, no group produces values of less than 1.00 on both indices). On the contrary, the data suggest that the SAT may in some instances be more of a power test for disabled than for nondisabled students.

## Reliability

☐ Table 7.3 also presents internal-consistency standard errors of measurement (SEMs) for handicapped and nonhandicapped students taking WSA3 and WSA5; these values are presented in terms of the number of items correct. For the reference group (NH), the raw-score SEM's are 3.74 for the 85-item Verbal and 3.12 for the 60-item Mathematical section. Without exception, the SEMs for all handicapped groups are virtually identical to these values, differing by only a few hundreths of an item.

## Unexpected differential item performance

☐ The study of Verbal and Mathematical cluster functioning involved the analysis of 162 pairs of cluster performances (9 groups × 18 clusters on each of two test forms). In these 162 performances, only five instances of deviant cluster functioning consistent across both SAT forms were detected; all were related to the Mathematical scale. Two instances, both involving visually impaired students taking the braille version of the test, were indicative of differential difficulty; that is, of students performing lower than expected on the basis of their total Mathematical scores. These instances occurred on a cluster composed of multiple-choice items containing graphics and on multiple-choice items classified as "miscellaneous" (items intended to assess relatively novel content, including elementary number theory, logic, new symbol systems, set theory, and newly defined functions and operations).

In addition to these two instances of differential difficulty, three occurrences of differential easiness were discovered. These instances involved a cluster composed of quantitative-comparison items with algebra content, which appeared unexpectedly easy for learning-disabled students using the cassette format and for hearing-impaired examinees using the regular-type format; and a cluster of items considered low in reading load because it was composed only of mathematical symbols, which was unexpectedly easy for the hearing-impaired group.

When the individual items composing these five errant cluster performances were analyzed, 22 of 61 item performances showed statistically significant effects consistent with cluster results. Ten differentially difficult items were associated with the clusters found unexpectedly difficult for visually impaired students taking the braille exam; 12 differentially easy items were linked to the clusters found easy for hearing-impaired and learning-disabled examinees. These items did not appear to dominate any particular cluster on both SAT forms, suggesting that no broad class of items posed a problem for handicapped students. However, the effects were of practical importance for most statistically significant items (19 of 22). The most serious effects were associated with items that were differentially difficult for visually impaired examinees.

What kinds of items produced negative effects for these

---

The results reported in this section are based on a reanalysis of data originally reported in Bennett, Rock, and Kaplan (1985). The reanalysis is fully described in Bennett, Rock, and Kaplan (1987).

students? The items had a variety of characteristics: some involved figures, while others presented special symbols; still others included potentially unfamiliar number systems or changes in translation from print to braille. For example, the item that showed the largest difficulty effect asked the examinee about the tally system. In this system, the number 5 is represented by four vertical lines crossed by a diagonal, 7 is denoted by the symbol for five followed by a group of two vertical lines, 10 is shown by two symbols for five, and so on. One plausible cause for the observed difficulty effect is that this symbol system is less familiar to blind students. A second probable contributing factor is that the versions presented to blind and sighted students were slightly different. Because the print symbol for five could not be represented easily as a raised-line drawing within the braille text of the item, it was denoted by a group of five *un*crossed braille symbols for the letter *l.* To reflect this modification, the text of the item was changed from "How many uncrossed tallies would be used in the representation of 29 in this system?" to the somewhat more complex "How many tallies *not in sets of five* would be used in the representation of 29 in this system?" (emphasis as in original). The added linguistic complexity of this modification and the novelty of the tally system are likely causes of the item's observed differential difficulty for blind students.

What produced the differential easiness effects for hearing-impaired and learning-disabled students? One possible explanation is that the implicated clusters were disproportionately loaded with items placed at the end of test sections. Clusters containing these items might be easier for hearing-impaired and learning-disabled students because extended time permitted them to reach these items in greater proportions than their nonhandicapped peers. When the individual items composing the clusters were examined, differential easiness was found to occur for some, but not all, of the items appearing at the ends of test sections, suggesting that extra time alone is not a sufficient explanation for differential operation.

A second possible explanation for this effect for hearing-impaired students is that they performed better on certain clusters because they are comparatively free of language.

## GRE results

Table 7.4 presents level of performance, test completion, and reliability statistics for handicapped students who took special and national administrations of the GRE General Test.

**Table 7.4 Performance level, test completion, and reliability averaged across sections for different groups of handicapped students taking the GRE**

| | *Verbal* | | | |
| Group | *Performance, in SD units from nonhandi- capped mean* | *Ratio of percent completing test* | *Ratio of percent completing 75% of test* | *Standard error of measurement, in items* |
|---|---|---|---|---|
| NH | .00 | 1.00 | 1.00 | 3.59 |
| PHN | −.03 | 1.02 | 1.00 | 3.61 |
| VIL | .12 | 1.06 | 1.02 | 3.60 |
| VIN | −.10 | 1.00 | 1.00 | 3.62 |
| | *Quantitative* | | | |
| NH | .00 | 1.00 | 1.00 | 3.07 |
| PHN | −.43 | .90 | .98 | 3.16 |
| VIL | −.11 | 1.04 | 1.01 | 3.10 |
| VIN | −.13 | .98 | 1.00 | 3.12 |
| | *Analytical* | | | |
| NH | .00 | 1.00 | 1.00 | 2.95 |
| PHN | −.31 | .91 | .93 | 2.97 |
| VIL | .28 | 1.12 | 1.03 | 2.89 |
| VIN | −.13 | .89 | .96 | 2.95 |

Note: Ratios are of handicapped to nonhandicapped students.

See Table 7.2 for an explanation of acronyms. For VIL, the reference group is composed of all nonhandicapped students taking General Test forms from October 1981 through June 1984, whereas for VIN and PHN, the group consists of nonhandicapped students taking C–3DGR3 in contemporaneous national administrations. For reliability and test completion, the reference group is nonhandicapped students taking C–3DGR3 in national administrations.

## Level of performance

☐ In Table 7.4, the performance of three handicapped groups on the Verbal, Quantitative, and Analytical scales of Form C–3DGR3 is compared to that of nonhandicapped students. Like those given for the SAT, the values indicate the difference between the handicapped and nondisabled students' means, expressed in units of the standard deviation of the nondisabled group. Because the group of visually impaired examinees taking the large-type exam (VIL) represents an accumulation of administrations given over the period October 1981 to June 1984, the performance of these individuals is compared to that of nondisabled students taking the General Test during the time span. The remaining two handicapped groups are derived from national administrations offered in October 1981 and April 1982; they are compared with nondisabled examinees taking contemporaneous administrations.

On the Verbal scale, the handicapped samples closely approximate reference-group performance. Mean scores for this scale range from –.03 (for PHN) to .12 (for VIL) standard deviation from the mean. For the Quantitative scale, only the physically handicapped–national administration group (PHN) evidences performance substantially below (by .43 standard deviation) the reference average. Finally, scores for Analytical sections are lower than average for the physically handicapped group (by .31 standard deviation) and higher than average for the visually impaired–large-type sample (by .28 standard deviation).

## Test completion

☐    Table 7.4 presents the ratio of each disability-group index to its reference-group counterpart. Each of these values is averaged across the two sections that compose each General Test scale (Verbal, Quantitative, and Analytical). Consideration of both indices supports several inferences. First, almost without exception, the handicapped group participating in the special administrations program (the visually impaired–large-type [VIL] sample) appears to complete the test (or three-quarters of it) in equal or slightly greater proportions than the reference group. For the Analytical scale in particular, it seems evident that this group had slightly more time than necessary to complete the test.

For the two national administration groups, however, the data are somewhat different. On the Analytical sections, slightly smaller proportions of the physically handicapped (PHN) and visually handicapped (VIN) samples than of their nonhandicapped peers reach the completion points. Less obvious because of the averaging of indices across sections within a scale are similar differences for the physically handicapped group on the first Quantitative section.

It is not possible to determine from the data why these groups completed the test in smaller proportions than their nonhandicapped peers did. On the one hand, the differences might be due to factors of speed unrelated to scholastic ability. For example, because of their motor impairments, physically handicapped examinees might take longer to record their answers, to perform the written computations necessary for some Quantitative problems, and to draw diagrams helpful in solving certain Analytical items. Similarly, visually impaired students might take longer to read test directions and items and to locate the correct boxes on the answer sheet.

As an alternative explanation, it is possible that differences in developed ability are responsible for the observed disparities in test completion. The sections in which completion differences appear belong to the scales on which both physically and visually impaired examinees score lowest. These groups may move more slowly through these sections simply because they are less adept in the abilities being measured. Data from construct and predictive studies presented in later chapters may shed some light on these competing hypotheses.

## Reliability

☐ Table 7.4 also presents internal-consistency standard errors of measurement for handicapped and nonhandicapped examinees taking C–3DGR3. For nonhandicapped examinees, the raw-score SEMs are 3.59 for the 76-item Verbal scale, 3.07 for the 60-item Quantitative scale, and 2.95 for the 47-item Analytical scale. Without exception, the SEM's for the handicapped groups are virtually identical to these values, differing in the worst case by only nine hundredths of an item.

Because internal consistency reliabilities can be spuriously affected by speed, standard errors derived from parallel-forms reliability coefficients were also computed. These values, too, suggested no differences of practical importance in measurement precision across groups.

## Unexpected differential item performance

☐ The analysis of Verbal, Quantitative, and Analytical cluster functioning involved the study of 63 cluster performances (21 clusters × 3 groups). Only one instance of deviant cluster functioning was found, for one of two clusters in the Analytical scale composed of logical-reasoning items. For the visually impaired students taking the large-type edition, the cluster was differentially easy.

When the four items composing the cluster were studied individually, two showed significant and practically important evidence of differential easiness. Since a second logical-reasoning cluster showed no indication of differential operation, the finding of cluster deviancy would appear to be attributable to these two isolated items, not to the general functioning of the item type. Analysis of the content of the two items did not reveal any obvious reason why they should be unexpectedly easy for visually impaired students; however, both were placed at the end of one of the Analytical sections. Given that this group's completion rates for that scale were higher (relative to the rates of nonhandicapped students) than for the other scales, the finding of differential easiness may result from extended time.

## SUMMARY

This chapter discussed four psychometric characteristics of the SAT and the GRE General Test for handicapped groups. Data on these characteristics are important in evaluating the comparability of scores for disabled and nondisabled examinees.

With respect to level of performance, the first characteristic described, handicapped groups varied widely. In general, visually impaired students achieved mean scores roughly comparable to those of other students typically taking the SAT and GRE. Whereas those with physical handicaps performed similarly to nondisabled students on special administrations of the SAT, a group with the same general disability classification taking a national administration of the GRE performed somewhat less well. Finally, learning-disabled and hearing-impaired students taking special SAT administrations performed least well of all the groups studied.

The second psychometric characteristic examined was whether disabled students finish admissions tests as often as their non-handicapped peers. For the SAT, no disability group was found to be disadvantaged by lack of time; on the contrary, there were indications that special administrations make the SAT more of a power test for handicapped groups under some circumstances. For the GRE General Test, physically handicapped and visually impaired students taking timed national administrations were slightly less likely to complete selected test sections, while visually impaired students taking a special administration were sometimes more likely to complete the test than were their nonhandicapped peers.

Analyses of the reliability of the SAT and the GRE General Test found measurement precision for all handicapped groups to be comparable to that of the reference population, suggesting that this potential type of score incomparability probably need not be of concern.

The final psychometric characteristic studied was unexpected differential performance, the analysis of which permits identification of broad item classes (based on features that might prove troublesome for handicapped people) that may not measure the ability assessed by the overall test. Differential performance was evaluated through a two-stage procedure in which the operation of groups of items was first investigated, and the individual items composing deviantly operating groups were then studied. This analysis revealed no indication of broad, general classes of items that functioned differently for handicapped students, though a number of individual items were identified that proved of serious differential difficulty for blind students taking the braille version of the SAT.

The localization of idiosyncratically operating items to visually impaired students taking the braille exam suggests that extra care should be taken in the development of test forms and their translation to braille. In addition, the possibility should be considered of pilot testing brailled exams before they are put into actual service. The aim of such testing would be to detect any items tapping inappropriate skills, confusing instructions, errors in brailling, or other irrelevant sources of difficulty. Pilot testing need not be carried out with large numbers of examinees; more desirable would be individual or small-group administrations in which examinees could discuss potential difficulties as they arise directly with test development staff. Finally, additional analyses of the operation of items on the braille exam should be considered in order to identify more definitely the critical dimensions of mathematical items that cause differential performance in this group.

# 8

# Construct Validity

☐ *Donald A. Rock,*
*Randy Elliot Bennett,*
*Bruce A. Kaplan, and*
*Thomas Jirele*

This study is primarily concerned with the comparability of test scores obtained by handicapped and nonhandicapped examinees on the Scholastic Aptitude Test and the Graduate Record Examinations General Test. *Comparability*, as used in this context, refers to the invariance of the respective tests' factor structure across handicapped and nonhandicapped populations. In addition to their implications for score interpretation, the results of this study provide evidence relevant to the appropriateness of the assumptions used in companion item-bias studies described in chapter 6. Those studies examined the extent of unexpected differential item performance when each of the handicapped groups was contrasted with a nonhandicapped group after matching on total Verbal, Quantitative, and (in the case of the GRE) Analytical scores. Under these conditions, similar performance across groups on individual items would be expected. This comparison of groups matched on total test score assumes that these scores have the same meaning for all groups. Otherwise, the finding of differential item performance may simply reflect the results of matching on different abilities.

The investigation of what a test measures and whether or not what it measures is invariant across different populations is a problem in construct validity. One standard method for empirically verifying the construct validity of a given test relies on the application of factor analytic methodology to either individual test items or item parcels.

Factor-analysis methodology is particularly appropriate for investigating the invariance of the "meaning" of test scores across populations because the ability factors that are assumed to underlie or contribute to variation among individuals are considered to be the more basic measures of the separable abilities that combine to yield the total scores. Therefore, if the relationship between the test items and their respective underlying factors remains the same across handicapped and nonhandicapped populations, and if the inter-relationship among the factors (basic abilities) themselves also is invariant across populations, then one can conclude that there is no internal evidence that the test scores mean different things in the different populations.

Rather than factoring individual items, in this study we scored *parcels* (groups of items arranged by type) and then used maximum-likelihood-confirmatory factor analysis to verify the stability of the factor structure of these parcels across populations. Scores based on item parcels rather than individual items were factor analyzed because relationships between dichotomously scored items tend to be non-linear and as a result yield more factors than are present in the data. These pseudofactors are sometimes called *difficulty factors*, since items with similar difficulty indices tend to cluster regardless of whether they are measuring the same constructs. Item parcels, however, provide continuous scores and tend to exhibit linear rela-tionships with one another.

It should be noted that a two-factor model was fitted to the SAT data, while a three-factor model was fitted to the GRE data. More complicated models could be, and have been, fitted using both the SAT and GRE (for example, see Rock, Werts, & Grandy, 1982). Given the relatively small sample sizes used in the present investigation, there easily could be a tendency to overfit (that is, to identify spurious or trivial factors). We have taken the approach of first defining a well overdetermined model based on the major factors and then inspecting the residual variances and covariances in order to identify any remaining method factors. The factor models will be well overdeter-mined since the verbal and quantitative factors in the SAT and the verbal, quantitative, and analytical factors in the GRE will be iden-tified or "marked" by several item parcels.

## Procedure

### SAT subjects

☐ From the fall of 1978 through July 1983, the Admissions Testing Program's Services for Handicapped Students offered two forms of the SAT, designated as WSA3 and WSA5, to handicapped students requesting special administrations throughout the United States. Data from both forms were used in this study. By using both data sets, we could focus attention on those findings that are replicated across forms. Such repeated occurrences are less likely than single instances to be artifacts associated with a particular test form or sample of subjects.

Students requesting special administrations of the SAT during the study period fell into five major disability groups: the visually impaired (VI), the physically handicapped (PH), the hearing impaired (HI), the learning disabled (LD), and the multiply handicapped. Types of special administrations offered included braille, large type, cassette, regular type, and cassette and regular type together. All special administrations included extra time. The reference group used in this study consisted of high school students taking Forms WSA3 and WSA5 under standardized (timed) conditions. Table 7.1 (page 85) shows the sample sizes and the acronyms used to denote each of the study groups.

## GRE subjects

☐ During the period from October 1981 through June 1984, the Graduate Record Examinations Program administered one form of the General Test, designated as C–3DGR3 in alternative formats. This form, in addition to 11 other regular-type forms, was also used for handicapped students requiring only extra time. In addition, it was administered (along with 18 others) under standard conditions to students participating in national administrations. Because of its use in both special and standard administrations, Form C–3DGR3 was selected for analysis in the current study and in a companion item-bias study (Bennett, Rock, & Jirele, 1986).

The nonhandicapped group used in this study consisted of 20,499 individuals taking Form C–3DGR3 under typical testing conditions in October 1981 and April 1982. The combined average scores of students taking these administrations are comparable to those of students generally taking the test in recent years (Bennett, Rock, & Jirele, 1986). Students whose levels of English proficiency were questionable were omitted from the analysis. Table 7.2 (page 85) lists the acronyms used to denote the groups selected for study. Also listed there are the sample sizes for each group.

## Factor models and methods

☐ Tables 8.1 and 8.2 show the factor models assumed to underlie the SAT and the GRE respectively. In the case of the SAT, a two-factor model based on verbal and quantitative factors was hypothesized and

**Table 8.1   Factor model underlying the SAT**

| | Factor | |
|---|---|---|
| *Marker variables* | *Verbal* | *Mathematical* |
| Antonyms–A | * | 0 |
| Antonyms–B | * | 0 |
| Antonyms–C | * | 0 |
| Sentence completion–A | * | 0 |
| Sentence completion–B | * | 0 |
| Sentence completion–C | * | 0 |
| Analogies–A | * | 0 |
| Analogies–B | * | 0 |
| Analogies–C | * | 0 |
| Reading comprehension–A | * | 0 |
| Reading comprehension–B | * | 0 |
| Reading comprehension–C | * | 0 |
| Quantitative comparison–A | 0 | * |
| Quantitative comparison–B | 0 | * |
| Quantitative comparison–C | 0 | * |
| Regular math–A | 0 | * |
| Regular math–B | 0 | * |
| Regular math–C | 0 | * |

* Factor loading to be estimated.

0 Variable has no loading on this factor.

tested. Similarly for the GRE, a three-factor model consisting of the Verbal, Quantitative, and Analytical sections of the General Test was hypothesized and tested. For both tests, the factors composing the models are marked by the item types that comprise the Verbal, Quantitative, and (in the case of the GRE) Analytical scales. For both Verbal scales, these types are antonyms, sentence completion, analogies, and reading comprehension. The SAT Quantitative scale is made up of quantitative-comparison items and regular math. The GRE Quantitative scale consists of quantitative-comparison, discrete-quantitative, and data-interpretation items. Finally, analytical-reasoning and logical-reasoning questions compose the GRE Analytical scale. These various item types are illustrated in Appendix B.

Each SAT item type is further subdivided into three parcels. This is also true of the GRE, with the exception of sentence completion, data interpretation, and logical reasoning, which are divided into two parcels each. Parcels within an item type are balanced for difficulty.

The asterisks in Tables 8.1 and 8.2 indicate that a factor loading is to be estimated. Conversely, the *0*s denote that the indicator variable

**Table 8.2  Factor model underlying the GRE**

| Marker variables | Verbal | Factor Quantitative | Analytical |
|---|---|---|---|
| Antonyms–A | * | 0 | 0 |
| Antonyms–B | * | 0 | 0 |
| Antonyms–C | * | 0 | 0 |
| Sentence completion–A | * | 0 | 0 |
| Sentence completion–B | * | 0 | 0 |
| Analogies–A | * | 0 | 0 |
| Analogies–B | * | 0 | 0 |
| Analogies–C | * | 0 | 0 |
| Reading comprehension–A | * | 0 | 0 |
| Reading comprehension–B | * | 0 | 0 |
| Reading comprehension–C | * | 0 | 0 |
| Quantitative comparison–A | 0 | * | 0 |
| Quantitative comparison–B | 0 | * | 0 |
| Quantitative comparison–C | 0 | * | 0 |
| Discrete quantitative–A | 0 | * | 0 |
| Discrete quantitative–B | 0 | * | 0 |
| Discrete quantitative–C | 0 | * | 0 |
| Data interpretation–A | 0 | * | 0 |
| Data interpretation–B | 0 | * | 0 |
| Logical reasoning–A | 0 | 0 | * |
| Logical reasoning–B | 0 | 0 | * |
| Analytical reasoning–A | 0 | 0 | * |
| Analytical reasoning–B | 0 | 0 | * |
| Analytical reasoning–C | 0 | 0 | * |

\* Factor loading to be estimated.
0 Variable has no loading on this factor.

will have a zero loading on that particular factor. For example, in Table 8.1 the Verbal antonyms–A parcel is expected to have a nonzero loading on factor one (the verbal factor) and a zero loading on factor two (the quantitative factor). From the sample covariance matrix, the maximum likelihood factor estimation procedure (Joreskog & Sorbom, 1984) is used to estimate the unknown factor loadings (those marked with asterisks) subject to the patterns of "zero" constraints and allowing the factors to be intercorrelated. This use of oblique (that is, intercorrelated) factors justifies setting zeros in the factor pattern even though the factor structures have nonzero loadings.

The primary question posed by the study is how well the above two-factor (three-factor, for the GRE) "simple structure" model fits the data on each handicapped population. By "simple structure" is meant that a given parcel is constrained to load only on its assumed underlying factor. Various measures of overall goodness of fit of the factor model were computed for each population, providing a measure of model fit. A reliability discrepancy procedure and the analysis of residual covariances were used to identify parts of the factor model that did not fit in any one population.

# SAT results

☐ ☐ The results for the SAT will be discussed separately from those for the GRE; a summary section will then discuss the similarities and differences found in the two analyses. The hypothesized two-factor verbal and quantitative model was found to fit the data reasonably well for each of the nine handicapped groups as well as for the non-handicapped group. In general, the quantitative factor tended to show a better fit to the population data than did the verbal factor. Averaged across both groups and forms, approximately 98 percent of the reliable mathematical parcel variance was explained by the single mathematical common factor. As Table 8.3 indicates, that figure varied little among handicapped groups.

In the case of the verbal factor, approximately 97 to 98 percent of the reliable variance in sentence completion and analogies parcels,

**Table 8.3  Percentage of performance variation on item-parcels that was accounted for by the hypothesized factor structure of the SAT and GRE—by handicap group**

| SAT group | | Verbal | Mathematical |
|---|---|---|---|
| HI—Regular | | 97 | 99 |
| LD—Cassette | | 92 | 97 |
| LD—Regular and cassette | | 94 | 98 |
| LD—Large type | | 93 | 98 |
| LD—Regular | | 94 | 99 |
| Nonhandicapped | | 96 | 100 |
| PH—Regular | | 96 | 100 |
| VI—Braille | | 98 | 100 |
| VI—Large type | | 96 | 100 |
| VI—Regular | | 95 | 99 |

| GRE group | Verbal | Quantitative | Analytical |
|---|---|---|---|
| Nonhandicapped | 95 | 92 | 97 |
| PH—National | 94 | 92 | 91 |
| VI—Large type | 94 | 93 | 89 |
| VI—National | 97 | 93 | 100 |

and 90 and 95 percent, respectively, of the reliable variance in reading comprehension and antonyms were explained by a single verbal factor. When averaged across item types, the percentage of reliable verbal parcel variance explained by a single verbal factor ranged from 92 to 98 percent for the various handicapped groups (see Table 8.3).

The verbal and mathematical factors tended to be less correlated for most of the handicapped populations than for the nonhandicapped population. This somewhat greater specificity in the handicapped population suggests the increased likelihood of achievement growth in one area independent of the other. This phenomenon may be due to a variety of factors, including selection bias, conditions secondary to the handicap itself, and the focus of special education programs.

There was some indication that the antonym item type was measuring something more than general verbal reasoning ability. This finding tended to apply somewhat to all groups, but it was particularly true for the learning-disabled cassette group. A similar but less pronounced situation was found to exist for the reading-comprehension items for the learning-disabled groups.

Finally, there was evidence that multiple-choice mathematical items led to different observed score-scale units for the learning-disabled cassette group than for the nonhandicapped group. This finding suggests that the mathematics scores may not have the same meaning for learning-disabled cassette individuals as they do for the nonhandicapped individuals. This finding, however, should be treated with caution because of the small sample sizes for this group.

# GRE results

☐ ☐ The three-factor model, based on verbal, quantitative, and analytical factors, provided a good fit in the nonhandicapped population, a moderately good fit for visually impaired students taking national administrations (VIN), and the least adequate fit for visually impaired students taking large-type, extended-time administrations (VIL) and for physically handicapped students taking standard administrations (PHN) of the GRE.

An estimate of the overall fit of the factor model was obtained by examining how much of the reliable variance in each of the item parcels was explained by the three-factor model when averaged across all groups. Approximately 95 to 98 percent of the reliable variance in the sentence completion, analogies, and reading parcels was explained by the single verbal factor. Ninety-one percent of the reliable variance in the antonym parcels was explained by the verbal factor. The single quantitative factor explained 98 percent of the reliable variance in the quantitative comparison and discrete quantitative parcels. However, only about 80 percent of the reliable variance in the data-interpretation items was explained by the quantitative factor. The analytical factor explained approximately 88 percent of the logical-reasoning parcels and almost all of the analytical-reasoning parcels' reliable variance.

For the VIL and the PHN groups, however, the analytical factor behaved differently than it did for other groups, with the item types composing it—logical reasoning and analytical reasoning—appearing to fit better as separate factors. Not only did these item types show relatively small relationships with each other, but they also exhibited different relationships with other factors. Table 8.3 shows the percentage of reliable parcel variance explained by a single verbal, quantitative, and analytical factor for the four GRE groups.

In addition to lacking fit with the single analytic factor, the scale units of the analytical parcels appeared different, suggesting that analytical scores may not have the same meaning for these two groups (VIL and PHN) as they do for nonhandicapped students. A hierarchical factor analysis supported this finding of differential item-type behavior.

The visually impaired (VIL) group also exhibited considerably lower intercorrelations between the verbal and quantitative factors than did the remaining groups, a type of specificity also found in the SAT analysis. This finding implies the increased likelihood of achievement growth for visually impaired students in one area independent of the other and suggests that the verbal and quantitative scores be interpreted separately rather than as part of a composite.

## SUMMARY

When one considers the number of possible comparisons carried out among the many handicapped groups and the one nonhandicapped group within each study, one has to conclude that the similarities found in factor structure far exceed the differences. It is particularly important, however, to note those differences that were replicated both within and across studies. One was the finding that the verbal and quantitative factors were more independent for almost all of the handicapped groups than for the nonhandicapped group. This potential specificity of skills among the handicapped should be noted by admissions personnel when evaluating individuals for admission or placement.

There was also some indication that the quantitative factor as a whole fitted all groups somewhat better than did the verbal factor. One notable exception was the learning-disabled cassette group (LDC), whose SAT quantitative scores would appear to have a somewhat different interpretation than those of the nonhandicapped group; admissions personnel might consider using caution in interpreting the quantitative scores of LDC individuals. Unfortunately, no GRE information was available for this group because of insufficient sample sizes. Since there could be no replication across studies, this finding must be considered exploratory.

Another finding replicated across both tests was that the antonym items tended to fit the verbal factor less well than did the remaining verbal item types. This result tended to be true for all populations, handicapped and nonhandicapped. The apparent fact that the antonyms have a greater tendency to form an item-type method factor is of only passing research interest and speaks little to any relevant policy with respect to handicapped individuals.

A result that was unique to the GRE analysis was the finding of an increased complexity for the analytical factor for most handicapped groups, but especially for visually impaired large-type (VIL) and physically handicapped standard-administration (PHN) individuals. For these two groups, the two item types composing the analytical score appeared to fit better as separate factors. This result suggests that admissions people should use caution in interpreting the analytical scores of students in these groups. This finding of a potentially different meaning for analytical scores when applied to VIL and PHN individuals is consistent with the findings presented in the companion chapter on differential GRE item performance.

# 9

# Predictive Validity

□ *Henry Braun,*
*Marjorie Ragosta, and*
*Bruce Kaplan*

As part of the research effort carried out by the College Board, Educational Testing Service, and Graduate Record Examinations Board, this study presents data on the validity of the Scholastic Aptitude Test and the Graduate Record Examination as predictors of college and graduate school performance for people in four disability classifications: hearing impairment, learning disability, physical handicap, and visual impairment. These data address the question of whether the SAT and GRE predict the academic performance of people with disabilities as well as they predict that of students in general. This chapter is based on two research reports (Braun, Ragosta, & Kaplan, 1986a and 1986b), which may be consulted for further information.

Although validity studies of the SAT and GRE have routinely been performed for the general population and for some special populations such as minority examinees, very few validity studies have involved specific handicapped groups (Bennett, Ragosta, & Stricker, 1984; Harrison & Ragosta, 1985; Jones & Ragosta, 1982). A major focus of the federal regulations implementing Section 504 of the Rehabilitation Act of 1973 was the validity of admissions tests for disabled test takers. The Panel on Testing of Handicapped People (Sherman & Robinson, 1982) also emphasized validity in its program of research. If it could be shown that all of the modifications made for handicapped people in a given test produced scores that predicted future performance as well as did scores on the regular version, then nearly all doubt about the appropriateness of the test would disappear. The panel noted the paucity of data and suggested studies of the effects of modifying tests and testing procedures. Recognizing the difficulty of finding enough disabled students within any single institution to provide data for a standard validity study, the panel recommended developing a validation technique that would facilitate the pooling of information across many institutions. With that charge in mind, a research design was developed, incorporating empirical Bayes methodology as the basis of the validation technique (Braun, Jones, Rubin, & Thayer, 1983; Rubin, 1980).

# The SAT study

During the four-year period from the fall of 1979 through the end of June 1983, more than fifteen thousand people took special SAT administrations. At the time of data collection, some proportion of them could be assumed to be in postsecondary educational institutions, and we needed to locate those people.

There was also a need for control data from nonhandicapped people who had taken regular administrations of the SAT and attended the same institutions as the handicapped students in the study. The solution appeared obvious. The College Board, through the Educational Testing Service, provides a free Validity Study Service (VSS) to educational institutions using the SAT in their admissions process (College Board, 1982). These validity studies traditionally use a measure of high school performance together with SAT Verbal and Mathematical scores to predict first-year college performance. During the four-year period from September 1980 through the summer of 1984, more than four hundred colleges and universities participated in more than eight hundred fifty validity studies.

There was also an interest in studying a second control group composed of disabled people who had taken regular administrations of the SAT. Since there existed no question concerning the presence of a disability in the Student Descriptive Questionnaire, these individuals were not easily located. Given the need for data on three kinds of students, an appropriate data-collection strategy was devised. Existing data files would be searched to determine which colleges or universities had received the largest numbers of score reports from special test administrations—that is, the largest numbers of disabled applicants. Those schools would be matched with schools having control data through participation in the VSS. Institutions that had both VSS data and relatively large numbers of disabled applicants would be asked to participate in the study.

## Data collection

☐ Initial contact was made by letter with 40 institutions in April, 1984, increased to 61 institutions by June 1984. The letter requested help in providing data on all three kinds of students for a series of validity studies. Follow-up phone calls were made shortly after the letters were sent and periodically thereafter. The requests for data were very well received; only two schools immediately declined to participate. Once schools became aware of the scope of the task, however, many found they did not have the resources to devote to the effort. Ultimately 31 schools provided data on handicapped students, but only 28 schools supplied data on students with scores from special test administrations.

When it became apparent that the data-collection strategy would not provide enough data from nonstandard test administrations, a second method was employed. Again the existing files were searched, and school-by-school printouts were obtained. For each institution, a four-year listing was obtained of disabled students whose scores from special test administrations had been sent to the admissions office, presumably as part of an application. Listings containing five or more names were sent to the corresponding 438 institutions, which were asked to return the forms with validity data for those students who might have attended. Many schools returned the listings indicating that none of the applicants had attended, but more than one hundred provided validity information on the few of their students who had taken special test administrations of the SAT. From this second round of data collection, however, no information was obtained on handicapped students with SAT scores from standard administrations.

With the information from the two rounds of data collection, a database was built. It contained information on handicapped students from special test administrations (Specials), handicapped students from regular test administrations (Regulars), and a random sample of at most fifty nonhandicapped control students from each of the institutions that provided data.

## Description of the sample

☐ From the full database, relevant data were drawn for a comprehensive validity study. This study required that all students have a high school grade-point average (HSGPA), both SAT–Verbal and SAT–Mathematical scores, and first-year college averages (FYA); a disability classification was also required for all handicapped participants. More than

**Table 9.1  Means and standard deviations for nonhandicapped and handicapped groups. SAT database**

|  | N | SAT–V $\overline{X}$ | (SD) | SAT–M $\overline{X}$ | (SD) | HSGPA $\overline{X}$ | (SD) | FYA (Stand.) $\overline{X}$ | (SD) |
|---|---|---|---|---|---|---|---|---|---|
| *Nonhandicapped* | 6255 | 465 | (99) | 509 | (107) | 3.19 | (0.55) | 0.00 | (1.00) |
| *Hearing impaired* | | | | | | | | | |
| Regular | 130 | 356 | (129) | 438 | (116) | 3.10 | (0.53) | –0.06 | (1.08) |
| Special | 84 | 315 | (97) | 429 | (117) | 2.87 | (0.61) | –0.24 | (0.96) |
| *Learning disabled* | | | | | | | | | |
| Regular | 99 | 385 | (88) | 452 | (98) | 2.90 | (0.53) | –0.38 | (1.12) |
| Special | 437 | 412 | (87) | 477 | (116) | 2.65 | (0.54) | –0.49 | (1.00) |
| *Physically handicapped* | | | | | | | | | |
| Regular | 198 | 473 | (108) | 494 | (121) | 3.21 | (0.59) | 0.00 | (0.95) |
| Special | 72 | 462 | (94) | 519 | (111) | 3.09 | (0.50) | –0.19 | (1.07) |
| *Visually impaired* | | | | | | | | | |
| Regular | 35 | 474 | (117) | 489 | (87) | 3.22 | (0.47) | 0.20 | (1.00) |
| Special | 171 | 452 | (92) | 502 | (123) | 3.00 | (0.58) | –0.11 | (1.06) |

six thousand control students and twelve hundred handicapped students were included in the comprehensive validity study. Of the handicapped students, 214 were hearing impaired, 536 were learning disabled, 270 were physically handicapped, and 206 were visually impaired.

Before the analyses were begun, the criterion data (the FYAs) were standardized with respect to the nonhandicapped students, so that within each institution the mean FYA was zero with a standard deviation of one. The purpose of this step was to achieve a comparable FYA scale across all institutions. Mean HSGPAs, SAT scores, and standardized FYAs are presented in Table 9.1.

Several features of the table are worth noting:

1. The numbers in some of the cells are small: there were only 35 visually impaired Regulars, only 72 physically handicapped Specials, and only 84 hearing-impaired Specials.

2. The data for this sample consistently show that Specials within any disability group earned lower mean grades in high school and college than their counterparts taking standard test administrations.

3. Specials (except for hearing-impaired students) earned higher scores than Regulars on at least one of the SAT scores, despite their lower grades.

**Table 9.2  Correlations among variables for nonhandicapped and handicapped groups. SAT database**

|  |  | SAT–V | SAT–M | HSGPA | FYA |  |
|---|---|---|---|---|---|---|
| *Nonhandicapped* |  |  |  |  |  |  |
|  | SAT–V | — |  |  |  |  |
|  | SAT–M | .61 | — |  |  |  |
| Regular | HSGPA | .40 | .45 | — |  |  |
|  | FYA | .26 | .25 | .37 | — |  |
| *Hearing* |  |  |  |  |  |  |
|  | SAT–V | — | .63 | .23 | .04 |  |
|  | SAT–M | .60 | — | .38 | .32 | Special |
| Regular | HSGPA | .31 | .45 | — | .21 |  |
|  | FYA | .26 | .31 | .35 | — |  |
| *Learning* |  |  |  |  |  |  |
|  | SAT–V | — | .61 | .22 | .09 |  |
|  | SAT–M | .58 | — | .36 | .10 | Special |
| Regular | HSGPA | .16 | .37 | — | .24 |  |
|  | FYA | .14 | .26 | .22 | — |  |
| *Physical* |  |  |  |  |  |  |
|  | SAT–V | — | .47 | .43 | .24 |  |
|  | SAT–M | .66 | — | .38 | .15 | Special |
| Regular | HSGPA | .38 | .45 | — | .40 |  |
|  | FYA | .37 | .28 | .42 | — |  |
| *Visual* |  |  |  |  |  |  |
|  | SAT–V | — | .50 | .49 | .19 |  |
|  | SAT–M | .52 | — | .46 | .17 | Special |
| Regular | HSGPA | .37 | .48 | — | .28 |  |
|  | FYA | .29 | .14 | .44 | — |  |

Correlations from regular administrations are to the lower left of the diagonals; correlations from special administrations are to the upper right.

4. Visually and physically handicapped students earned higher mean SAT scores than did learning-disabled students, who in turn earned higher scores than did hearing-impaired students. Those findings are consistent with patterns found in other studies (Bennett, Ragosta, & Stricker, 1984; Bennett, Rock, & Kaplan, 1985; Ragosta & Kaplan, 1986).

Table 9.2 presents the correlations among the variables. Those between SAT scores and standardized FYAs pooled over schools are really part correlations and should be interpreted with care (Gulliksen, 1950). Correlations for scores derived from standard and from special test administrations are presented for each disability group. The correlations between, for example, SAT–V and SAT–M ranged from

.52 to .66 for handicapped candidates in regular test administrations and from .47 to .63 in special administrations, compared to a range of .25 to .61 for nonhandicapped test takers.

In the nonhandicapped population, the lowest correlations occur between SAT–M and FYA (.25) and between SAT–V and FYA (.26). If we look at those relationships for handicapped test takers, we note several that are markedly less. The SAT–M/FYA correlation for visually impaired Regulars is only .14, and similarly low correlations appear for learning-disabled (.10), physically handicapped (.15), and visually impaired Specials (.17). Note that for hearing-impaired Specials and Regulars, the correlations between SAT–M and FYA are the strongest in the table (.32 and .31, respectively).

With regard to the SAT–V/FYA correlations, smaller values occur for learning-disabled Specials (.09) and Regulars (.14). An interesting result is evident for hearing-impaired test takers: although the SAT–V/FYA correlation for this group is only .04, for hearing-impaired Regulars it is .26. The difference between those correlations suggests that different populations of students are being measured—a point that requires a closer look.

More than other handicapped people, the hearing-impaired students in this study tended to cluster at specific institutions. One group was located at an institution established especially for such students. Since there were no control students at that location, the data were not used in the empirical Bayes analysis. In another institution, where all hearing-impaired students routinely attended classes with their hearing counterparts in a *mainstream* program, mean SAT scores for Specials were 307 Verbal and 407 Mathematical. In a third institution, a *separate* two-year school for hearing-impaired students within a much larger technical institute, mean SAT scores for 41 Specials were 291 Verbal and 413 Mathematical. The remaining 21 hearing-impaired Specials, located in institutions across the United States, earned mean SAT scores of 369 Verbal and 484 Mathematical—far higher than that of their clustered counterparts.

Means for hearing-impaired Regulars followed the same pattern, with lower means for students clustered in the mainstream and separate institutions and much higher means for students distributed across all other institutions. In fact, the hearing-impaired Regulars in all other institutions had mean scores only 9 to 20 points lower, on the average, than nonhandicapped people. Clearly, the hearing-impaired students who took regular SAT administrations and who distributed themselves across many institutions were not academically at risk.

The comprehensive database just described was the basis for three sets of analyses: one using SAT test scores and high school performance to predict college grades, a second using only test scores for the prediction, and a third using only high school performance.

In the data analysis, we focus our attention on the following questions: Do regression equations based on data from nonhandicapped students predict the performance of handicapped and nonhandicapped students about equally well? If not, are there any particular patterns of under- or overprediction that are worthy of note?

Before these questions are addressed, we need to point out that the first-year grade-point average may have some deficiencies as a criterion measure. If, for example, college students with disabilities are not given adequate test time for final examinations, their FYAs might be lower than anticipated. On the other hand, grades may sometimes be inflated if disabled students are more likely to seek tutoring assistance. Noncomparability of FYAs might also result from differences in the number and kinds of courses taken by handicapped and nonhandicapped students. Therefore, patterns of over- or under-prediction may result in part from peculiarities in the criterion measures themselves, as well as in the predictors. In this report we cannot speak to the adequacy of the criterion measures and will concentrate instead on the adequacy of the predictors: SAT scores and high school GPA. It is well to keep in mind, however, that the criterion itself is far from an ideal measure.

## Validity of SAT scores and high school grades

☐  To study the validity of test scores and high school grades for predicting the college grades of handicapped students, it is essential to have an appropriate baseline. In the present analysis, this baseline is provided by samples of nonhandicapped (control) students attending the 145 institutions for which we have data on handicapped students. For each school, FYAs were standardized to have a mean of 0 and a standard deviation of 1. Then for each school a separate regression equation was established to predict FYAs from the high school grade-point average (HSGPA) and the SAT scores. These prediction equations were estimated using the empirical Bayes paradigm (see Appendix A of Braun, Ragosta, & Kaplan, 1986a). Using this paradigm, data from all the colleges influence the estimate for each individual college. Regression equations obtained in this manner and typically more stable and perform better in cross-validation (Braun & Jones, 1985).

A predicted FYA was obtained for each handicapped student by substituting his or her high school grades and test scores in to the prediction equation for the college attended. The difference between

Table 9.3 Using HSGPA and SATs to predict FYA. SAT database

| | | Disabilities | | | | | | | |
| | | Hearing | | Learning | | Physical | | Visual | |
| Row | Nonhandicapped controls | Standard | Special | Standard | Special | Standard | Special | Standard | Special |
|---|---|---|---|---|---|---|---|---|---|
| 1 Number | 6255 | 130 | 84 | 99 | 437 | 198 | 72 | 35 | 171 |
| *Means* | | | | | | | | | |
| 2 Actual FYA | 0.00 | −0.06 | −0.24 | −0.38 | −0.49 | 0.00 | −0.19 | 0.20 | −0.11 |
| 3 Predicted FYA | 0.00 | −0.31 | −0.51 | −0.41 | −0.42 | −0.04 | −0.08 | 0.06 | −0.16 |
| 4 Residual | 0.00 | 0.25 | 0.27 | 0.03 | −0.07 | 0.04 | −0.11 | 0.14 | 0.05 |
| *Residuals* | | | | | | | | | |
| 5 Low predicted | .03 | .52 | .74 | .12 | .14 | .15 | .21 | .28 | .31 |
| 6 Med. predicted | −.07 | .02 | .25 | .04 | −.03 | −.03 | −.26 | −.20 | .02 |
| 7 High predicted | .04 | .21 | −.20 | −.07 | −.31 | .02 | −.23 | .27 | −.18 |
| *Standard deviations* | | | | | | | | | |
| 8 Actual FYA | 1.00 | 1.08 | 0.96 | 1.12 | 1.00 | 0.95 | 1.07 | 1.00 | 1.06 |
| 9 Predicted FYA | 0.50 | 0.56 | 0.60 | 0.50 | 0.50 | 0.54 | 0.52 | 0.40 | 0.55 |
| 10 Residual | 0.87 | 1.00 | 1.01 | 1.07 | 0.96 | 0.82 | 1.01 | 0.93 | 1.00 |
| *Correlations* | | | | | | | | | |
| 11 Actual and predicted FYA | .49 | .39 | .23 | .33 | .34 | .50 | .35 | .37 | .37 |

the actual FYA earned by the student and the predicted FYA is called the *residual* (for that student): Residual = Actual FYA − Predicted FYA.

If the control equations yield fair predictions of the performance of all handicapped students, then the distribution of residuals for each subgroup of handicapped students should be centered at about 0, the mean residual for the control students. Ideally, the variances of these distributions of residuals should also be comparable to that of the distribution for control students.

The means and standard deviations of the residuals for non-handicapped and handicapped students are presented in Table 9.3, rows 4 and 10. A positive mean residual indicates that students do better than expected; that is, that the control prediction equation tends to underpredict performance. A negative mean residual indicates poorer performance than expected; that is, overprediction. Except for the hearing-impaired group, the mean residuals for the different subgroups are reasonably close to 0 when measured against the size of the standard deviations of the distributions. There is a suggestion in the data that the performance of handicapped students who took standard administrations tended to be underpredicted, while that of students who took special test administrations tended to be overpredicted. The mean residuals for the hearing-impaired groups are strongly positive, indicating severe underprediction. This underprediction merits closer attention and will be discussed below.

It is also of some interest to compare the correlations between actual and predicted FYAs across the different groups (row 11 of Table 9.3). These correlations, obtained by pooling data over schools, tend to be lower for the handicapped groups than for the controls, demonstrating that test scores and high school grades do not predict the college performance of handicapped students as well as that of controls. This result is buttressed by the finding that the standard deviations of the distribution of residuals for the handicapped groups were some 10 to 15 percent higher than that of the control residuals (row 10 of Table 9.3). However, one would expect somewhat attenuated correlations and larger standard deviations, since the disabled students did not contribute to the estimation of the prediction equations.

While these gross comparisons have been informative, a more detailed analysis of the distributions of residuals is possible. We first note that there does not appear to be an association across groups between the mean predicted FYA and the mean residual (compare rows 3 and 4 of Table 9.3). That is, the typical level of preparation of a particular group of handicapped students (as measured by predicted FYA) relative to the group of controls is not related to their being over- or underpredicted as a group. We look next for associations between predicted FYA and the residuals *within groups.*

To this end, the individuals in each disability group were ranked on predicted FYA and divided into three roughly equal sections (low, medium, and high predicted FYAs). The mean residual for each section was calculated, and the data are displayed in rows 5, 6, and 7 of Table 9.3. There is a clear tendency in the special test administration groups for the mean residual to decrease as the mean predicted FYA increases. In fact, the higher the predicted FYA for a disabled individual, the more likely it is that his or her actual FYA will fall below the prediction (be overpredicted). For example, in all four special test administration disability groups, the mean residuals in the sections with the highest predicted FYAs are negative.

It is noteworthy that these four groups of disabled test takers differ in mean predicted FYA by nearly half a standard deviation. So, again, the pattern does not depend on the relative standing of the group. For those who took a standard administration, this pattern is evident, only weakly, if at all. There is no such pattern for the controls.

The described pattern in the residuals, which is observed in subsequent analyses as well, has at least one major implication, namely, that the prediction plane for students with any disability is very unlikely to be parallel to the prediction plane for nonhandicapped students in the same school. Because of prohibitively small sample sizes, it would appear to be theoretically or practically impossible to make simple adjustments to either the predicted FYA or the predictors to obtain unbiased predictions for disabled students at all levels of achievement.

## The validity of test scores alone

By dropping the HSGPA's from the previous data, new regression equations were formed based on SAT Verbal and Mathematical scores. Again, empirical Bayes methods were employed, and the resulting prediction equations were used to generate new residuals for the handicapped students on the basis of the use of SAT scores alone.

The means and standard deviations of the residuals by group are presented in rows 4 and 10 of Table 9.4. Except for the hearing-impaired groups, the mean residuals are all somewhat lower than the corresponding means shown in Table 9.3, using predictions based on both test scores and high school grades. The largest decrease occurs for learning-disabled students taking the special test administration. On the other hand, the standard deviations are little changed. Thus,

**Table 9.4  Using only SATs to predict FYA. SAT database**

| | | Disabilities | | | | | | | |
| | Nonhandicapped controls | Hearing | | Learning | | Physical | | Visual | |
| Row | | Standard | Special | Standard | Special | Standard | Special | Standard | Special |
|---|---|---|---|---|---|---|---|---|---|
| 1 Number | 6255 | 130 | 84 | 99 | 437 | 198 | 72 | 35 | 171 |
| *Means* | | | | | | | | | |
| 2 Actual FYA | 0.00 | -0.06 | -0.24 | -0.38 | -0.49 | 0.00 | -0.19 | 0.20 | -0.11 |
| 3 Predicted FYA | 0.00 | -0.37 | -0.50 | -0.32 | -0.15 | -0.01 | 0.00 | 0.05 | -0.05 |
| 4 Residual | 0.00 | 0.31 | 0.26 | -0.05 | -0.33 | 0.01 | -0.18 | 0.15 | -0.05 |
| *Residuals* | | | | | | | | | |
| 5 Low predicted | .03 | .32 | .60 | .16 | -.14 | .09 | -.11 | .55 | .07 |
| 6 Med. predicted | -.04 | .56 | .08 | -.39 | -.30 | -.03 | -.24 | -.27 | -.09 |
| 7 High predicted | .01 | .05 | .11 | .07 | -.53 | -.02 | -.19 | .08 | -.13 |
| *Standard deviations* | | | | | | | | | |
| 8 Actual FYA | 1.00 | 1.08 | 0.96 | 1.12 | 1.00 | 0.95 | 1.07 | 1.00 | 1.06 |
| 9 Predicted FYA | 0.37 | 0.46 | 0.43 | 0.39 | 0.39 | 0.39 | 0.39 | 0.34 | 0.39 |
| 10 Residual | 0.93 | 1.03 | 0.98 | 1.08 | 0.98 | 0.89 | 1.04 | 0.99 | 1.01 |
| *Correlations* | | | | | | | | | |
| 11 Actual and predicted FYA | .37 | .31 | .19 | .29 | .22 | .36 | .22 | .22 | .31 |

we conclude that inclusion of high school grades in the prediction equation slightly reduces the chance of overprediction for disabled students.

As one would expect, the correlations between actual FYA and predicted FYA (row 11 of Table 9.4) are all lower, by about 25 percent, than the corresponding values in Table 9.3. This is true for both the controls and the disabled students. The correlations between the residuals and the two predictors are all negative for the special test administration groups but mixed for the standard test group. Thus, at least for the former group, the two SAT scores are again not as strongly related to college performance as they are for controls.

Each disabled group was divided into three approximately equal sections on the basis of predicted FYA, and the mean residual for each section was computed. These are displayed in rows 5, 6, and 7 of Table 9.4. As it was in Table 9.3, a strong negative association is evident for the special test administration groups. In fact, the FYA's for most of the disabled students in those groups (with the exception of the hearing impaired) would be overpredicted by a control equation based on SAT scores alone.

## The validity of high school grades alone

☐ It is of some interest to compare the performance of high school grades as a sole predictor of college performance with that of test scores. Table 9.5 contains the relevant data. For visually impaired and physically handicapped as well as learning-disabled students, neither predictor dominates the other with regard to the size of the mean residual or the variability of the residuals. Perhaps the most dramatic difference occurs for learning-disabled students taking special test administrations, for whom the mean residual is only –0.10 using high school grades but –0.30 using test scores. Correlations between observed and predicted college grades (row 11) tend to be somewhat higher in Table 9.5 than in Table 9.4, though comparison with Table 9.3 shows that the addition of test scores to high school grades generally improves the correlations.

## Validity for hearing-impaired students

☐ The underprediction of college FYA for hearing-impaired students (who show large positive residuals) referred to earlier can best be studied by dividing them into three groups: the first comprises individuals attending an institution in which they are mainstreamed but are offered excellent support services; the second, those attending a

**Table 9.5  Using only HSGPA to predict FYA. SAT database**

|  |  | Disabilities | | | | | | | |
|  | | Hearing | | Learning | | Physical | | Visual | |
| Row | Nonhandicapped controls | Standard | Special | Standard | Special | Standard | Special | Standard | Special |
| 1 Number | 6255 | 130 | 84 | 99 | 437 | 198 | 72 | 35 | 171 |
| *Means* | | | | | | | | | |
| 2 Actual FYA | 0.0 | -0.06 | -0.24 | -0.38 | -0.49 | 0.00 | -0.19 | 0.20 | -0.11 |
| 3 Predicted FYA | 0.0 | -0.06 | -0.23 | -0.23 | -0.38 | -0.04 | -0.10 | 0.03 | -0.17 |
| 4 Residual | 0.0 | 0.00 | -0.01 | -0.15 | -0.10 | 0.04 | -0.09 | 0.17 | 0.06 |
| *Residuals* | | | | | | | | | |
| 5 Low predicted | .03 | .22 | .56 | -.02 | .04 | .08 | .26 | -.05 | .33 |
| 6 Med. predicted | -.04 | -.06 | -.24 | -.10 | -.05 | .04 | -.61 | .64 | -.01 |
| 7 High predicted | .01 | -.19 | -.36 | -.31 | -.30 | .01 | .14 | -.03 | -.14 |
| *Standard deviations* | | | | | | | | | |
| 8 Actual FYA | 1.00 | 1.08 | .96 | 1.12 | 1.00 | .95 | 1.07 | 1.00 | 1.06 |
| 9 Predicted FYA | .43 | .47 | .57 | .45 | .47 | .50 | .44 | .37 | .48 |
| 10 Residual | .91 | 1.03 | 1.02 | 1.10 | .97 | .85 | 1.00 | .94 | 1.02 |
| *Correlations* | | | | | | | | | |
| 11 Actual and predicted FYA | .41 | .32 | .19 | .25 | .30 | .44 | .36 | .35 | .32 |

separate school within a large technical institute; and the third, those scattered among fifty-odd mainstream institutions. Test scores of these three groups have already been discussed.

An examination of the residuals from the three groups of students taking special test administrations makes it evident that the underprediction observed for hearing-impaired students as a whole in Table 9.3 is due to severe underprediction at the separate school (mean residual = 0.73), which is only partially offset by moderate overprediction at the mainstream school. Students in the third group have an average residual that is essentially 0. For individuals taking the standard administration, the results are rather different. While the performance of students at the mainstream institution is fairly predicted on average, those of students in the special institution and in the third, heterogeneous group are quite strongly underpredicted, with mean residuals of 0.43 and 0.44 respectively.

The data for the heterogeneous group of hearing-impaired students are most nearly comparable to those available for the other disabled groups, at least with regard to distribution. Comparing that group's data to those for the other three disability groups, we find that the only anomaly occurs for the hearing-impaired regular test administration students, who are strongly underpredicted.

# The GRE study

☐ ☐ In the GRE validity study, the implementation of empirical Bayes methods was impeded by the lack of data for nonhandicapped students from the departments in which the disabled students in the study were enrolled. Consequently, a rather elaborate strategy was developed in order to obtain estimates of the prediction equations for those departments. The procedure is described in some detail in Appendix A of the original report (Braun, Ragosta, & Kaplan, 1986b). Briefly, data from 99 departments that participated in the Validity Study Service of the GRE were used to calibrate a model that related certain departmental characteristics to the prediction equation for each department. This model was then applied to the departments in the study, for which the values of these characteristics have been obtained. Because the process does involve substantial extrapolation, the residuals that are derived from these prediction equations must be interpreted with great caution. Moreover, it must be borne in mind that the population of interested, handicapped graduate students who have taken special administrations of the GRE, forms a minuscule fraction of the total population of graduate students; and while our sample represents a substantial fraction of that population, it is a nonrandom sample.

During the period from the fall of 1981 through the end of June 1984, more than eight hundred fifty examinees took special administrations of the GRE. At the time of data collection, some proportion of those students could be assumed to be in graduate institutions. Others perhaps had never attended graduate school, while still others may have attended and dropped out. Before we could collect data for the validity studies, we needed to locate those people who had been admitted to specific departments of graduate schools after taking special administrations of the GRE. A further consideration was the interest in studying a second control group, composed of disabled people who had taken regular administrations of the GRE and attended the same departments in the same graduate institutions.

Faced with the need for data on two kinds of students, we devised an appropriate data-collection strategy. Existing data files would be searched to determine which graduate schools had received score reports from special test administrations. For all such institutions, current data files were searched for individuals who had taken regular administrations of the GRE and who had reported having a disability. Lists of the identified individuals were produced for every graduate school to which students taking special test administrations had applied.

## Data collection

☐ Initial contact with 432 graduate institutions was made by letter in June 1985. The letter requested help for a series of validity studies and included listings of disabled individuals who had sent their GRE scores to the school being addressed. The listings of students taking special administrations typically contained only one or two names. Those of disabled students taking regular administrations were much longer, often running to several pages. To assure a good response, no more than one or two pages of names (selected randomly) were sent to any schools for review.

Of the 432 schools that were contacted, 339 responded—a response rate of 78 percent. One hundred and eighty-eight of them had no information on students taking special GRE administrations. The 151 schools that did report the presence of students taking special administrations provided the data for the current study. Of those, only 63 provided information on disabled students taking regular test administrations, and almost half of those data came from just 10 departments. Because there were many fewer data on Regulars—despite the fact that Regulars are a proportionately much larger group than Specials—and because those data were not well distributed across the departments in our sample, inferences are more difficult to make for this group than for others.

## Description of the sample

☐   The comprehensive validity study required that all participants have an undergraduate GPA, GRE–Verbal and Quantitative scores, and a first-year graduate GPA. For a small number of participants, the first-year GPA was not available, and a cumulative graduate GPA was employed instead. The study also required a disability classification for all Specials. Hearing-impaired and multiply handicapped students were dropped because only a small number of them could be identified. The resultant database contained three categories of students taking special test administrations, one category of handicapped students taking regular test administrations, and nonhandicapped controls. (Note that the controls attended departments that were, in general, different from those attended by the handicapped students.) The means and standard deviations for these five groups on the four variables of the comprehensive validity study are presented in Table 9.6. We note that in the studies reported below, the FYAs were not standardized in any way; raw FYAs on a 0 to 4 scale served as the criterion.

The test scores of this sample of disabled students taking special administrations of the GRE are, on the average, lower than those of the nonhandicapped controls. The 19 learning-disabled students in the comprehensive data set had GRE–Verbal and Quantitative scores

**Table 9.6   The comprehensive data set means and standard deviations for non-handicapped and handicapped groups. GRE database**

|  | N | GRE–V | | GRE–Q | | UGPA | | FYA | |
|---|---|---|---|---|---|---|---|---|---|
|  | N | $\overline{X}$ | SD | $\overline{X}$ | SD | $\overline{X}$ | SD | $\overline{X}$ | SD |
| *Nonhandicapped* | 2025 | 519 | 106 | 543 | 124 | 3.26 | .44 | 3.48 | .42 |
| *Specials* | | | | | | | | | |
| Learning disabled | 19 | 469 | 95 | 472 | 142 | 3.01 | .35 | 3.49 | .46 |
| Physically handicapped | 48 | 514 | 116 | 481 | 129 | 3.18 | .55 | 3.46 | .55 |
| Visually impaired | 105 | 492 | 107 | 457 | 126 | 3.09 | .53 | 3.31 | .54 |
| *Regulars* | 184 | 482 | 122 | 454 | 128 | 3.02 | .48 | 3.40 | .50 |

about one-half of a standard deviation lower than those of the non-handicapped controls. The GRE–V scores of the 48 physically handicapped students were similar to those of control students, but their GRE–Q scores were, on the average, half a standard deviation lower. The 105 visually impaired students' GRE–V scores were one-quarter of a standard deviation lower, and their GRE–Q scores were more than two-thirds of a standard deviation lower. Despite their lower scores, the disabled Specials had overall graduate grade-point averages close to the mean for nonhandicapped students. The exception was visually impaired individuals, whose grades were more than one-third of a standard deviation lower. Once the database was built, we investigated three families of prediction equations: one employing both GRE scores and UGPA, one GRE scores only, and one UGPA only.

## Validity of GRE scores and undergraduate grade-point average

☐ The residual analysis was possible only after substantial effort had been expended in obtaining an estimate of the prediction equation for each department. This effort was made necessary by the lack of data on nonhandicapped students. Since the prediction equations obtained resulted from an extrapolation of a model based on data from other departments, it should be expected that the residuals are at least somewhat more variable than they would have been had relevant control data been available. In fact, we show below that the standard deviations of the residuals for the different handicapped groups are typically about 50 percent larger than that of the pooled residuals for the nonhandicapped students that were used to estimate the model parameters. This finding should be compared to the study of the SAT, in which the corresponding increase is in the range of 10 to 15 percent. Of course, in that instance, relevant control data were available.

It will also be apparent that while the correlations between predicted and actual FYA are not negligible in most cases, the standard deviations of the residuals are comparable in magnitude to those of the FYAs. Thus there is considerable variability in the residuals, which may mask whatever systematic patterns exist in the data. Some of the excess variability results from the manner in which the prediction equations were estimated; some is undoubtedly due to the facts that the groups of handicapped students we study are very heterogeneous and that we have no information on the process by which they matriculated at a given department or on the course of study followed. Accordingly, in drawing inferences from these data, we will

**Table 9.7  Residual analysis derived from predictions based on test scores and UGPA. GRE database**

|  | Nonhandicapped | Regular | Handicapped | | | |
|---|---|---|---|---|---|---|
|  |  |  |  | Special | | |
|  |  |  | Total | Learning | Physical | Visual |
| 1. Number | 2025 | 184 | 216 | 19 | 48 | 105 |
| *Means* |  |  |  |  |  |  |
| 2. Actual FYA | 3.48 | 3.40 | 3.38 | 3.49 | 3.46 | 3.31 |
| 3. Predicted FYA | 3.50 | 3.46 | 3.47 | 3.42 | 3.50 | 3.47 |
| 4. Residual | −0.02 | −0.06 | −0.09 | 0.07 | −0.04 | −0.16 |
| *Mean residuals* |  |  |  |  |  |  |
| 5. Low predicted | −0.06 | 0.10 | −0.04 | 0.10 | −0.08 | 0.06 |
| 6. Medium predicted | −0.00 | −0.10 | −0.02 | −0.31 | 0.12 | −0.11 |
| 7. High predicted | 0.02 | −0.15 | −0.20 | −0.22 | −0.16 | −0.28 |
| *Standard deviations* |  |  |  |  |  |  |
| 8. Actual FYA | 0.42 | 0.50 | 0.52 | 0.48 | 0.55 | 0.54 |
| 9. Predicted FYA | 0.23 | 0.20 | 0.20 | 0.20 | 0.16 | 0.20 |
| 10. Residuals | 0.33 | 0.49 | 0.51 | 0.53 | 0.49 | 0.53 |
| *Correlations* |  |  |  |  |  |  |
| 11. Actual and predicted | 0.63 | 0.24 | 0.27 | 0.23 | −0.04 | 0.29 |

rely on the similarity of the findings to those of the SAT study.

Table 9.7 displays the results of the first family of prediction equations. For nonhandicapped students, the equation employed for each department is the empirical Bayes estimate, using the applicant data to provide covariate information. The fit is very good. The mean residual is close to 0 (line 4); moreover, division of these students into three equal groups according to the level of predicted FYA—low, medium, and high—yields only a slight upward trend in the mean residuals (lines 5, 6, and 7). While the correlation between actual and predicted FYA is 0.63, a rather substantial figure, it should be recalled that this correlation is obtained from a pooled sample drawn from 99 different departments.

For the disabled students, the prediction equations for each department are obtained from a two-stage empirical Bayes model. The mean residuals are somewhat more negative, −0.06 and −0.09 respectively, and the correlations between actual and predicted FYA are much more modest. Perhaps most important, the pattern in the mean residuals by level of predicted FYA is reminiscent of those observed in the analysis of SAT data: increasing predicted FYA is accompanied by increasing overprediction. The trend is quite strong, inasmuch as the standard error of one of the subgroup means is approximately 0.06, while the difference in means between the low-predicted group and the high-predicted group is approximately 0.25 (regular administration) or 0.16 (special administration).

Visually impaired students form the largest subgroup among those taking special administrations, and their results mirror those for the disabled group as a whole. Physically handicapped students form the next largest subgroup, and their results (with the exception of the trend in the mean residuals [lines 5–7]) are similar to the others'. The results for the learning-disabled group are somewhat anomalous, with a positive mean residual and a negative correlation between actual and predicted FYA. However, the sample size is so small that it is difficult to lend much credence to these findings.

## Validity of GRE scores alone

☐ Table 9.8 presents the results for predictions based on GRE scores only. For the nonhandicapped students, the effect is to increase the

**Table 9.8  Residual analysis derived from predictions based on test scores alone. GRE database**

|  | | Handicapped | | | | |
|  | | | | Special | | |
|  | Nonhandicapped | Regular | Total | Learning | Physical | Visual |
|---|---|---|---|---|---|---|
| 1. Number | 2025 | 184 | 216 | 19 | 48 | 105 |
| *Means* | | | | | | |
| 2. Actual FYA | 3.48 | 3.40 | 3.38 | 3.49 | 3.46 | 3.31 |
| 3. Predicted FYA | 3.50 | 3.50 | 3.50 | 3.48 | 3.51 | 3.51 |
| 4. Residual | −0.02 | −0.10 | −0.12 | 0.01 | −0.05 | −0.20 |
| *Mean residuals* | | | | | | |
| 5. Low predicted | −0.12 | 0.02 | −0.07 | 0.02 | −0.03 | −0.07 |
| 6. Medium predicted | −0.01 | −0.11 | −0.11 | 0.28 | −0.03 | −0.04 |
| 7. High predicted | 0.07 | −0.19 | −0.25 | −0.39 | −0.09 | −0.37 |
| *Standard deviations* | | | | | | |
| 8. Actual FYA | 0.42 | 0.50 | 0.52 | 0.48 | 0.56 | 0.54 |
| 9. Predicted FYA | 0.23 | 0.17 | 0.14 | 0.13 | 0.13 | 0.13 |
| 10. Residuals | 0.35 | 0.50 | 0.53 | 0.51 | 0.57 | 0.55 |
| *Correlations* | | | | | | |
| 11. Actual and predicted | 0.56 | 0.15 | 0.12 | −0.12 | 0.04 | 0.11 |

**Table 9.9 Residual analysis derived from predictions based on UGPA alone. GRE database**

|  | Nonhandicapped | Regular | Handicapped | | | |
|  |  |  | Special | | | |
|  |  |  | Total | Learning | Physical | Visual |
| 1. Number | 2025 | 184 | 216 | 19 | 48 | 105 |
| *Means* |  |  |  |  |  |  |
| 2. Actual FYA | 3.48 | 3.40 | 3.38 | 3.49 | 3.46 | 3.31 |
| 3. Predicted FYA | 3.50 | 3.46 | 3.48 | 3.44 | 3.51 | 3.48 |
| 4. Residual | −0.02 | −0.06 | −0.10 | −0.05 | −0.05 | −0.17 |
| *Mean residuals* |  |  |  |  |  |  |
| 5. Low predicted | −0.04 | 0.02 | −0.06 | 0.15 | −0.12 | −0.06 |
| 6. Medium predicted | −0.02 | −0.04 | −0.15 | 0.03 | −0.02 | −0.30 |
| 7. High predicted | 0.01 | −0.18 | −0.10 | −0.04 | −0.06 | −0.14 |
| *Standard deviations* |  |  |  |  |  |  |
| 8. Actual FYA | 0.42 | 0.50 | 0.52 | 0.48 | 0.56 | 0.54 |
| 9. Predicted FYA | 0.22 | 0.17 | 0.17 | 0.11 | 0.17 | 0.18 |
| 10. Residuals | 0.34 | 0.49 | 0.50 | 0.48 | 0.52 | 0.53 |
| *Correlations* |  |  |  |  |  |  |
| 11. Actual and predicted | 0.59 | 0.21 | 0.29 | 0.04 | 0.36 | 0.24 |

positive trend in the mean residuals with increasing predicted FYA. The effect for disabled students is to make the mean residuals more negative and to further reduce the correlations between actual and predicted FYA, a trend that is particularly striking for the learning-disabled group.

## Validity of undergraduate grade-point average alone

☐ Table 9.9 presents the results for predictions based on UGPA only. The pattern of residuals for handicapped students taking both regular and special administrations indicates substantial overprediction, though the correlations between actual and predicted FYA are substantially higher than those shown in Table 9.8.

# Discussion: The SAT study

☐ ☐ Across all disability groups there were several trends in the data. Test scores and high school grades did not predict the performance of disabled people as well as that of nonhandicapped controls. Correlations between actual and predicted college performance were lower for students taking special test administrations, and the standard deviations of residuals tended to be higher. Near-zero average residuals often masked important over- and underpredictions.

**High school performance**   One pattern of over- and underprediction is evident in the data based on high school performance alone. The performance of students earning the lowest HSGPAs was more likely to be underpredicted, while that of those earning the highest HSGPAs was more likely to be overpredicted. Although the trend is only slightly evident for the students who elected to take standard SAT examinations, it is much stronger for those who earned lower grades and who elected to take special administrations of the SAT. The most severe over- and underprediction occurred for hearing-impaired students taking special test administrations: low grades underpredicted college performance by more than half a standard deviation, and high grades overpredicted it by more than one-third of a standard deviation. An examination of why this phenomenon occurs is beyond the scope of the current study. One hypothesis for the finding is that handicapped students in special schools with strong support services may earn higher grades than those (perhaps less handicapped) students who are mainstreamed into more competitive environments.

**SAT scores**   A second pattern emerges from the predictions based on SAT scores alone. Except those for hearing-impaired students, SAT scores from special administrations have a strong tendency to overpredict the college performance of students with disabilities. This effect is strongest for relatively high-scoring learning-disabled students, whose college grades are overpredicted by more than half a standard deviation. (For low-scoring hearing-impaired students taking special administrations, SAT scores underpredict college performance by more than half a standard deviation.) One possible explanation for these results is based on the policy of extending unlimited time to persons taking special test administrations. An earlier study of handicapped people who had taken both standard and special administrations of the SAT (Centra, 1986) showed that greater score increases were associated with greater amounts of extra time. There is some indication that gain occurs for students whose disability necessitates the extra time: those who need the time most gain most by it. But there is also an indication that more capable students are taking longer amounts of time. That finding, together with the current findings on overprediction, leads to the conclusion that, in general, special test administrations need to become more standardized. This conclusion is supported by the *Standards for Educational and Psychological Testing* (American Psychological Association, 1985), which recommends that empirical procedures be used whenever possible to establish time limits for testing handicapped people.

**SAT scores and high school performance**  Using both high school grades and SAT scores to predict the college performance of students taking special test administrations results in good overall predictions, but only because overprediction in some areas is offset by underprediction in others. Overprediction on the basis of the high school grades of the strongest third of the handicapped student group is balanced by underprediction of the weakest third.

Overprediction arising from the practice of allowing unlimited time on standardized tests has the effect of reducing the validity of those test scores and decreasing the correlations between predicted and actual scores. Overcompensation is also unfair to those non-handicapped students who do not have time enough to complete the test. By accommodating the needs of handicapped students in this way, we decrease the potential for obtaining special test administration data with validity as high as that for standard test administrations. To increase validity, a more accurate match needs to be made between the extra time needed to compensate for disability and the amount of time given.

# Discussion: The GRE study

□ □    For the GRE, data on students taking special administrations are much more representative than those on disabled students in regular administrations; therefore, we will concentrate on the Specials.

**Undergraduate grade-point average**  The undergraduate grade-point average is the best single predictor of graduate performance for disabled students. Although UGPA has a slight tendency to overpredict grades, there is no pattern of under- and overprediction associated with the level of prediction, as there was for high school grade-point average.

One reason may be that in colleges there is less variation in grading standards than there is in the special schools and the mainstream environments of the nation's high schools.

**GRE scores alone**  The GRE scores alone show a tendency toward overprediction, associated strongly with high predicted graduate school grades. If better control data had been available, the scope of the overprediction might have been even greater.

**GRE scores and undergraduate grade-point averages**   The pattern of increasing overprediction associated with increasing predicted scores reinforces the findings of the comprehensive validity study of the SAT. Because of the similarity in findings, we emphasize the recommendation that, insofar as is possible, the timing of special test administrations become more standardized.

## GENERAL DISCUSSION

One method of determining the appropriate amount of time for a special test administration is by empirical analysis. If, for example, 80 percent of nonhandicapped students can finish the SAT in the standard time, how much time is needed for 80 percent of blind students taking the braille SAT to finish? Some such empirically derived administration times might be reasonably fair to most test takers using the braille version. This method of setting time limits is perhaps more problematic for some types of handicaps such as learning disabled, where degree of impairment and accuracy of identifications may vary widely.

Another systematic method of establishing reasonable time limits for SAT special administrations is to make use of the Individualized Education Program (IEP) committee. An IEP is established by law for all special education students, and the committee that establishes or oversees the IEP is sometimes responsible for determining the conditions under which the student is tested. For example, in states with minimum competency tests for high school graduation, the IEP committee may decide whether or not an individual should be in the high school track leading toward a diploma or in the one leading to a lesser award such as a certificate of attendance. The committee may also make recommendations about the conditions under which the minimum competency test will be administered. Although the IEP system is currently in place nationwide and might be used to establish testing guidelines, it may be more reasonable to use the IEP committee only in cases where prescribed standards derived from empirical data are clearly not suitable for the individual being tested.

Underprediction has more serious consequences than overprediction for the student in that it can result in denial of admission to an institution in which the student could succeed. Further work should be done to investigate those groups of individuals for whom underprediction is most severe: hearing-impaired students with low grades and low test scores (whether or not they take special test administrations) and low-scoring handicapped students generally. If, for example, strong underprediction consistently occurs for specific groups of students (for instance, deaf students whose primary mode of communication is sign language) one might recommend that the SAT not be used for those populations. At minimum, admissions officers should be alerted to the fact that disabled people who may appear to be poor risks for college tend to perform better than expected.

Further research might also help to explicate the conditions behind the over- and underprediction resulting from the use of high school grades. A clearer understanding of this phenomenon would be of practical importance to admissions offices and could lead to stronger demonstrations of the validity of the SAT for disabled students taking special administrations.

As we stated previously, the general finding of over- and underprediction implies that no simple rescaling of the predictors (test scores or high school grades) will achieve the goal of unbiased predictions for disabled students. Consequently, it appears that the issue of flagging scores from special test administrations cannot be resolved easily by appealing to a statistical adjustment of the obtained scores. Moreover, the small sample size in this study and the heterogeneity of conditions, even within a particular class of disabled students, make it unlikely that a suitable transformation of test scores can be estimated reliably.

# 10

# The Feasibility of Rescaling

☐ **Donald E. Powers and Warren W. Willingham**

A central concern of the National Research Council Panel on Testing of Handicapped People was the establishment of comparable tests (and scores) for handicapped and nonhandicapped test takers. This concern was fueled by the desire to avoid the need to flag scores obtained from nonstandard test administrations. Basically, flagging is intended to insure the objectivity and fairness of testing procedures—to inform test-score recipients that certain scores were obtained under conditions that deviated in some way (test format, construction, administration, timing) from the uniform standards for the test in question. The modifications made for handicapped examinees constitute deviations in either construction or administration, for which flagging is deemed appropriate. Flagging presents a dilemma, however, because it is desirable to protect an applicant from having to reveal the existence of a disability against his or her wishes.

The panel considered various means of eliminating the need to flag the test scores of handicapped examinees. It observed that it is not feasible to use standard procedures to equate scores obtained on tests modified for and administered to special populations to those obtained on regular forms administered to a different population. To use such procedures fairly, we would have to establish either that the modification did not affect what the test measured or its difficulty, or that the two populations were equivalent with respect to the ability being measured. Neither of these conditions can be expected to apply, however. Establishing even the less rigorous conditions of test comparability—that is, providing the same scale for tests of different psychological functions—was not possible because of the need to administer tests to equivalent groups of test takers. Consequently, after much deliberation, the panel proposed that

> the establishment of a relationship between scores from modified tests and the kind of performance in school or employment that serves as the validity criterion for standard tests can, in effect, serve to define comparability of test scores on modified and standard forms. (p. 114)

Under this rationale, if the modified and standard versions of a test were to predict the performance of interest equally well for handicapped and nonhandicapped applicants, then the two versions could be considered comparable, and there would be no need to flag scores for modified versions of a test. However, if equivalent prediction were not the case, then either new modifications would have to be made or else the scores from modified test forms would need to be transformed in some way so as to yield equivalent prediction of the criterion.

A similar type of criterion scaling was carried out some years ago by a team of researchers headed by Ernest Primoff of the Civil Service Commission (1956). The project involved the development of tests for placing blind workers in trades and occupations. Several features of the study, though different from the present situation, were critical in rendering it theoretically attractive as well as practical: in an employment context, it was possible to test different skills for blind than for sighted employees, assign workers to jobs that used their special skills, and change job specifications in accordance with the skills available.

The argument here for scaling is related to the function of a standardized test. The purpose of standardization—establishing uniform conditions for all examinees—is to insure that test scores will have the same meaning for, and thus be fair to, all examinees. The purpose of test-score flagging is to indicate that some aspect of standardization has been breached. Scaling or adjusting test scores from modified test versions can restore the desired comparability.

The objective of this chapter is to examine the technical feasibility of scaling, or transforming the test scores of handicapped examinees through adjusting their relationship to a criterion. The question of feasibility turns on whether or not there is a reasonable basis for assuring that any such scaling adjustments would be acceptably accurate and thus fair to individual examinees. This judgment involves technical matters, but it does not rest strictly on psychometric considerations or operational convenience.

# Assumptions

☐  ☐  Adjusting the test scores of handicapped students on the basis of predicted criterion performance rests on several specific assumptions:

1. That there is empirical evidence of systematic over- or underprediction of college performance associated with nonstandard test scores (otherwise, there is nothing to correct);

2. That there are sufficient data to develop stable score adjustments (otherwise, the adjustments would be plagued by indefensibly large random errors; they might also be unfair to individuals because of systematic over- and undercorrection for particular groups);

3. That the criterion is adequate as a scaling measure (otherwise, adjustments may contain an unacceptable level of random error or systematic bias);

4. That scale transformations can be developed for the several handicapped groups accurately reflecting important differences among them (otherwise, an individual's test score may be altered arbitrarily, possibly incorrectly); and

5. That the disabilities of individual examinees can be identified accurately (otherwise, an individual may be incorrectly classified with other students whose situations and score adjustments may be quite different).

Each of these assumptions is examined in turn.

**Equivalent prediction**   The first assumption is that the current modified and standard versions of a test provide equivalent prediction for handicapped and nonhandicapped examinees. Braun, Ragosta, and Kaplan (1986a) have examined the prediction systems for several classifications of handicapped examinees to determine how well the different versions of the Scholastic Aptitude Test predict the first-year college averages of each group. Although the results are difficult to summarize briefly, the investigators found generally that:

1. Test scores and high school grades predicted the college performance of handicapped people relatively well, but not quite as well as they predicted that of nonhandicapped people.

2. SAT scores from special test administrations, when used as the sole predictor, had a strong tendency to *over*predict the college

performance of learning-disabled students. This overprediction differed for high-scoring and low-scoring examinees (.56 versus .18 standard deviation unit, respectively). By contrast, *under*prediction was noted for hearing-impaired students.

3. When both high school grades and SAT scores were used to predict performance, there was little evidence overall of consistent prediction errors.

These results suggest that, while in some respects predictions of the college performances of handicapped and nonhandicapped students can be treated as being similar, there is also evidence of some important differences, especially for some subgroups. It is not clear whether those differences result from systematic measurement error. Furthermore, much of the prediction error appears to result simply from the apparent fact that the performance of handicapped students is less predictable (from scores or previous grades) than that of others, and it is not clear that unpredictability should be considered a basis for flagging scores. These differences do nonetheless suggest that exploring the feasibility of test-score scaling is desirable.

**Data sufficiency**    A major determinant of the feasibility of scaling test scores is the ability to collect sufficient data to perform psychometrically defensible adjustments. Adjustments disaggregated to take account of subgroup differences have considerable potential for error even with large databases. As Cohen (1986) has demonstrated, statistical uncertainty quickly overwhelms the possible value of the adjustment. The result is to increase rather than reduce prediction errors. In the case of handicapped students, samples are typically small at the outset and must be further divided to take account of wide diversity within handicap category or type of educational program.

In their study, Braun, Ragosta, and Kaplan (1986a) were able only with extraordinary effort to collect enough data to study the validity of SAT scores for handicapped students. Their effort was successful only after two rounds of data collection, using a full four years of data from the College Board's Validity Study Service. Even though listings of test takers were accumulated for individual institutions over four years, they frequently contained only two or three names. At many schools, disabled student services personnel, while universally recognizing the need for the study, were unable to devote the time needed to search student data files.

Braun, Ragosta, and Kaplan (1986a) were able to gather data at least minimally sufficient for the purposes of their study; however, numbers were quite small even for the total group in some categories of handicapped examinees. For example, only 72 physically handicapped students and 84 hearing-impaired students could be found for whom high school grade-point averages, first-year college grades, and SAT scores from special administrations were available. Furthermore, these subgroups are far from homogeneous, representing many different kinds of physical disability and degrees of hearing impairment. An added complication is that the information needed to identify the subgroups in order to determine and apply adjustments is largely unavailable. The same heterogeneity is likely for the somewhat larger numbers of learning-disabled test takers; and for some groups, such as the visually impaired, the numbers are clearly very small.

Hearing-impaired students clustered at specific institutions, which at first blush would seem encouraging for data-collection efforts. However, as Braun, Ragosta, and Kaplan (1986a) found, at these institutions there may not be any appropriate groups of non-handicapped students that could serve as control (or, in the case of scaling, that would help determine scaling parameters).

Thus, the experience of Braun, Ragosta, and Kaplan was encouraging only in the sense that it demonstrated that, with some significant effort by schools and test sponsors, minimally sufficient data might be gathered to permit scaling of the scores of some undifferentiated groups of handicapped students. But what is discouraging is that despite the extraordinary effort, the quantity of the data appears only partly sufficient in the case of the SAT—by far the largest testing program administered by ETS. This finding suggests that for smaller (though still very large) testing operations like the GRE program, it would be even less feasible to collect the needed data. Graduate departments are generally characterized by small numbers of students, and many traditionally are unable to collect enough data to conduct a validity study based on *all* of their students, undifferentiated even by major subgroups.

Recent developments in empirical Bayes methodology (Braun, Jones, Rubin, & Thayer, 1983; Braun & Jones, 1980 and 1985; Raudenbush & Bryk, 1985; Rubin, 1980), which greatly facilitates statistical estimation with small samples, sometimes prove invaluable. However, as has been noted in other contexts, even empirical Bayes methods have minimum data requirements. Given the fragmented nature of data on handicapped examinees, these methods are pushed beyond reasonable limits even in the case of the SAT. Regardless of the statistical methodology, it is clear that for particular subgroups of handicapped examinees, nationwide score adjustments would have to be based on tiny quantities of data—a highly questionable procedure.

**Adequacy of the criterion** When alternate forms of a test are equated, one design often employed involves the administration of each form to a different group of examinees, usually along with a smaller set of items given to both groups. The common items, quite reasonably assumed to have the same meaning for both, serve as the basis for adjustments in the means and variances of the two groups, thus allowing the equating of both forms as though they had been given to equivalent groups. Performance on this common-item test typically bears a very strong relationship to that on each of the other test forms, a situation that permits precise scaling. In comparison to common-item equating tests, typical criteria of success in academic and employment settings have critical shortcomings. Because, for example, grade-point averages are usually based on different sets of courses for different students, and because those who assign grades have varying standards, the averages are not strictly comparable for different students—certainly not as comparable as common test items. For handicapped and nonhandicapped students, they are likely to have even less comparability because of possible differences in the ways their academic performances are evaluated. Indeed, Braun, Ragosta, and Kaplan (1986a) documented dramatic differences in over- and underprediction for hearing-impaired students in different programs, differences very likely associated with variations in criteria. Furthermore, support services, which may have a direct effect on grades, may be differentially available to handicapped students, constituting another component of noncomparability. And it is well known that grading standards vary across institutions and among different fields of study within the same institution.

Thus, there is no assurance that the criterion according to which test scores would be scaled is itself comparable for handicapped and nonhandicapped test takers: that it has the same meaning and contains no systematic bias favoring one group. This condition is critical because the phenomenon of over- or underprediction may suggest either over- or undermeasurement (by the special test administration) or over- or underachievement on the criterion (resulting from such factors as special support services or extraordinary student effort). Because these components are so thoroughly confounded and because there may be many reasons why a particular group of students might make better or worse grades than predicted, there is no compelling basis for assuming that over- or underprediction is necessarily the result of measurement error in the test. When we scale test scores through criterion performance, however, the assumption is made that they should reflect any and all observed between-group differences in performance, regardless of the reasons for those differentials, even if the criterion may reflect a bias against some groups of students.

In addition, the relationship between aptitude test scores and first-year academic performance is typically much more tenuous than that between a common-item test and the test forms that are to be equated. While it is not unusual for correlations between test forms and a common-item test to run in the .80s or higher, test performance and first-year grades typically correlate below .50. Thus, any scaling adjustment made on the basis of this relationship would contain a significant error component, compounding the errors resulting from small samples. Under these circumstances, it is conceivable that the error the adjustment introduces might be as large as its practical effect—a situation that would be difficult to defend as fair to individuals, since even greater accuracy is needed for adjusting individuals' test scores by subgroup membership than for equating alternate forms of a test. Therefore, the adequacy of the criterion as a scaling variable must be seriously questioned.

**Feasibility of scaling transformations** There is no strong evidence that modified and standard version of admissions tests differ in their precision of measurement (reliability and scale units) for handicapped and nonhandicapped examinees. For such a situation, a suitable transformation probably would not exist. The findings of Rock, Bennett, and Kaplan (1985) suggest no dramatic differences in the precision with which abilities are measured for various groups of handicapped and nonhandicapped students. Provided that both sufficient data and an adequate criterion (scaling variable) were available, the task of defining a defensible and fair scaling transformation could be undertaken.

The findings of Braun, Ragosta, and Kaplan (1986a) suggest, however, that the required transformation does not simply entail adding or subtracting a constant to the scores of each member of an examinee subgroup. Rather, because overprediction was sometimes noted at some points in the test-score range and underprediction at others, the appropriate transformation would require an adjustment of prediction equation *slopes* as well as intercepts. While this situation does not preclude the possibility of defining a suitable transformation, it does complicate matters, since slope and intercept differences are more difficult to estimate precisely than intercept differences alone. Further complications arise because the adjustments can be applied either when test scores are used as the sole predictor or when they are used in combination with one or more other predictors. The data of Braun, Ragosta, and Kaplan (1986a) show that the transformations would differ for these various combinations. Thus, the test-score adjustments would depend on the particular combination of predictors used by a school. Unless score users were willing to agree on the use of a particular, common set of predictors (and to interpret the scores for the same purpose), *several* adjusted scores, corresponding to each combination of predictors, would need to be reported for handicapped students. Such a procedure would be tantamount to flagging the test scores of these examinees.

It is important to add that, as Linn (1978) has noted, equal correlations between a predictor and a criterion do not necessarily imply equivalent prediction systems for two groups of examinees, nor do equivalent prediction systems (equal slopes, intercepts, and errors of estimate) imply equal correlations. The findings of Braun, Ragosta, and Kaplan (1986a) suggest that predictor-criterion correlations are likely to differ for handicapped and nonhandicapped examinees as well as for subgroups of handicapped test takers. One consequence of these differences, as Lord (1980) has pointed out, is that any scaling transformation will typically vary from group to group, effectively precluding the identification of a single transformation that would be fair to every handicapped group.

**Adequacy of identification procedures**    Finally, adjusting individual scores would require that handicapped students be identified and classified accurately as to type and, probably, severity of handicap, to insure not only that scaling parameters are computed without bias, but also that the right adjustments are applied for individual examinees. Bennett and Ragosta (1984) have documented in some detail the inherent difficulty in defining handicapping conditions and the unreliability of individual classifications.

Under current procedures, the test scores of handicapped examinees are flagged, not adjusted. The need to verify handicapping conditions is less critical now, since verification serves only to permit a student to take a nonstandard version of a test and does not directly affect either a given handicapped individual's test score or those of other handicapped students, as it would if test scores were to be scaled.

## Broader concerns: Social, educational, and measurement issues

☐    Several other, somewhat broader, issues are also suggested by the scaling proposition; two in particular would appear to require some consideration. One is the question of scaling scores of other relevant subgroups. If the practice of adjusting scores through the criterion can be justified for handicapped examinees, it can be argued that such adjustments may be desirable for innumerable other subgroups in order to render their scores comparable in meaning to those of the majority of test takers. While such analogies may break down at some point, they do serve to raise the possibility of adjusting or scaling the scores of other subgroups. (Incidentally, for some of these groups, particularly those that exhibit below-average test performance, the phenomenon of *overprediction* has been extensively documented. For these students, a scaling through the criterion of first-year averages would actually result in lowering test scores.)

In this regard, the Braun, Ragosta, and Kaplan (1986a) findings are of interest because the first-year performance of some handicapped students was overpredicted and that of others was underpredicted. Thus, if the method of scaling through the criterion were to be implemented on the basis of these results, the test scores of members of one handicapped subgroup would be raised and those of another would be lowered. Shaky adjustments based on small samples seem even harder to justify when the effect may be to lower the likelihood of admission for some groups.

One particular handicapped group requires some additional consideration. Looking at the data of Braun, Ragosta, and Kaplan (1986a), it is clear that if scaling were undertaken in an effort to make scores equally predictive, by far the most frequent adjustment would be to lower substantially the scores of learning-disabled students. But it is not certain to what extent, if at all, the pattern of LD students' overpredicted college grades is due to some miscalibration of test scores.

In fact, there is evidence that the pattern of overprediction has another explanation altogether. As has been described elsewhere (Willingham, 1986), federal criteria for determining LD status emphasizes aptitude-achievement discrepancy; schools commonly identify LD students on that basis; such a pattern is strongly evident in the SAT scores and school grades of LD students who take special admissions tests; and finally, that same pattern is apparent when college grades and SAT scores are compared. Thus, the overprediction for LD students may result simply from the way that group is identified, in which case scaling down their test scores could be quite misleading and unfair.

## SUMMARY

Each of the dual goals of providing measurement conditions that do not penalize examinees for some disability and insuring by protecting their identities that handicapped students are neither favored nor penalized in admissions is certainly desirable. However, for the reasons discussed earlier, using criterion performance as a basis for scaling the scores of handicapped examinees does not appear to represent a feasible or defensible strategy for achieving these goals. Further, the additional problems introduced by such a strategy would, in our opinion, outweigh any potential advantages.

Our objective was to examine the feasibility of the scaling proposal advanced by the Panel on Testing of Handicapped People. While this report fulfills that narrow purpose, an unfavorable assessment of one method does not put the problem to rest. The dilemma of the incompatible dual goals remains. Is it possible through some other means to bring the modified tests to a condition of sufficient comparability to warrant removing flags? We think it is important to continue searching for a workable solution. One possible avenue may be improved methods of establishing fair time limits for tests administered to handicapped examinees. Another possibility is adjusting scores to take account of gains resulting from unlimited time.

An important principle to encourage, we believe, is a more individualized admissions process for handicapped students, a process wherein care is taken to collect pertinent information and weigh the circumstances of each case. This principle can be furthered by carrying out periodic validity studies for handicapped subgroups of examinees and disseminating the results of those studies to ad-missions officers. Whether or not certain groups of handicapped test takers tend to be systematically over- or underpredicted would develop over time as useful background information for test-score users.

Finally, it is recommended that further research be conducted along two lines: exploring the development of other possible score adjustments or the kinds of test modifications that might deviate less from standardized procedures (and thus obviate the need to flag scores); and determining the nature of any over- or underprediction that is observed for handicapped students (i.e., whether discrepancies result from an over- or underestimate of ability or from a systematic bias in the evaluation of subsequent performance). The work of Rock, Bennett, and Kaplan (1985) suggests that systematic bias is a some-what more probable explanation. This research would help to deter-mine the appropriateness of any scaling of test scores. It seems unlikely, however, that even with this better understanding, a purely mechanical adjustment of test scores could be defended. Even if a scaling procedure were technically feasible, any such corrections would call for careful evaluation of side effects and the interests of other groups of test takers. These important considerations have not been examined here in any detail since they lie beyond the scope of this report.

# 11

# Discussion and Conclusions

## ☐ *Warren W. Willingham*

In the previous chapters we have described a number of individual studies undertaken over the past four years and their principal results. The purpose of this chapter is to integrate those findings in order to see more clearly what answers they suggest for the three key questions posed at the outset of this report:

1. When admissions tests are modified for handicapped people, to what extent are the nonstandard tests and the resulting scores comparable to those of the regular national program?
2. Might the comparability of such tests be improved? If so, how?
3. What implications might be drawn concerning possible resolutions of the flagging problem?

The following two sections are concerned with the question of comparability, first looking at different aspects of score and task comparability, then examining comparability from the standpoint of different groups of handicapped examinees. Next we take up the issue of flagging and possibilities for improving the comparability of tests modified for disabled people. This chapter and the report end with a brief summary of what we take to be the main conclusions and implications of this series of studies. As a preface to this discussion, it may be useful to reflect briefly on several aspects of research on this topic that seem to us important in interpreting the results and considering their possible implications for testing programs and test users. These observations come from our experience over the past few years and from work recently completed elsewhere.

Availability of data on handicapped examinees has always been recognized as a troublesome issue. If anything, the problem now appears to be worse than imagined a few years ago. Obtaining adequate data for visually impaired, hearing-impaired, and physically handicapped examinees is especially difficult. Each of these groups numbers only a few hundred nationally each year for a major test like the SAT. Furthermore, these groups divide into subgroups that differ substantially in character or degree of disability. Disabled examinees take different forms of the test under different conditions and then fan out into hundreds of institutions. Without Bayesian methods developed quite recently (Braun & Jones, 1985; Braun, Jones, Rubin, & Thayer, 1983; Rubin, 1980), most of the prediction work reported here would have been quite impossible. Aside from operational difficulties in obtaining data and the lack of confidence one feels in interpreting results from small samples, many questions simply cannot be addressed because the relevant subgroups are too small. That is even more true for smaller-volume tests.

That handicapped students enroll in many different colleges or graduate programs is related to another problem—the comparability of the grade information used to evaluate the comparability of the test scores. Comparability of criterion data is always an uncertainty in predictive validity studies; its main effects are usually to add noise and lower validity coefficients (Goldman & Slaughter, 1976). Noncomparable criteria can also produce systematic differences when subgroups have different educational experiences. Many handicapped students, particularly those with hearing impairments, are enrolled in special college programs designed to meet their particular educational needs and provide support services as necessary. It would not be surprising if both grading standards and admissions standards were different in such programs. Our data (reviewed in chapter 9) suggest that both assumptions are correct. The effect is to give an impression of noncomparable test scores when noncomparable criteria are a more likely explanation: the test is the same, but grading practices are developed independently in different programs. We will come back to this problem in discussing the findings of the prediction studies. It also bears on the scaling suggestion of the NAS panel.

Another problem is accuracy of classification—an essential assumption in any analysis of comparability of tests across groups. Reliable identification, particularly as to severity of disability, is a significant issue within each of the four types of handicap, but learning disability poses by far the most perplexing problem. As Figure 1.2 shows, this group represents a large and rapidly expanding proportion of all disabled people taking nonstandard SAT's. This rapid expansion is evidently connected with the way LD students are identified.

In Chalfant's (1984) view, the problem of identification starts with the fact that, in defining operational criteria for actually determining which students are classified as learning disabled, federal regulations omit reference to any psychological process, such as a perceptual deficit. Initially the regulations (Dept. of Health, Education, and Welfare, 1977c) did define specific learning disability as "a disorder in one or more of the basic psychological processes involved in understanding or in using language" (for example, perceptual handicaps, dyslexia, developmental aphasia) (p. 65083). But in a report of a special work group appointed by the Department of Education (Reynolds, 1985), the development of federal guidelines for identifying LD students is described along the following lines:

> For many years but particularly since the passage of public law 94–142 the diagnosis and evaluation of learning disabilities has presented major problems. . . . When the rules and regulations for PL–94–142 were being developed, many experts testified in Office of Education hearings, wrote numerous papers, and were convened for discussion and debate. . . . The only consensus regarding the characteristics of this "thing" called learning disability was that it resulted in a major discrepancy between what you would expect academically of learning disabled children and the level at which they were actually achieving. (p. 452)

Thus, federal regulations stipulate two operational criteria for determining the existence of a specific learning disability: whether a child's achievement is commensurate with his or her age and ability (assuming appropriate educational experiences); and whether the child displays a severe discrepancy between intellectual ability and achievement in one or more of seven areas related to communication and mathematical abilities (Dept. of Health, Education, and Welfare, 1977c, p. 65083).

A recent survey of state and local education agencies shows the influence of the aptitude-achievement discrepancy in current definitions of learning disability (Chalfant, 1984). It seems reasonable to assume, then, that such discrepancies are not uncommon among LD students who take an extended-time version of the SAT, since it is school documentation of the LD condition that establishes eligibility for the special administration of the SAT. Our data confirm that assumption. Relative to those of other groups, the SAT scores of LD students were substantially higher than their high school grades (see chapters 6 and 9).

When college grades of LD students were predicted on the basis of their scores on a nonstandard SAT, performance was overpredicted to a much greater extent than was true of any other handicapped group. Does this mean that the nonstandard version of the SAT is seriously biased *in favor of* LD students? A more plausible explanation would be that many students in this group had been identified as underachievers earlier and continued that pattern in college. But the picture is even more complicated.

An extensive study in Colorado (Shepard, Smith, & Vojir, 1983) revealed that more than half of the students labeled "LD" failed to meet even a weak criterion for that classification. The misclassified students proved to have a variety of other problems: language difficulties, emotional problems, absenteeism, slow learning rate, or average learning rate in high socioeconomic districts. Elsewhere, Shepard (1983) described two motives at work: first, the strong interest of many parents in having their low-achieving children labeled "learning disabled" in the belief that the label is more socially acceptable than other alternatives; and second, the professional interest of teachers and program administrators in moving pupils into this category.

Certainly many LD students do have the specific learning disabilities or marked aptitude-achievement discrepancies cited in federal guidelines, but as Chalfant (1984) notes, "prevalence data reported by state and federal agencies indicate that many students are being inappropriately classified as learning disabled" (p. 4). Chapter 2 provides other references to the growing literature of the misclassification problem. Congress recently mandated a federal interagency committee to determine the nature and extent of learning disabilities and to recommend research that might be helpful in clarifying the apparent confusion (Landers, 1986).

Meanwhile, LD classifications have risen dramatically, increasing every year since the federal government first required states to count students in special education programs funded under Public Law 94–142. In 1976–77 there were about eight hundred thousand LD students; in 1982–83 the number was 1.7 million. During this period the number of students classified in several other categories, including mentally retarded, actually declined (*Education of the Handicapped*, June 29, 1983; January 8, 1986). Undoubtedly, "learning disability" is a valid signal that a student needs help, but from a scientific standpoint, the LD classification as it is now employed seems to be a moving target, representing a diverse collection of students with quite different educational problems.

These various observations regarding the amount and quality of data available and the ambiguity in interpreting a designation of handicapped status all call for caution in evaluating the results here reported. Furthermore, our results obviously do not pertain to individuals not represented in these studies. It is impossible to say how many people with what disabilities never take admissions tests, either by choice or because they are no longer in the educational system. We believe that these studies have added significantly to what was known about how admissions tests work with handicapped students, but obviously there are severe limitations in the extent to which one can expect even a conscientious research effort to provide definitive answers to the questions posed. We move now to the findings.

# Eight marks of comparability

☐ ☐   The first objective of this research was to determine to what extent admissions tests administered under nonstandard conditions are comparable to the regular tests offered in national administrations. As was discussed in chapter 1, the validity and fairness of admissions tests depend upon their comparability for handicapped and nonhandicapped examinees, and the tests should be examined with respect to comparability of the task as well as of the scores.

Taking an admissions test is not likely to be seen as a comparable task from the perspective of most handicapped students. It is not remotely similar for someone who is blind, someone who cannot hold a pencil, someone who is deaf and does not normally converse in standard English. For a student who has great difficulty in reading or has a problem with motor control, taking such a test can require enormous effort and perseverance. For example, reading a test in braille takes some two and a half times as long as sight reading. Earning a score commensurate with their ability is disproportionately hard work for many disabled students. From this viewpoint, the task may seem hardly comparable to that faced by a nonhandicapped person, and it may be just as difficult to see how the scores could be comparable.

This view would be accurate if one took "comparable" to mean "identical." Comparable scores do not necessarily imply the same average score for handicapped and nonhandicapped groups because there is no way to know whether the groups are either representative of students generally or comparable in their learning experience. Scores should, however, have comparable meaning in several respects, as indicated in chapter 1 and examined in the studies reported. Nor can the test-taking task necessarily be identical. The important objective is to make the task as comparable as possible by removing irrelevant sources of difficulty.

In thinking about what constitutes irrelevant difficulty in the task and what provides a reasonable basis for ascribing comparable meaning to the scores, it is helpful to consider the test-taking process from an additional perspective. Three levels of the process can be distinguished: the *sensory-motor process* involved in "reading" the test content and recording the answers (i.e., the input-output mechanism); the *encoding process* required to recognize test material and make it available for higher-order processing; and the *cognitive process* that involves comprehension and reasoning. These processes obviously overlap, and test performance reflects all three to some degree. But the primary purpose of the admissions test is to assess the higher-level processes—the cognitive abilities.

Least critical to this end would be the sensory-motor process. That a nonstandard test engages a different sensory modality (e.g., hearing a cassette rather than seeing a page) is less important in measuring verbal comprehension than that the test material is presented in a manner accessible to the examinee and consistent with her or his educational experience. That change in modality clearly changes the surface character of the task as well as the perceptual skills involved and the demands on short-term memory. It is normally assumed that the underlying cognitive abilities that the test is mainly intended to assess are probably not thereby altered, but that the change in modality does require changing the timing lest a more lengthy task artificially depress scores.

For the purposes of this discussion, *encoding processes* refers to any of a number of lower- to intermediate-level skills such as connecting word sounds and syllables, using short-term memory, attaching meaning to words and phrases, and so forth. A disabled person may encounter various types of encoding difficulties: for example, a blind examinee who has limited experience with graphical material, a deaf examinee who does not ordinarily use some elements of standard English in routine communication, a learning-disabled examinee who consistently misinterprets words that are similar in appearance. Such encoding problems may or may not have a significant effect on test performance. They may or may not represent a specific disability separate from what the test is intended to measure. It may or may not be possible to avoid such difficulties in the test. They may or may not be avoided or compensated for in the course of academic work.

It is assumed that the *cognitive abilities* assessed by a test (e.g., verbal comprehension, quantitative reasoning) are reflected directly in the examinees' answers to the test questions. Studies of the pattern of those answers (factor analysis, analysis of differential item functioning) give an indication of whether differences in sensory-motor or encoding processes have any effect on the *structure* of cognitive abilities. The predictive studies provide external evidence as to whether those differences have distorted score *levels.*

We move now to a discussion of study results that bear on the comparability question. In interpreting these results, it is important to keep in mind the different levels of the test-taking process. These distinctions are helpful in deciding whether a nonstandard test poses a comparable task and whether it measures similar cognitive abilities at comparable score levels for a handicapped group, even though it may appear different in some obvious ways.

Table 11.1 summarizes key findings. It serves a limited purpose: to provide an overview of comparability from two perspectives. Looking across each of the eight rows, one gains a summary view of different aspects of comparability. That is the focus of this section. Looking down the four columns, one sees a summary view of the degree of comparability for each type of disability. In the following section we look at the findings from that second perspective.

When one considers each of these types of comparability, it is useful to note that standard and nonstandard tests differ largely in conditions of administration, not in content. In three nonstandard administrations out of four, handicapped students use identical tests but with extended time. The remaining nonstandard administrations involve different test formats (e.g., braille) but only minor changes in items or in the way they are presented.

Many of the results cited here are based only on the SAT. This is because the much larger amount of SAT data permitted more detailed analyses and because during the past four years there have been additional studies of SAT data (reported in chapters 4 and 6) beyond those included in the jointly sponsored series. The GRE and the SAT are similar tests; the results here reported tend to be similar wherever they can be compared. In this discussion we have tried to avoid tedious detail, but we do indicate where important findings are based on one test or two and when results are confirming or inconsistent.

## Reliability

☐ The reliability of individual subscores reported for the regular SAT and GRE tends to run about .91 to .92, which is normally considered high. Our data indicate that the reliability of these tests administered to disabled students was at that level, or somewhat lower if the handicapped group was restricted in range. A preferred measure, largely insensitive to range variation, is the standard error of measurement. For all of the handicapped groups examined, the error of measurement was essentially identical to that of the regular

**Table 11.1  Summary of key findings concerning the extent to which nonstandard tests for handicapped examinees are comparable to those regularly administered to nonhandicapped students**

| | Nonstandard tests administered to examinees who were: | | | |
|---|---|---|---|---|
| | Hearing impaired | Learning disabled | Physically handicapped | Visually impaired |
| *Score comparability* | | | | |
| 1. Reliability | Comparable reliability. | Comparable reliability. | Comparable reliability. | Comparable reliability. |
| 2. Factor structure | Comparable overall—V and M less highly related. | Comparable overall—V and M less highly related (math ability may be underestimated with cassette form). | Comparable overall—V and M less highly related. | Comparable overall—V and M (or Q) less highly related (GRE Analytical behaved differently in large format). |
| 3. Differential item difficulty | Little evidence of differential item difficulty. | Little evidence of differential item difficulty. | Little evidence of differential item difficulty. | Some SAT math items differentially difficult in braille format. |
| 4. Prediction of GPA | GPA less accurately predicted from grades or test. GPA underpredicted from SAT—but only in special program. | GPA less accurately predicted from grades or test. Overall, slight GPA overprediction—more from high grades or scores (esp. scores). | GPA less accurately predicted from grades or test. Overall, slight GPA overprediction—by SAT or grades. | GPA less accurately predicted from grades or test. Overall, slight GPA underprediction with grades plus SAT. GPA overpredicted by high GRE scores and grades. |
| 5. Prediction of admissions decisions (undergraduate) | Selection process comparable—but more admitted than predicted. | Selection process comparable—but a few less admitted than predicted. | Selection process comparable—but in smaller colleges, a few less admitted than predicted. | Selection process comparable—but in smaller colleges, a few less admitted than predicted. |

*Task comparability*

| | | | | |
|---|---|---|---|---|
| **6. Test content** | Internal statistics indicate good comparability. | Internal statistics indicate good comparability. | Internal statistics indicate good comparability. | Internal statistics indicate mostly good comparability. |
| | Examinees report difficulty with Verbal—V and M scores confirm. | Examinees report difficulty with Verbal—V and M scores do not confirm. | Most examinees report no items difficult because of disability. | Examinees report difficulty with reading and graphical material—latter partly confirmed in item analysis. |
| | SAT scores lower for manually fluent examinees. | No differential item difficulty due to reading load. | | |
| **7. Test accommodations** | Most examinees satisfied. | Most examinees satisfied. | Most examinees satisfied. | Most examinees satisfied. |
| **8. Test timing** | More likely than nonhandicapped to complete SAT. | More likely than nonhandicapped to complete SAT. | More likely than nonhandicapped to complete SAT. | More likely than nonhandicapped to complete SAT and GRE. |
| | Some SAT items easier near the end of the test. | Some SAT items easier near the end of the test. | GPA overpredicted by SAT and grades for examinees taking more time. | Near end of the test some items easier on SAT and GRE. |
| | | GPA overpredicted by SAT for examinees taking more time—not true for grades. | | |

SAT data were available for all cells of the table. GRE data were available only for visually impaired examinees for lines 1, 2, 3, and 7; for all groups except the hearing impaired for line 4; and in limited quantity for all groups in line 6.

test (see Table 7.4). These are internal estimates; that is, they are based upon test performance at one point in time. The fact that Centra (1986) found quite high correlations when handicapped students took the SAT under timed and untimed conditions suggests that retest reliability over time would be high as well.

These results demonstrate that the tests are comparable with respect to the amount of score fluctuation one would observe if the student took the test a second time. That is, the tests measure what they measure with the same precision for handicapped and non-handicapped examinees. That begs the question, do the tests measure the same thing?

## Factor structure

☐ A standard method for determining whether a test measures the same thing for different groups is to analyze its factor structure. Factor analysis determines empirically whether the ability factors that are assumed to underlie the variation among individuals are actually the same across groups. The main finding (presented in chapter 8) was that the structure was comparable overall for each of the handicapped groups where data permitted the analysis. This finding was based on the fact that typically some 95 percent of the reliable variation in scores was accounted for by the ability factors that the test is assumed to measure.

As Table 11.1 shows, there were two minor exceptions to that overall comparability and one difference between the standard and nonstandard tests that ran through all handicapped groups for SAT and GRE; that is to say, verbal and quantitative ability were somewhat less highly related for handicapped examinees than for others. That finding may mean that these abilities develop in a somewhat more differentiated manner among handicapped students because, in compensating for a disability, they tend to lean more heavily on one skill or another. Or the difference could result from the fact that on the standard timed test a speed factor common to the Verbal and Mathematical sections is more pronounced. Such a factor would tend to increase their intercorrelation for nonhandicapped examinees. In either event, the effect of the lower correlation between the sections may be to make the scores of handicapped students somewhat more useful for diagnostic purposes.

The similarity in the tests' factor structure for handicapped and nonhandicapped examinees supports the assumption that the nonstandard test scores represent comparable cognitive abilities and that they have not been distorted by the student's disability (e.g., use of a different sensory-motor or encoding process in taking the test). One possible implication is that scores are more likely to be useful in predicting academic performance. But predictive accuracy is determined by many factors and is directly testable (discussion following and in chapter 9). A more important implication of these findings concerning factor structure is that the tests have comparable meaning in such other contexts in which the scores may be used as self-assessment of strengths and weaknesses, course placement, and educational advisement. In these situations, test scores provide additional information that is often helpful in assessing the reasonableness of a planned course of action or in identifying areas of endeavor that may require extra work or assistance. For that reason comparable meaning, as indicated by comparable factor structure, is an important attribute of the scores.

## Differential item difficulty

☐ Even though a nonstandard test measures similar cognitive abilities to those assessed by a standard test, it is still quite possible that it contains inappropriate items. Inappropriateness might be indicated by certain types of items being especially difficult. If an item or type of item is hard for a given subgroup, that difficulty does not in itself signify a problem. For example, if a subgroup scores low on verbal ability, it would tend to find most such items difficult.

Whether generally low performance on a test is an accurate representation of a group's ability cannot be assessed by looking at individual items; the answer to that question requires other information, such as whether the test tends to over- or underpredict academic grades. The question at hand is only whether some items are differentially difficult (or easy) considering how the group performed on the test overall. If some items are discovered to be *differentially* difficult, the next step would be to look at the content of the items to see whether they were arguably unfair, perhaps because they require skills tangential to the ability that the test is intended to measure (Shepard, 1982b).

The content of one form of the GRE and two forms of the SAT were analyzed for various subgroups of handicapped examinees, first in clusters representing classes of items, then as individual items within aberrant clusters. Overall, there was little evidence of differential item difficulty. The few differentially difficult items identified were primarily associated with the braille version of the mathematics section of the SAT. Several of these items involved figures, providing partial empirical confirmation of blind students' reports of difficulty. But other items of this sort were not differentially difficult. Nor has examination of the content of the difficult items thus far revealed why some items proved problematic for blind students.

The fact that there was little evidence of differential item difficulty for the hearing-impaired students might appear inconsistent with the well-known fact that verbal material in standard English is difficult for deaf students. The apparent explanation is that all (rather than some) of the items within the verbal section of the SAT tended to be relatively difficult for this group, and that finding shows up in line 6 of Table 11.1. The analysis of mathematics items reported by Bennett, Rock, and Kaplan (1985) does suggest that problems requiring little reading were relatively easier for hearing-impaired students than those with more reading.

The content of the braille version of the SAT Mathematical test deserves further study. In general, however, these results indicate that the SAT and GRE are largely free of aberrant items that are more difficult for handicapped students than other items measuring the same ability. This finding suggests that present test-development procedures are largely successful in eliminating such items.

## Prediction of academic performance

☐ The NAS panel viewed the accuracy of grade predictions as a critical aspect of comparability, and with good reason. The validity issue is whether one can safely make the same inference as to future academic performance when looking at test scores from nonstandard and regular administrations. Do the nonstandard scores predict performance accurately? Are they useful to the college and fair to the students?

There were two prominent findings from the studies reported in chapter 10 and summarized in Table 11.1. One important finding was that when academic performance was predicted on the basis of test scores and prior grades, there was little consistent over- or under-prediction for the great majority of handicapped students. The small group of students in special college programs for deaf students was an exception that needs to be considered separately. For all other groups, however, the average residual (actual grade minus predicted grade) was near 0. This is an important finding because it indicates that if admissions officers follow the standard advice and usual practice of using previous grades as well as test scores in estimating future performance, those estimates will not, on average, be either too high or too low.

A second prominent finding was that the academic performance of handicapped students proved to be less predictable than that of others from test scores, from previous grade-point average, or from both combined. This finding was common to students at both the undergraduate and graduate levels. The less predictable performance of handicapped students was reflected as a systematic pattern in most of the residual analyses: those with low test scores or previous grades tended to achieve better than expected (thus were underpredicted); those with high test scores or previous grades tended to do more poorly than expected (thus were overpredicted). Why was this pattern so consistently observed? Why would the performance of disabled students tend to be less predictable?

One possibility is that other factors (such as financial problems, problems with managing the disability, poor quality of support services, dissatisfaction with the educational program) are more likely to intervene if a student has a disability. Another possibility is that the effectiveness of educational programs for disabled students may vary widely, as may grading standards among those programs in which handicapped students tend to matriculate. At the secondary level, as many as one handicapped student in three may be enrolled in a special program for disabled individuals (Harris, 1986). And at the college level, about one-third of the students taking nonstandard SAT's applied to institutions purporting to have a special program relevant to their disability (Willingham, 1986). No doubt, those programs differ a great deal in character and quality.

The performances of three of the four groups of handicapped students studied were significantly under- or overpredicted when forecasts were based on test scores alone. The situation was quite different for each group. Hearing-impaired students were substantially *under*predicted by the SAT—even, to some degree, when predictions were based on test scores and previous grades. Closer analysis, however, disclosed that underprediction was associated exclusively with students who were enrolled in a separate special program for deaf students. When the academic performance of hearing-impaired students in regular college programs was predicted on the basis of both test scores and previous grades, there was no evidence of significant over- or underprediction (see p. 122 of this report and Table 3.9 in Braun, Ragosta, & Kaplan, 1986a).

With the available data, it is not possible to be sure why there was such a discrepancy between the average predicted GPA and the average actual GPA of deaf students in special programs. One possibility is that the academic performance of students who are consistently taught with a manual language may be underestimated by a test administered solely in English. Another is that deaf students in special programs may be graded on a curve that is not necessarily comparable with grades in other college programs. In any event, any such consistent pattern in the performance of deaf students in special programs should be taken into account in score interpretation. Local norms could serve that purpose when it is clear that applicants are handicapped. That would normally be the situation in a program for deaf students, regardless of flagging practices.

The test *over*predicted the college performance of two other groups—those who were physically disabled and those who were learning disabled. For physically handicapped students, that over-prediction was not unique to the test, nor was it very large overall.

The learning-disabled group presents a very different picture. It was substantially overpredicted by the SAT and at all score levels. Is that overprediction because LD students (or a misclassified subset of LD students) earn higher scores with extended time? Before that question is examined, it is important to note a potentially quite misleading aspect of this overprediction from the SAT. The LD group was not overpredicted to any consequential degree when forecasts were based on test scores and previous grade-point averages; the big overprediction associated with the SAT alone is attributable to the fact that, relative to nonhandicapped students, the LD group had notice-ably higher test scores than high school grades.

As noted in chapter 1, federal regulations specify that learning-disabled students be identified on the basis of poor school per-formance in relation to ability. It would seem to make little sense to evaluate score comparability for this group on the basis of over- or underprediction (from test scores alone) when a discrepancy in the test–school achievement relationship is precisely the basis upon which the group is identified! Finally, calibrating the scores against subsequent college GPA (without taking school grades into account) does not necessarily make the scores comparable for the other uses to which they might be put. For example, achieving that calibration for the learning-disabled group would mean substantially lowering test scores and perhaps seriously misrepresenting the individual's ability for other uses of the score such as educational advising, career guidance and so on.

There was one other important type of prediction discrepancy: the effects of extended time. It was in the learning-disabled group that the data most clearly suggested that providing longer amounts of time may raise scores beyond the level appropriate to compensate for the disability. Those LD students who spent several extra hours on the test earned scores that more seriously overestimated their actual per-formance in college than did LD students who took only one extra hour. These data provide no experimental control, and there may be other explanations for the finding. For example, LD examinees who took more time may have been more anxious and done less well in college for that reason. However, the same students showed no such pattern when predictions were based on high school grades, suggesting that the increasing overprediction with increasing time was more likely due to the test timing than to some characteristic of the examinee.

We see important implications in these research findings. One is obvious: that admissions applications must be evaluated with special care when they are known to come from handicapped individuals. It is very important to take account of previous grade record along with test scores. The scores can provide useful additional information, but focusing only on them can lead to serious over- or underestimation of performance in college or graduate school.

Furthermore, the finding that the academic performance of disabled students is less predictable than that of others on the basis of either previous grades or test scores certainly suggests caution in relying too heavily on those measures and calls for careful appraisal of other information in the student's background. These considerations offer an argument for a preadmissions inquiry regarding handicapped status (for example, flagging scores) in order to increase the likelihood that such care is taken. Such inquiries might occur more often if better interpretative information were made available to admissions officers. However, the NAS panel saw both positive and negative effects of identifying handicapped individuals (Sherman & Robinson 1982, pp. 22–24). Such lower predictability for other subgroups (for example, Hispanic students) has not been seen as sufficient cause to flag scores.

It is also apparent that there are shortcomings in the prediction model for evaluating and considering possible improvements in the comparability of nonstandard tests:

1. An empirical approach is dependent on the availability of sufficient data, and we commented on that serious problem earlier.

2. To emphasize predictive accuracy as a basis for comparability is to assume that any discrepancy in predictions results from the test. In fact, there are a great many reasons why members of a particular group might earn higher or lower grades than expected in college (e.g., they are less well prepared, they study more, they receive inadequate support services, etc.).

3. To rely on predictive accuracy is to assume one has a good criterion that is comparable across different groups of students. There is always reason to doubt criterion comparability—all the more reason

in this case, considering that handicapped students are often enrolled in special programs. Our data on hearing-impaired students seem to be a good illustration.

An important implication of these observations is that there are serious limitations in the extent to which comparability of non-standard tests can be established on the basis of empirical studies alone. The comparability of the task is also an important consideration, especially when adequate data are not likely to be obtainable. We address that topic in a later section.

## Admissions decisions

☐ A final aspect of score comparability concerns test use. Previous paragraphs have examined the appropriateness of inferences that users *might* draw about nonstandard scores on the basis of the relationship of the score to academic performance after admission. It is equally important to know what inferences are *actually* drawn. It seems doubtful that there is any practical way of knowing how admissions officers interpret and act on nonstandard scores, but it is possible to examine the outcome of those actions; that is, whether the scores of handicapped and nonhandicapped students tend to yield comparable admissions decisions.

Such evidence is an important aspect of score comparability because the score for handicapped examinees is different in one obvious respect: it comes with a flag. If there is a tendency to interpret these scores differently or to act on disabled students' applications differently, a flag could facilitate that inclination. That danger is one factor to weigh when testing programs develop score reporting policies. The study of admissions decisions reported in chapter 6 was undertaken in order to better assess the possible extent of that danger.

Broadly speaking, two outcomes of that study merit attention. First, the data indicated that the nature of the selection process was generally comparable for nonhandicapped applicants and handicapped applicants submitting flagged scores, insofar as one can judge from analyzing decisions against test scores and school grades. The probability of admission tended to increase in very like fashion as scores and grades increased, and the weight placed on those measures in reaching decisions was quite similar for both groups. Handicapped applicants were not less likely to be admitted when their test scores were relatively higher than their school grades—a result inconsistent with any assumption that colleges act negatively on suspicion that nonstandard scores are unduly high.

The second finding concerns an aspect of comparability that is arguably more important, the discrepancy between the number of applicants actually admitted and the number predicted to be admitted on the basis of their school grades and test scores. There were such differences   probably real differences, both positive and negative   but the effects were quite small. There is no evidence to connect these discrepancies with test-score flags per se; but, as we said before, that possibility must be weighed.

## Test content

☐   In considering the comparability of test content for handicapped and nonhandicapped examinees, it is important to note that the two groups take essentially the same test. The question is whether the test represents a comparable task in light of the nature of an examinee's disability. We have three types of information that are useful in judging whether the task is comparable:

1. internal statistical analysis of items and factors;
2. the impressions of handicapped examinees; and
3. relative performance on different sections of the test. The internal statistical analyses indicated good comparability in that the factor structure was generally quite similar and there was little evidence of differential item difficulty for handicapped examinees.

Several groups of handicapped examinees taking either the SAT or the GRE reported special difficulty with the vocabulary and amount of reading material on these tests. This reaction is not uncommon among nonhandicapped students. Except for hearing-impaired students, most handicapped groups taking various forms of the SAT and GRE actually scored higher (relative to nonhandicapped examinees) on the Verbal than on the Mathematical section of these tests (Table 7.3). For some deaf students, however, the task may not be comparable because of their deficit in English-language communication skills. Those who are manually fluent tended to do especially poorly. This observation raises the question, would a test translated into sign language (on a rationale similar to that for the braille form for blind examinees) possibly give a more valid assessment of the ability of these students? The feasibility of such a test should be examined.

The comparability of test content that leans heavily on reading is a question of special importance for learning-disabled students. A principal rationale for giving them extra time in nonstandard administrations is the concern that difficulty in reading will prevent LD students from performing well on the test. Consistent with that assumption, they are far more likely to cite problems with the verbal portions of the test than with mathematics items (Ragosta & Kaplan, 1986). Might it be fairer to give these students tests that have a lower reading load or perhaps provide an additional score for the mathematics section based on items with little reading?

A careful look at the test performance of this group does not make these suggestions appear promising. Relative to nonhandicapped examinees, all of the LD groups had *higher* average scores on the Verbal than on the Mathematical section of the SAT (Table 7.3). Is it possible that the extra time available in the nonstandard administration allows the LD students to compensate for their reading problem and pull up the verbal scores more than the mathematical scores? Evidently not. Learning-disabled students who took both a timed and an untimed test did gain 38 points on the untimed version of the verbal section—but they gained 38 points on the mathematical section as well (Centra, 1986). A study by Evans (1980) demonstrated that nonhandicapped examinees made little if any gain on verbal or mathematical scores with extra time.

One other result is pertinent. A special analysis of mathematics items rated according to reading load showed no evidence that LD students found items more difficult if they contained more reading material (Bennett, Rock, & Kaplan, 1985). For the overall group of LD students studied here, these several lines of evidence are not consistent with the assumption that reading poses a special problem that prevents them from performing well on the SAT. There likely is a subgroup of LD students who do have a serious, specific reading problem, but how many such examinees there may be and how they might be reliably identified in an operational testing program is not clear.

The task posed by an admissions test is certainly more difficult for some disabled students than it is for students generally. Overall, these data suggest, however, that for the great majority of handicapped examinees, the content of the test appears to be comparable in the sense that it provides a fair assessment of the cognitive abilities it is intended to measure. Two possible exceptions need to be examined: the feasibility of a manual translation for deaf students and, as discussed earlier, better ways to avoid some mathematical items that may be unduly troublesome to blind students taking a braille test. In general, we find little evidence that the content of the tests is inappropriate.

A test-development procedure recently adopted at ETS is designed to make the content of a nonstandard form as nearly identical as possible to that of the standard form. This objective is accomplished by identifying before the test is assembled which form will be used as a braille or cassette version, permitting review of the content with special consideration for its appropriateness to students whose disability is sufficiently severe to necessitate a different test format. The results on comparability of test content appear to support this procedure.

## Testing accommodations

☐ Our information concerning the adequacy of testing accommodations came from a survey of handicapped students (described in chapter 5). The data are quite useful but should be interpreted with some caution because the response rate was low. The principal finding here is that the great majority of handicapped examinees expressed satisfaction with SAT (94 percent) and GRE (86 percent) testing arrangements. For particular groups of disabled students, 88 percent to 91 percent said that they were satisfied. There was, of course, a variety of very specific complaints (such as technical problems with a cassette or a braille translation, inadequate assistance from a reader) voiced by some individuals.

The one aspect of special accommodations that may be somewhat lacking is the quality and extent of supplementary information services. For example, disclosed tests are not now uniformly available in braille, cassette, and large-type formats. Also, respondents complained that they are unable to take advantage of the so-called disclosure service whereby nonhandicapped examinees can obtain a copy of their marked answer sheet and test booklet. A surprising 68 percent of the respondents who took the nonstandard SAT (and 19 percent of the GRE respondents) reported not having heard that nonstandard administrations were available at the time they first took the test. These figures certainly suggest that the word is not getting out uniformly. Note, however, that if these SAT respondents are representative and understood the question, the implication is that at least 68 percent of the handicapped examinees taking a nonstandard test also took a standard test. Actual program data, based on all examinees taking the nonstandard SAT, indicate that only 29 percent also took the standard form (Centra 1986), so the 68 percent figure is misleading. We do not know, however, how many eligible students may have taken only a standard test because they never heard of the nonstandard administration.

An additional measure of the adequacy and comparability of special testing accommodations is to contrast those arrangements with testing practices that are common in the college classroom.

Respondents to this survey were more likely to use a reader for college tests than for the admissions test, but twice as many examinees reported having a separate testing room for SAT (72 versus 34 percent). And among the large group of learning-disabled students, twice as many reported having extra time on the admissions test (90 versus 45 percent). The corresponding percentages for GRE examinees were similar. Also, for both SAT and GRE examinees, alternate test formats were more common in the admissions test than in college testing. Although there are significant areas of possible improvement, the general implication of these survey responses is that present testing accommodations achieve a reasonable standard of comparability. That conclusion seems justified by the generally high level of satisfaction expressed by examinees and the favorable comparison of typical practices in admissions testing and college testing.

## Test timing

☐ In a standard national administration, students are allowed some two and one-half hours for those portions of the SAT and the GRE that are scored. Most nonstandard test administrations involve time extended beyond that limit. The present policy of the testing programs is to give the students whatever time they need (up to 12 hours on the SAT and 6 hours on the GRE) rather than attempting to specify particular time limits for different handicapped groups.

Before addressing the question of whether this policy creates a comparable task, it is interesting first to ask how much score gain handicapped students realize from the present extended-time policy. Centra (1986) examined this question in some detail. As it turns out, some 3 in 10 handicapped students who take the SAT in a nonstandard administration also take the nationally administered standard version. Centra examined the records of 3,282 such students during the period 1979–82. He refers to the standard administration as "timed" and the nonstandard administration as "untimed"—not strictly accurate, but a reasonable characterization since very few students take the full 12 hours.

By comparing scores from the so-called timed and untimed administrations (taking into account the normal practice effect), it was possible to estimate how much various groups of students gained with how much testing time. The average difference in SAT scores (both Verbal and Mathematical) between timed and untimed administrations was as follows, by disability group: hearing impaired, 30 points; learning disabled, 38; physically handicapped, 31; visually impaired, 35. The timed-untimed score difference, according to amount of extra time taken, was as follows: one hour, 33; two hours, 41; three hours, 55.

There are obviously limitations to this sample. All examinees taking nonstandard administrations are not likely to be faithfully represented by the 29 percent who took both the standard and the nonstandard test. Nonetheless, one interesting question is how to interpret the increasing gain associated with increasing amounts of extra time. One explanation is that students who take more time need more because of a more severe disability and that the larger gain illustrates the importance of their having that extra time. Another explanation might be that the more time a student takes, the more likely he or she will earn a higher score than would be earned under an appropriately determined comparable time. Which interpretation is more accurate?

There is no direct answer to the question, but there are three types of data that bear on it; they are summarized in the last line of Table 11.1. One type of evidence is the speed with which handicapped examinees complete the test. The SAT and GRE are timed so that most but not all examinees are able to consider all items. The proportion completing the test is therefore an indication of how speeded it is for any particular group. Our data indicate that the test was less speeded for all handicapped groups (Table 7.3).

Another indication that the nonstandard test tends to be less speeded is that some items near the end of the GRE and SAT proved differentially easy for three of the four handicapped groups studied. The apparent explanation is that having more time increased the likelihood of reaching those late items and getting some right, even though they tend to be the most difficult.

A third and quite different type of evidence comes from the prediction studies reported in chapter 9. Predicted versus actual performance in college was examined for students who took a short, medium, or long period of extra time on the SAT. One critical finding of that analysis is that the more time the LD students (by far the largest group) took on the test, the more their test scores overpredicted college performance. The second critical point was that no such pattern was found when those same students' grades were predicted on the basis of their high school records. This suggests that the SAT scores of some LD students are higher than they would be if earned with a comparable time limit.

Such timing effects are visible in two other groups. Physically handicapped examinees showed a similar pattern, but the interpretation is unclear because for the physically handicapped examinees who took a long time with the test, college grades were overpredicted from high school grades as well. This may mean that the physically handicapped students who took more time are likely to underachieve in college for reasons having nothing to do with the accuracy of their SAT or high school GPA. For example, because of automobile accidents or athletic injuries, some students are not handicapped in high school but are in college. Hearing-impaired students showed a somewhat similar shift in scores with increasing time on the test, but their situation is very different because college grades for this group are underpredicted.

The conclusion one must reach from the foregoing discussion is that the nonstandard versions of the SAT and the GRE are not comparable to the standard test with respect to timing. Because of the difficulty in determining degree of handicap, the testing programs have not attempted to establish time limits for disabled students that would be comparable in light of their disability. That fact alone would not be sufficient to warrant the conclusion that the timing is noncomparable. Three types of data do indicate, however, that the present policy gives disabled students more time to consider more test questions, and the effect is evidently to raise their scores at least somewhat beyond the level they would achieve with comparable time. That effect obviously varies from group to group and person to person.

# Comparability for handicapped examinees

In the previous section the results of this series of studies were reviewed with respect to eight aspects of score and task comparability. This section examines the findings from the standpoint of handicapped examinees generally and for different types of disability. One purpose of this section is to distinguish important differences in the results and their implications for the four groups of handicapped examinees.

It is important to remember that there is enormous variation in the extent and nature of disability among and within the four principal groups. How can one judge on any common basis, for example, whether a test is comparable for an LD student who has a mild reading problem and another who uses an audio cassette because he is unable to read? The distinctions previously drawn among sensory-motor, encoding, and cognitive processes should be borne in mind. By *comparable*, we do not mean that the testing experience or score levels attained are necessarily the same. The question is whether the assessment process yields a reasonably accurate estimate of the cognitive abilities that it is primarily intended to measure. The eight aspects of comparability all address that question.

With these important qualifications in mind, we first review the overall comparability of the SAT and GRE for handicapped students by briefly summarizing the most significant points of the previous discussion.

## Overall comparability

☐ The findings regarding overall comparability of the test can be summarized with the following five points. SAT and GRE results were generally consistent, though more information is available on the SAT.

1. The nonstandard tests appear to be generally comparable to the standard test with respect to three important internal characteristics: similar reliability, similar meaning of scores as to the cognitive abilities represented, and little evidence of differential item difficulty that would suggest inappropriate questions or item types.

2. Little systematic over- or underprediction of academic performance occurred when predictions were based on test scores and previous grades. Except in the unique case of hearing-impaired students in special programs, average residuals (actual minus predicted grades) were near zero. This result suggests that predictions are comparable for handicapped and nonhandicapped students when the tests are used along with previous grade record, as advised. The major source of error in grade predictions resulted from the fact that the academic performance of handicapped students is less predictable from either test scores or grades. As previously discussed, this finding has important implications for admissions practice, but it does not necessarily mean that the test scores are not comparable. When neither predictor works as well as usual, the more likely explanations are associated with characteristics of the students or the educational program.

3. One source of prediction error did appear to be associated with the test; namely, overprediction for examinees who took more time, especially in the learning-disabled group. These results indicate some degree of noncomparability in present timing practices. As suggested in chapter 9, a more accurate match between disability and time limits would improve test validity. Lack of comparability in timing is also supported by the analysis of the number of examinees able to complete the test and their degree of success on items that came later in the test.

4. Admissions officers appear to use the SAT in much the same way with handicapped as with nonhandicapped applicants. Small

groups of handicapped students, however, were less likely to be admitted than their test scores and previous grades would indicate. These results may represent a potential lack of comparability in test use that could disfavor some handicapped students.

5. The data indicate that accommodations in test administration are reasonably comparable for handicapped examinees.

Several ways in which testing practices could possibly be improved are discussed in a following section. Such modifications could work to improve comparability of the test, especially with respect to timing for some groups. With that exception and with the important qualifications previously stated as to the meaning of comparability, the overall picture presented by these results is that the tests are generally comparable and that the scores have similar meaning for handicapped and nonhandicapped examinees. Necessarily, that broad conclusion takes on a somewhat different interpretation when we consider individual handicapped groups. We turn to that task now.

## Hearing-impaired examinees

☐ Developing comparable admissions tests for hearing-impaired individuals is especially difficult when the hearing loss is severe. There are two important factors to consider. First, when total deafness occurs prior to language acquisition, there is a deficit in language development for most individuals. It is well established that deaf people show a full range of nonverbal intellectual functioning but the verbal skills are clearly less well developed (Myklebust, 1964). Second, as it has been put, being deaf is more than not hearing. The American Sign Language used by many deaf people is not based on standard English. For example, the verb "to be" does not exist; there are no standard tenses; signs do not readily distinguish such common pronouns as "he," "she," "her," or "his." Consequently, reading standard English is exceedingly difficult for many deaf people.

Given those facts, how can an admissions test that leans heavily on verbal skill be comparable for deaf people? Perhaps there are two answers. The results described here suggest that the test is comparable because it measures the same cognitive abilities in the same way: the items within sections of the test are similarly interrelated; and there is little evidence of differential item difficulty within the major sections of the test (that is, Verbal and Mathematical).

Another answer is that the test cannot be comparable because there is no hope of disentangling the effects of disability on the skills—particularly verbal—that it intends to measure. This view recognizes that the verbal skills are important in academic work and that that is why they are strongly represented in the test. From the limited amount of data available, predictions based on the nonstandard test plus high school average do not appear to misrepresent performance in mainstream college programs (though the regular test may). This result suggests that the test probably measures accurately the English-language skills of mainstreamed hearing-impaired people, recognizing that these students are less handicapped than those who use primarily manual communication.

What are the possibilities for improving admissions tests for students whose hearing impairment interferes markedly with verbal performance? In a recent review, Johanson (1986) concludes that there have been improvements in testing hearing-impaired people, but no breakthroughs. For example, at the Office of Personnel Management, test performance of deaf examinees was improved by reducing verbal content, allowing more time, and providing an interpreter for test instructions (Nester & Sapinkopf, 1982). The last two modifications are already available for SAT and GRE examinees; the reduction of verbal content raises questions regarding validity.

Nonverbal tests are often used with deaf students, but as Darnell (1980) argues, nonverbal abilities do not give a full view of intellectual functioning. Such a test would not likely prove as useful as a verbal one for student guidance and admission in a highly verbal environment. Another possibility is to translate an admissions test into a manual language, which could make it more comparable for deaf students who are taught with a manual language throughout their school and college years. A recent study (albeit of children) has shown improvement in the test performance of deaf examinees using added sign communication (Sullivan, 1982). This mode may not prove workable with a test as difficult as the SAT or GRE, but a feasibility study seems worthwhile. Finally, it may be that the national admissions tests should not be used at all for students whose primary mode of communication is a manual language.

## Learning-disabled examinees

☐ Equitable testing for learning-disabled examinees poses very difficult problems, but they are of a different sort from those just discussed. LD students form a very large and heterogeneous group. All professionals seem to agree that learning disability is a poorly defined term; the research literature has encompassed a wide variety of perceptual and cognitive disabilities. Functionally, LD is most frequently associated with problems in reading, but it can affect other skills such as listening or writing.

*Dyslexia*, the most widely cited form of learning disability, refers specifically to reading disability, which is presumably the reason most LD students qualify for testing under extended time conditions. Dyslexia has often been associated with defects in visual processing. One manifestation traditionally cited is the inability to process letters in their proper sequence; for example, an LD student might read "was" for "saw." Such perceptual explanations have been attractive because they offer the prospect of specific instructional intervention. Currently, theories of specific visual deficit find less favor, in part because such perceptual difficulties as word reversals appear to be common among all poor readers (Stanovich, 1986). Researchers and theorists now tend to attribute reading disability to dysfunction in low-level cognitive abilities such as poor-short term memory or an inability to encode words phonologically (Spear & Sternberg, 1986; Stanovich, 1986; Torgesen, 1985; Vellutino, in press; Wagner, 1986). In educational practice, the term *dyslexia* is often used loosely to signify nearly any kind of reading problem, ranging from no reading to near-normal reading ability. The deficit is sometimes estimated to affect 10 percent or more of the population (van Rijn, 1976). Highly capable individuals such as Nelson Rockefeller, Thomas Edison, and Woodrow Wilson are often given as examples of people who overcame dyslexia or learned to live with it.

The rationale for extended testing time would seem to rest on the assumption that learning disability is a specific dysfunction that distorts scores. There is recent debate in research literature, however, as to whether it is specific and different from the general verbal reasoning measured by tests like the SAT and the GRE (Stanovich, 1986). To complicate matters further, learning disability is actually not typically defined in the schools as a specific dysfunction or even a reading problem; as discussed at the beginning of this chapter, LD students are identified on a variety of grounds, particularly on the basis of their doing more poorly in school work than their tested ability would predict. One must assume that students so identified do indeed have academic handicaps and that there is sound reason for providing them special assistance in local and federal programs in keeping with Section 504 and other provisions of the 1973 Rehabilitation Act.

It does not clearly follow, however, that all LD students should have extended time on admissions tests. Our data appear inconsistent with the assumption that this group, as a whole, suffers on test performance because of a reading problem. These students' test performance is in fact not poorer but typically much better than their school performance. And as Table 11.1 indicates, LD examinees scored as well on the Verbal as on the Mathematical section (relative to nonhandicapped examinees). In addition, there was no evidence of their having special difficulty with mathematical items that have a heavy reading load.

Finally, it is mainly in the learning-disabled group of examinees that our research findings suggest an association between longer SAT testing and overpredicted college performance. It is possible that the college performance of some LD students is constrained partly because their disability is less visible than others, and therefore they are less likely to receive adequate support services. Also, it is possible that a four-year college grade-point average would give a fairer picture than the freshman average. But the performance of LD students generally was not overpredicted—only that of those who took the longest amount of testing time was. It seems certain that seriously disabled LD students (particularly those who take the large-type or cassette version of the test) need extra time in order to obtain an accurate score. These students seem to be a small segment of the total group, however, and there is at present no attempt made to differentiate them from a far larger group of LD examinees who evidently have no special problem with verbal as opposed to other types of material.

These results suggest that testing programs need to reevaluate their policies regarding extended time for LD students, especially as to how much time should be allowed and whether it is possible to improve present practices concerning eligibility for the nonstandard examination. It is important to reemphasize, however, that the group of examinees presently identified as learning disabled is quite heterogeneous and has been changing in character. Consequently, generalizing these results to all LD students now or to LD examinees a few years hence may be hazardous.

## Physically handicapped examinees

☐ Physical handicaps include a wide variety of orthopedic and neuromuscular disabilities. White (1978) provides a typography with comments on testing adaptations, based in part on the severity of upper-body limitations. The most important accommodations concern access to the testing room and adequate work space, assistance in handling test materials, and the provision of extended time.

Table 11.1 suggests that admissions tests are generally quite comparable for physically handicapped examinees. Since most physical handicaps do not ordinarily involve sensory or cognitive disability, the amount of time available to take the test is ordinarily the matter of primary consequence. Our data on test completion and grade prediction show some evidence of excessive time (see last line of Table 11.1), though it is not as clear as that for learning-disabled examinees. Determining appropriate time limits appears to be the main need in improving comparability of tests for physically handicapped examinees. Due to the wide variety of physical disabilities, that task is likely to prove more difficult than with other handicapped groups.

## Visually impaired examinees

☐   There is considerable division of opinion within the blind community about separate tests and separate standards for visually impaired people (Spungin, 1980). Some blind people object strongly to being compared only with other blind individuals, while others feel that comparisons are fair only within the blind population. These attitudes influence opinions about conditions of testing, whether there should be any modification of the content of tests, and so on. Spungin (1980) quotes a blind professional as follows:

> If I can't do something because I can't see, I still can't do it and there's no sense in either eliminating it from a test, or giving me compensatory credit for it on a test, because, if it was important enough to test for in the first place, then, somebody better recognize my need to be taught how to do it, or else, to be taught some way of living adequately without it. (p. 4)

Nonetheless, it is evident that there are types of items and particular concepts that can make a test spuriously difficult for blind or visually impaired people. Material that assumes visual experience (e.g., color discrimination, depth perception) may or may not be a necessary component of a test. Also, it is obvious that an examinee can not get through a braille or cassette test without a considerable time extension. Since it does take time to cover the material and decipher the various symbols, figures, and so on, it is not surprising that items involving reading and graphics were reported to be especially difficult for the visually impaired. We did not find, however, that these examinees performed more poorly on items that contained reading; evidently, the entire test is difficult in that respect.

There was indication that items involving graphics are sometimes especially difficult, particularly if "graphics" is interpreted broadly to include unusual symbols. But not always: test development specialists report that blind examinees often show surprising facility with visually related material. The total visually impaired group scored generally quite well on both the Verbal and Mathematical sections of the SAT, but those taking the braille version did score lower on the Mathematical section. Visually impaired students also scored well on the GRE Verbal but noticeably lower on the Quantitative section. When visually impaired students were asked about the test, one-fourth of those who had taken the SAT reported difficulty with graphic material. Twice as many GRE examinees reported such difficulty. More work needs to be done to determine what types of items may pose an unfair task for blind examinees.

These data showed only limited evidence of excess time for tests administered to visually impaired examinees. Prediction errors were not large for this group. One exception was visually impaired graduate students with above-average test scores and undergraduate grades, who did earn noticeably lower graduate GPAs than expected. But overall, the test seemed to be reasonably comparable for visually impaired examinees except for the problem with some mathematics items on the braille version.

# The flagging issue

☐ ☐ Whether to flag (that is, to identify) nonstandard scores for test users is a critical issue and one important reason for undertaking these studies. It is useful to review the issue briefly in order to connect the results that were just discussed with the flagging dilemma described in chapter 1.

First, why is flagging a problem? One obvious answer is that it is seen to be inconsistent with the spirit if not the letter of the 504 regulations (now in temporary abeyance), which prohibit inquiry about handicapping conditions. The prohibition is based partly on respect for the right to privacy and partly on the desire to protect disabled students from possibly biased treatment. Aside from these important considerations, there is another negative aspect to flagging. To many handicapped people, it is inherently objectionable to be told that one must go through the testing process because it is important and then to hear that the score must be flagged because the test sponsor is not sure what it means.

A second question is, Why flag, anyway? What are the main arguments that individual scores should be identified as nonstandard? One rests on the comparability issue: that is, if the test sponsor cannot guarantee standard conditions, it is under obligation to tell users that the comparability of the score is uncertain. Professional standards endorse that action by suggesting that users be cautioned about nonstandard scores (American Psychological Association, 1985, p. 79). The standard is not specific as to when it is appropriate to use a strong caution such as flagging individual scores versus a weaker caution such as explanatory statements in users' manuals.

A related argument concerns the credibility of the testing process and fairness to examinees generally. If it is understood that an examination is given under standard conditions, then all examinees deserve reasonable protection from the possibility of others taking unfair advantage. If there is no flag on the nonstandard score, what would stop many students from seeking the advantage of extended time? Some admissions officers suspect that the nonstandard test administrations are already abused. If flags were removed from scores obtained under nonstandard conditions, it might prove necessary for testing programs to undertake more stringent central monitoring of access to the nonstandard administration in order to avoid compromising the program. The practicality and desirability of such monitoring is an important factor to consider in determining flagging policy.

Clearly, these different points of view on the benefits of flagging and the problems with it engage quite different value issues. In both cases the objectives may be socially positive; unfortunately, they may also be contradictory. The studies reported here have some bearing on various aspects of these issues, but the results are especially pertinent to the technical questions concerning score interpretation. Obviously, a program policy and practice concerning nonstandard scores cannot be decided on technical considerations alone.

## Implications of research results

☐   What can we now say about the meaning of nonstandard scores? They evidently have much the same meaning as do standard scores regarding the abilities measured. Their meaning is also much the same in the respect that students with higher scores are more likely to do better in a given college than are those with lower ones. But several lines of evidence suggested noncomparability in the timing of nonstandard administrations, a discrepancy that appears to be the main evidence of noncomparability. In theory, it is correctable.

Errors in predicting the grades of handicapped examinees stem mostly from the fact that their performance is less predictable than that of their able-bodied peers from either scores or previous grades. Predictability undoubtedly varies for other groups as well (for example, Hispanic students; see Duran, 1983). The fact that a group is less predictable has never been a basis for identifying individual scores as being of doubtful comparability. It is even possible that if scores were disaggregated on the basis of other factors (especially the nature of the college program), they might prove *more* valid than is typically true for nonhandicapped students! For example, if grading standards vary in two departments, it is readily demonstrable that pooled data are likely to yield lower validity coefficients than those found in each department separately.

Are flagged scores used in a comparable manner? Is there real danger of flags working against handicapped students in the admissions process? The findings of the study reported in chapter 6 do not tend to support that worry. However, that study does suggest that some groups of handicapped students may be at a slight disadvantage is selective admissions. If flagging of nonstandard scores is judged to be necessary, it would be useful to study further its possible effects. Asking admissions officers about their practices with respect to flagged scores might be useful; more informative would be a double-blind study in which the same "applications" were run through the admissions process with and without flags.

Is flagging effective? Some of our data may have a bearing on that question. Though flags may be intended to caution users, there is little evidence that users take that caution to mean that less weight should be placed on test scores in making admissions decisions. Our finding was that test scores and previous grades received much the same weight in selection decisions for handicapped as for non-handicapped applicants.

Would it be desirable to use different flags to discriminate among different types of nonstandard test administrations? Such a procedure may have merit. At present, a flag signals a handicap but does not provide information that is particularly helpful to the institution or the student. If scores are flagged, more specific information concerning the conditions of testing and/or nature of handicap could be helpful, particularly if backed up by a manual for admissions officers that would help them interpret the scores and suggest appropriate test use.

Does flagging nonstandard scores inhibit students from exercising the option of taking nonstandard administrations? Program statistics do not seem to indicate that such is the case. The learning-disability category is most subject to ambiguity as to who is eligible, but that category has quadrupled in membership since 1979—a much faster increase than that of the number of LD students in the schools. It is possible, of course, that the increase would have been even faster without flagging.

To summarize what we now know, there is little evidence that tests are measuring substantially different abilities for handicapped and nonhandicapped examinees. The scores do not predict grades as well for the handicapped, but that is true of previous GPA as well. There is arguably enough evidence of noncomparable timing to warrant flagging, but that problem may be correctable. The next question is, Through what means?

## Scaling and other options

☐ Searching for a way to make the scores of handicapped and non-handicapped examinees more comparable, the NAS panel suggested the possibility of rescaling test scores according to how handicapped students performed in college or graduate school. The feasibility of this possibility was examined on the basis of predictive validity data for the SAT (Braun, Ragosta, & Kaplan, 1986a) because far more data were available for the SAT than for the GRE. Chapter 10 describes in some detail the theoretical and practical problems such scaling would encounter and concludes that the procedure is not technically feasible.

Upon examination, a variety of problems arising from such scaling became apparent, but the first and insurmountable roadblock was the unavailability of adequate data. Despite a considerable data-collection effort, the samples were small, scattered, and heterogeneous with respect to the nature of handicapping condition as well as to educational program. To complicate matters further, it became clear that the necessary adjustments would not simply involve adding a constant to the scores of a particular group of handicapped examinees: different observed slopes called for more complex adjustments, which in turn called for more data, which were not available.

It was concluded that rescaling scores was not technically feasible for the SAT. Needless to say, it would be even less feasible for the GRE because the GRE database is approximately one-fourth that of the SAT. Even had there been sufficient data to make the scaling technically feasible, there were other serious problems as well. For example, were SAT scores to be rescaled in this manner, the most frequent and largest corrections would entail substantially lowering the scores for learning-disabled students. But for reasons already discussed, overprediction for this group on the basis of SAT scores seems much more likely to result from the way the group is identified in the secondary schools than from some miscalibration of scores.

Thus, such rescaling would likely have the effect of systematically misrepresenting the ability of LD students and distorting interpretation of scores outside the specific application of predicting grades.

Finally, we note again that the main prediction errors were due to the generally lower predictability characteristic of handicapped students. Were correcting those errors technically feasible and without negative side effects, there could be some benefit in it. But as noted, unpredictability has many causes and does not in itself call for adjusting or flagging scores.

Overall, the data reported here suggest that the scores of handicapped students can be interpreted in much the same way as those of nonhandicapped examinees. It is true that there are variations in testing procedures that may cause some variation in scores. But the main effect of such variations seems to result from excessive time, and that problem may be correctable in large part. If such correction were successful, then comparability of scores would be largely attainable. In that event, the question of flagging versus not flagging becomes less a technical issue and more a matter of program policy, in which the interests of all students and institutions must be weighed.

What are the options for correcting the evident overprediction associated with unlimited time? One possibility would be to give all examinees the standard time allowance (say, only three hours) but to increase the scores of handicapped students by adding a disability allowance based on a prior determination of the amount of score gain typically achieved during the extended time by students with different handicapping conditions. This option has the advantage of improving standardization, but it would involve changing scores and necessitate a difficult determination of the nature and severity of handicap for individual examinees.

Another option would be to allow handicapped students essentially unlimited time but to subtract from their scores the amount that would normally be gained with unlimited time by nonhandicapped students scoring at the same level. This option has the advantage of treating all handicapped students the same way but the obvious disadvantage of reducing their scores.

A third option is to leave the scores alone altogether and focus attention on the source of the problem—namely, the fact that the time limits are not comparable. Developing comparable limits would not be simple and straightforward, but there are several approaches to the problem that could be evaluated. Such score adjustments as just described may be worth exploring, but improving the comparability of timing seems a preferable first step.

# Possibilities for improving comparability

☐ ☐ In the previous discussion we concluded that the nonstandard SAT and GRE are largely comparable to the regular tests in most respects for most handicapped examinees. The major source of noncomparability is timing, but a variety of additional possibilities for improving the comparability of the task for handicapped students have been suggested by findings of these studies. We comment specifically in this section on the timing problem and then list a number of other steps that might improve comparability and warrant further consideration.

These suggestions are offered in the following spirit: The purpose of standardizing the testing task is to make it more objective and fair—to increase the likelihood that all examinees have an equal opportunity to demonstrate their knowledge and skills. The task has extraneous sources of difficulty for some examinees because of their disability, without some adjustment, the test would be unfair. So standardization in this case means comparable, not identical, conditions.

The goal should be to neutralize extraneous sources of difficulty insofar as possible; that is, to standardize the test in a manner that fits the conditions of disability. It is important to remember that test standardization means not only controlling variation in testing conditions but also providing comparable information about the test to all examinees in order to put them on an equal footing in that respect.

A word of caution is in order if the intention is to time tests according to the conditions of disability. The nature of disabling conditions varies widely, as do their consequences for appropriate test timing. Setting fair time limits, therefore, implies not only developing defensible guidelines but also administering them fairly; that is, determining what timing condition is appropriate for individual examinees. It is not a foregone conclusion that such a procedure would prove equitable and workable in practice.

For example, present practices regarding nonstandard SAT administrations are based on local determination of handicapped status and what accommodations are needed. The only verification normally necessary is a written statement from a school or college official or a health care professional that the student requires a nonstandard administration. GRE practices vary because many candidates are not in school at the time of examination. Should differentiated timing be deemed to necessitate verification and documentation of individual disabilities by the testing program directly, such procedure would go considerably beyond the present practice.

It is also important to take a balanced view of what constitutes adequate standardization. Certainly testing conditions—possibly even timing—inadvertently vary to some degree in regular administrations, from center to center and from individual to individual. It is possible to standardize beyond detection of any difference. The objective should be to achieve an acceptable degree of comparability that is fair to all, with adequate safeguards to insure that flexible arrangements are not abused.

Finally, improving comparability is a continuing process. In the past few years there have been special efforts at ETS resulting in a number of improvements in test accommodations for handicapped students. Some of the suggestions mentioned here are already being considered.

## The timing problem

☐ There are a number of reasons why timing of nonstandard tests is a critical issue. Seven in 10 students taking a nonstandard test use the regular form, with extended timing usually being the only variation of any consequence. For all examinees, one would assume that timing is the modification most likely to depress or inflate scores. For that reason, it is a highly visible issue. Most nonhandicapped students taking the standard test are much aware of the time constraint, and they rightly or wrongly assume that they could improve their score if only more time were available. Also, the testing programs have a clearly different policy on the timing of standard and nonstandard tests.

The present policy regarding nonstandard testing is not intended to provide comparable time to handicapped examinees. Those who administer nonstandard tests are instructed to allow examinees sufficient time to finish the test, up to a limit of 12 hours on the SAT and 6 on the GRE. "To finish" means to consider all items, not necessarily to answer every item. ETS test-development guidelines regarding the length and speed of tests like the SAT and GRE are *not* based on the assumption that all examinees will finish the test. The target is to insure that approximately 80 percent of the examinees have an opportunity to try all the items (Swineford, 1974). Thus, the standard test is somewhat speeded for most people.

Why are admissions tests speeded, even moderately so? One practical but important reason is that providing sufficient time for all to finish causes distraction and confusion when large numbers of students are taking the test in the same room. If all examinees had ample time, however, problems of test anxiety might be reduced for some students, and the timing problem for disabled students would become moot. It may be time to reevaluate the pros and cons of extended timing for all examinees—particularly on tests designed for individual, computer-based administration. In any event, such a change is not likely to come quickly.

Meanwhile, how to determine fair time limits for disabled candidates is a difficult problem, largely beyond the scope and purpose of this report. An obvious difficulty comes from the fact that the time an individual student needs depends on the nature and severity of disability, which may vary a great deal, sometimes even within the same handicapped grouping. A key element in setting fair time limits, therefore, is to identify groups that are relatively homogeneous as to handicap; that is, examinees for whom the task posed by the test is relatively similar. This would provide a basis for determining the amount of time in which approximately 80 percent of handicapped examinees would have an opportunity to try all items, a timing standard that would be comparable to that faced by nonhandicapped examinees.

Table 11.2 is a starting point. It shows how many hours different groups of handicapped students worked on the extended-time version of the SAT before "finishing." Several aspects of the table are noteworthy. Very few of the disabled students finished the test in three hours, a bit over the normal time allotment. Most but not all finished within one day (six hours). The College Board has an experimental program in which learning-disabled students can now take the SAT in regular national administrations with a limited amount of extra time. Those students have available approximately four hours' actual working time on scored sections of the test. Table 11.2 indicates that, typically, about half of the examinees in an extended-time administration work on the test for more than four hours. It is clear that visually impaired students taking the braille or cassette version require considerably more time than other handicapped examinees.

Blind students taking the braille form probably face a sufficiently similar task so that one time limit could be established for that group as a whole. Some other groups might be similarly treated, while some groups would have to be further subdivided as to time limit. It would be desirable that any timing policy allow for exceptional cases that do not fit any category, though that provision may prove difficult to implement without flagging such scores.

An obvious shortcoming of the data in Table 11.2 for deciding how much time might be appropriate for examinees with a particular type of handicap is the fact that the test takers on whom the data are based were working under the assumption that ample time was

**Table 11.2 Percentage of handicapped examinees who worked on the SAT for different amounts of time under extended-time conditions (1979–83)**

| Type of test and handicap | Total N | Cumulative percent working for: | | | |
|---|---|---|---|---|---|
| | | *3 hours* | *4 hours* | *5 shours* | *6 hours** |
| *Visual* | | | | | |
| Braille | 337 | 3 | 19 | 41 | 62 |
| Large type | 1542 | 16 | 50 | 75 | 88 |
| Cassette | 200 | 2 | 29 | 55 | 74 |
| Regular | 572 | 15 | 51 | 80 | 92 |
| *Physical* | | | | | |
| Regular | 729 | 15 | 51 | 78 | 91 |
| *Hearing* | | | | | |
| Regular | 590 | 25 | 70 | 90 | 97 |
| *Learning* | | | | | |
| Large type | 446 | 15 | 49 | 71 | 88 |
| Cassette | 1065 | 12 | 50 | 77 | 91 |
| Regular | 7053 | 18 | 56 | 81 | 95 |

From Packer (1986).

*For the SAT, the maximum time is 12 hours.

available if needed. It would be useful to have additional data comparing the performances of handicapped and nonhandicapped students under different timing conditions on different formats (such as large type or regular).

One result from earlier work on timing effects for nonhandicapped examinees may prove significant. Evans (1980) found that various subgroups of nonhandicapped examinees lose score points from reduced time, but gain little from a modest time extension. This finding needs to be replicated, and the effect would presumably vary with score level. Nonetheless, the study suggests that a limited amount of extra time granted to a handicapped student might result in a score increase only if the standard time was, in fact, unduly short in light of the student's disability. If confirmed, this finding could be useful in developing timing guidelines that give benefit of doubt but do not run great risk of unfair gain. Any fair and workable method of using differentiated time limits depends, of course, on practical means of screening and documenting which examinees should have which time condition.

## Other possible improvements

☐ In addition to better regulation of timing, the following possibilities for improving the comparability of nonstandard tests are recommended for consideration:

1. A special effort is warranted to duplicate for handicapped examinees, insofar as possible, the various ancillary test materials that are available to nonhandicapped test takers. It is particularly important to insure that information about nonstandard administrations is widely available and that test familiarization and practice materials are available in braille, large type, and cassette format.

2. Standard instructions and checklists should be provided to administrators of nonstandard tests whenever possible. These individuals are sometimes inexperienced in this task and may need help in understanding areas of sensitivity and in avoiding administrative mishaps.

3. Standard scripts and procedures should be developed for readers who describe graphic material for blind examinees. Examinees responding to a survey indicated too much variability at present in the competence of readers to perform this task well. Similarly, guidelines for essay recorders would be helpful.

4. It would be useful to provide handicapped students with an evaluation form to facilitate their reacting to testing conditions and giving suggestions. This procedure could be helpful in monitoring test administrations as well as in soliciting ideas for improvement.

5. The practice of identifying, before test assembly, regular test forms that will later be converted to nonstandard format should be used whenever possible. Study results confirm that this procedure is a key element in developing comparable tests for handicapped examinees.

6. In addition to present test-development procedures for reviewing the content of nonstandard tests, all forms of the SAT and GRE should be checked routinely for items that may be confusing or unnecessarily difficult for handicapped examinees. Items that require visual or hearing experience may not always be necessary on regular test forms that are taken by many handicapped people.

7. Further studies of differential item difficulty should be undertaken using operational procedures presently being developed at ETS. More detailed studies at the item level may provide information helpful to test-development staff in recognizing material that may be troublesome for individuals with particular disabilities.

8. Additional work is needed to identify types of mathematics items that cause unusual difficulty for blind students. From previous experience it has been reasonably clear to test-development staff that items involving three-dimensional figures are often troublesome, and for that reason such items are typically avoided in tests with non-standard formats. These results suggest that there may be other sources of special difficulty in mathematical items presented in braille. Blind candidates may need a scratch-paper equivalent for mathematics items.

9. The feasibility of translating the admissions test into American Sign Language (or developing a new one) should be examined. If practical, such full communication could provide a fairer test for hearing-impaired students, especially those applying to programs in which classroom lectures are routinely signed either by the professor or by an interpreter.

10. Institutions should be encouraged and assisted in carrying out validity studies on the basis of academic performance over four years as specified by the 504 regulations (Section 84.42d). There are several reasons why such studies can provide a better basis for determining the long-term success of handicapped students. In the upper division, disabled students may be better able to cope with the demands of college life, better able to play up their strengths, and better able to demonstrate higher-order skills than they are when faced with the factual emphasis of academic work in the lower division in many college programs.

11. It is desirable to implement Bayesian statistical procedures in all validity studies that are routinely performed on behalf of institutions. Having the benefit of statistical methods used in the studies reported here would provide test users with better means of monitoring admissions practices regarding small groups of applicants.

12. Norms should be provided for hearing-impaired students applying to special programs. Since these students earn grades in such programs substantially beyond those predicted on the basis of test scores, appropriate norms could be helpful in insuring comparable score interpretation.

13. Guidelines should be developed for translating these results and suggestions, as appropriate, to smaller testing programs. There may be alternative methods of modifying tests or conditions of administration that are more financially feasible in small programs and also operationally satisfactory when the number of examinees is limited.

14. In addition to improving current admissions tests, it would be useful to provide admissions officers with better information than is currently available on other important characteristics to look for in identifying students with academic promise.

15. More attention should also be given to the development of better means of assessing educational needs and monitoring progress (Messick, 1984). The College Board and ETS are currently developing a major computer-based program for diagnosing learning problems in mathematics, writing, and reading and study skills. Adaptation of this program for handicapped students is a promising possibility.

## Summary of conclusions and implications

□  □     1. *Conclusion.* The quantity and quality of data on handicapped examinees are severely limited. The possibilities for establishing comparability of nonstandard tests on the basis of empirical studies alone are correspondingly curtailed.

> Implication. It is necessary to work toward improving the comparability of tests for handicapped students on two fronts: through studies of score comparability and through evidence of what constitutes a comparable task, taking into account the disabling condition.

2. *Conclusion.* The measurement characteristics of the SAT and GRE are much the same in nonstandard and standard form. Good reliability is obtained, and similar abilities are represented.

> Implication. In these respects the scores appear to have similar meaning, undistorted in any obvious way by conditions of disability.

3. *Conclusion.* There is little evidence that the SAT and GRE contain particular types of items that are more difficult for handicapped students than the complete subtest (Verbal, Quantitative, etc.) in which they are included.

> Implication. Given the abilities that the tests measure, their content is appropriate. The recently adopted ETS practice of using essentially identical items in standard and nonstandard tests appears to be largely sound.

4. *Conclusion.* Some mathematical items in braille format may be an exception to the conclusion jut stated.

> Implication. Further work is needed to determine what causes special difficulty for blind examinees on some mathematics

items. Such items should be avoided if they are not essential to the character of the test.

5. *Conclusion.* Special test accommodations were judged satisfactory by the great majority of SAT and GRE examinees queried, and they compared favorably with the experiences of these students in college testing. Supplementary services of the testing programs might be an exception.

> Implication. Testing programs should review the availability of comparable bulletins of information, practice materials, and related services for handicapped students.

6. *Conclusion.* Prediction errors are typically smaller when both test scores and previous grade-point average are used than when only one of these measures is employed. Use of one predictor can result in substantial errors, but there is little indication of any consistent over- or underprediction for any handicapped group when both measures are used (see paragraph 10, below, for an exception).

> Implication. Admission officers should be careful to consider both test scores and previous grades in advising students and in reaching admissions or placement decisions.

7. *Conclusion.* Compared to that of nonhandicapped examinees, the academic performance of handicapped students is generally less predictable from either test scores or previous GPA. Lower predictability does not necessarily represent any miscalibration of the test score, nor does rescaling of test scores appear to be technically feasible. Lower predictability should not be seen as a negative consideration in evaluating a handicapped applicant for admission.

> Implication. Testing programs should provide a handbook or special materials for admissions officers and other score recipients regarding types of disability, nonstandard testing conditions, and principles of good practice in proper score interpretation. Users should be cautioned to give less weight to traditional predictors and to take special care in reviewing the background and personal characteristics of individuals known to be handicapped.

8. *Conclusion.* Test scores and school grades appear to be related to undergraduate admissions decisions in much the same manner for handicapped and nonhandicapped applicants.

> Implication. A positive aspect of this finding is that it shows comparable use of test scores. A negative aspect, however, is that other factors that may be important in evaluating

handicapped applicants are evidently not getting as much attention as they may deserve.

9. *Conclusion.* To a small extent, there are groups of handicapped applicants who are apparently less likely to be admitted than their school grades and test scores would suggest. In the absence of a controlled experiment, there is no way to determine whether test-score flags play a role in such decisions, though it does not appear that flagged scores that are high in relation to school grades attract any special attention.

> Implication. In time it would be wise to replicate these findings. Any significant change during a period when nonstandard testing is receiving special attention could signal trouble for handicapped applicants. Reporting national norms for handicapped groups might be helpful in counteracting any tendency for these groups to fare less well than others in admissions.

10. *Conclusion.* Deaf applicants to special college programs are underpredicted but also overadmitted. Results of this study are consistent with those of much previous research; they show that verbal scores of deaf students are frequently lower than their scores on other types of ability tests.

> Implication. A test translated into a manual language (if feasible) might better assess the academic potential of deaf students, particularly those entering special programs where sign language is used. If admissions tests are used in such programs, special norms for deaf students could be helpful.

11. *Conclusion.* The results reported here and other recent research give reason to question whether extended time is warranted for all learning-disabled students.

> Implication. Testing programs should review policies regarding the qualifications necessary for nonstandard testing and consider whether there are ways to better differentiate handicapped students who do and do not need extended time.

12. *Conclusion.* There is no apparent way to disentangle some conditions of handicap from the verbal, quantitative, and reasoning skills required by admissions tests. There seems little prospect of developing a valid test that does not include these or similar skills, because they are requisite to much academic work in colleges and graduate schools.

Implication. It can be expected that some students, because of their disability, will not score as high on admissions tests as they otherwise might. More emphasis should be placed on research and development of diagnostic instruments that would be useful in improving the educational experience of handicapped people.

13. *Conclusion.* The primary source of noncomparability that is directly associated with test scores is the extended time available in nonstandard test administrations. Several types of evidence suggest that in some cases the extra time is excessive and results in noncomparable scores.

Implication. Programs should review their policies on extended testing time and consider adjustments that could standardize testing arrangements to fit fairly the conditions of an individual's disability.

14. *Conclusion.* Assuming success in establishing test time limits that take proper account of disabling conditions, the tests would then be largely comparable from a technical perspective.

Implication. In that event, present flagging policies should be reevaluated, taking into account the intended purposes of flagging, what is fair to handicapped and nonhandicapped students, and the interests of institutions and others who may use test scores.

# Appendix A

# Services for Handicapped Students

## ATP SERVICES FOR HANDICAPPED STUDENTS: 1985–86 Information for Counselors and Admissions Officers

The Admissions Testing Program (ATP) provides the Scholastic Aptitude Test (SAT), Test of Standard Written English (TSWE), Achievement Tests, and other services for students who plan to continue their education beyond high school.

Since 1939, the College Board has sought to provide special testing arrangements for handicapped students in order to minimize the effects of their handicaps on their test performance. These special arrangements currently consist of special editions of the SAT and TSWE in braille, large type, or on cassettes; extended testing time; flexible testing dates and administration at the student's high school rather than at an ATP national test center; separate test rooms; or individualized supervision or instructions.

### New Services

In 1985–86, ATP will add new services, available only to students with *documented* learning disabilities who can use regular-size type and who require extended testing time of up to an additional one and one-half hours. These students will have the option of registering to take the SAT at national test centers on two national test dates—November 2, 1985, and/or May 3, 1986. (The Achievement Tests are not available under this option.) Students registering for the November 2 or May 3 administration will be able to request the SAT Question-and-Answer Service.

### Eligibility for nonstandard testing

The presence of a physical handicap should not necessarily result in a student's registration for nonstandard test arrangements. If visual or writing abilities are not impaired and if extended testing time is not needed, students should be encouraged to participate in the standard, timed national testing program. Moreover, an undocumented disability does not qualify a student to participate in services for the handicapped.

Best served through special testing arrangements is the student with an Individual Educational Plan that states the nature and effect of the disability and the modified testing arrangements required. This plan should be in effect for the student for whom you are requesting special testing arrangements.

In the absence of the documented plan described above, the student may obtain two signed statements describing the disability and the need for special testing arrangements from any of the following: physician(s), psychologist(s), child-study team(s), or learning disability specialist(s). Both statements cannot be from the same individual or team.

The Individual Educational Plan or the two statements should be retained in the school file unless requested by ATP Services for Handicapped Students.

**Temporary disabilities.** Students with temporary disabilities should be advised to register for a later date in the national testing program unless an admissions application deadline requires immediate action. College admissions officers or scholarship programs may be receptive to an extension of the deadline. However, the student and counselor are responsible for making sure that the test date is early enough to satisfy the deadlines of colleges and scholarship programs.

## Selecting the appropriate option

Students who are eligible to take ATP tests at a nonstandard administration should consult with their guidance counselor prior to registering. Since each service—current and new—has distinct features, the chart on page 192 is provided to assist you in counseling students about which service would best minimize the effect of their handicap on their test performance.

As you review the chart, please note that under the new service: only the SAT is offered and only on two national test dates; the test is administered at an ATP national test center; only the regular-size type test book and standard machine-scannable answer sheet are available; only limited extended testing time is given; aids are not permitted; and the student may request the SAT Question-and-Answer Service.

## Current services (special administration)

Any secondary school counselor or other designated school administrator can arrange to administer special editions of the SAT, TSWE, and/or Achievement Tests at his or her own high school to students who have documented visual, physical, hearing, or perceptual handicaps.

The tests may be given any time from September 1 through June 30. All arrangements for special test administrations must be requested at least one month in advance of the test date. The test date agreed on must be indicated on the Test Order Form.

Braille, large type, regular-size type, or cassette editions of the SAT, and regular-size type editions of the Achievement Tests may be administered. (See the section following for test formats.) Responses may be recorded on machine-scannable or large-block answer sheets. A reader, a manual translator, or an amanuensis may be used.

The tests may be administered over two consecutive days. A test day may consist of no more than six hours of testing time, excluding rest periods and lunch. It is not necessary to use the entire 12 hours, but they are available if needed. Complete instructions for administering the tests are given in the *Supervisor's Manual: Instructions for Nonstandard Administrations of the Admissions Testing Program,* which is sent to the test administrator with the test materials. Upon arrival, test materials should be thoroughly checked to avoid any last-minute problems.

Under current service rules, students may take special administrations of the SAT and Achievement Tests twice in a school year. (To administer the Latin Achievement Test, special arrangements must be made with ATP Services for Handicapped Students. The English Composition Test with Essay will be given only on the December 7, 1985, test date at a national ATP test center. Special arrangements for this test must also be made, by November 1, 1985, with ATP Services for Handicapped Students.)

Because of the unusual expense of providing the current services for handicapped students, no honorarium can be paid to test administrators.

**Test formats.** Four special editions of the SAT and the TSWE are available for special administrations:

□ *Regular-size type.* Students who are able to read regular-size type at their own speed may test the regular-size type edition (contained in a single test book).

□ *Large type.* Students unable to read a regular-size type edition at their own speed may take the large-type edition (each of the five test sections is in a separate test book).

□ *Braille.* Students unable to read either the regular-size or large-type edition at their own speed may take the braille edition. The SAT Verbal sections are available in regular grade 2 braille; the mathematical sections are in the 1972 revised Nemeth code.

□ *Cassette.* Visually handicapped or learning-disabled students who cannot read braille may work with cassettes. the mathematical portions must be administered with either the regular- or large-type edition of the SAT.

Braille diagrams are available for the mathematical portions for those students who can read braille but who would perfer to use the cassette edition for the verbal portions.

The Achievement Tests are available in regular-size type only.

## New services (national administration)

Students with documented learning disabilities who can use regular-size type and a standard machine-scannable answer sheet but who require limited extended testing time may take the SAT at a national test center on two national test dates—November 2, 1985, and/or May 3, 1986. (The Achievement Tests are not available under this option.) Up to one and one-half hours of extended testing time will be allowed. Students registering for the November 2 or May 3 administrations may also participate in the SAT Question-and-Answer Service.

Please note that the late registration deadlines in effect for the standard national administrations are not applicable under the new service—students will not be able to transfer from the regular national administration to the new service with extended testing time after the regular registration deadline of September 27 (for the November test date) or March 28 (for the May test date).

## Registering for nonstandard administrations

To obtain student registration material for either the current services or the new services, write or phone ATP Services for Handicapped Students. You will be sent a Registration Form, two Additional Report Request Forms, a Test Order Form for current services, an Eligibility Statement for new services, a *Registration Bulletin*, and *Information for Students with Special Needs*.

**For the current services.** To register a student for the SAT or Achievement Tests at your high school, instruct the student to:

□ Complete the Registration Form using the special instructions outlined in *Information for Students with Special Needs*.

□ Sign the Test Order Form to indicate acceptance of the conditions that are specified. (If the student cannot sign, a parent or guardian should sign.)

□ Make out a check or money order to ATP Services for Handicapped Students for the test fee, $11.50 for the SAT or $18.50 for Achievement Tests (in New York State, $12.00 or $19.00, respectively). If a student cannot afford the test fee, you should ask the appropriate College Board Regional Office for a fee-waiver card. (See back cover.)

□ Return the completed Registration Form, the Test Order Form, and the check or fee-waiver card to you.

Whey you have received the materials from the student, you should:

□ Complete and sign the Test Order Form. The test date and test site must be indicated on the Test Order Form.

□ Return all appropriate materials in the

envelope provided to ATP Services for Handicapped Students. The registration materials and Test Order Form must be *received* at least four weeks before the test date.

**For the new services.** To register a student to take the SAT with extended testing time at a national test center on November 2, 1985, and /or May 3, 1986, instruct the student to:

□ Complete the Registration Form following instructions in the *Registration Bulletin.*

□ Sign the Eligibility Statement to indicate acceptance of the conditions that are specified.

□ Make out a check or money order to ATP Services for Handicapped Students for the test fee, $11.50 for the SAT (in New York State, $12.00). If a student cannot afford the test fee, ask the appropriate College Board Regional Office for a fee-waiver card. (See back cover.)

□ Return the completed Registration Form, the Eligibility Statement, and the check or fee-waiver card to you.

When you receive the materials from the student, you should:

□ Complete and sign the Eligibility Statement.

□ Return all appropriate materials to ATP Services for Handicapped Students in the envelope provided. The envelope containing the materials must be *postmarked* no later than September 27 for the November 2, 1985, test date or March 28 for the May 3, 1986, test date.

## Refunds

Students unable to take the test for any reason can request a refund of the test fee (less the $8.50 service fee). The refund request must be made within 60 days after the test date. Students who have received an Admission Ticket should return it to ATP Services for Handicapped Students with their refund request. Students registered under current services should ask you to request their refund.

## Changing test dates

**Current services.** The test date on the Test Order Form is the one for which the student is registered. If the student wants to take an ATP test on another date, another Registration Form and fee must be submitted.

**New services.** The test date on the Admission Ticket is the one for which the student is registered. If the student wants to take an ATP test on another date, another Registration Form and fee must be submitted.

Please note that regular registration deadlines in effect for the standard national administrations must be met for the new services; late registration deadlines do not apply. Students cannot transfer from the regular national administration to the new services with extended testing time after September 27 (for the November 2 test date) or March 28 (for the May 3 test date). Also, a student may not register as a standby on the day of the test.

| Checklist of materials to be returned | |
| --- | --- |
| **Current services** | **New services** |
| Deadline: received 4 weeks prior to test date | Deadline: postmarked by September 27 for November 2 test date and by March 28 for May 3 test date |
| Check for test fee or fee-waiver card | same |
| Test Order Form | Eligibility Statement |
| Registration Form | same |
| Additional Report Request Form (if needed) | same |

## Interpreting scores from nonstandard administrations

Whether testing occurs at a special administration in the student's own high school or at a national administration with extended testing time, the student's ATP score report will include the notation "Nonstandard Administration." The individual circumstances that require special test arrangements are so diverse and the methods of administration vary so widely that the College Board is not able to provide meaningful interpretive data for scores earned in nonstandard administrations.

The *ATP Guide for High Schools and Colleges* is the basic reference for score interpretation and should be consulted for further information. However, please keep in mind that the effects of differences in test format, time limits, and mode of administration for a given candidate are not measurable; for example, it cannot be determined how someone who took a test in braille would have done had the person been able to take the test in print. Thus, the usual caution that test scores should be considered only one factor in the assessment of a student's academic potential is especially applicable to students with handicaps.

**For further information** or to request the booklet *Information for Students with Special Needs*, contact:

> ATP Services for Handicapped Students
> CN 6400
> Princeton, NJ 08541-6400

Telephone (8:00 a.m.-4:00 p.m., EST, Monday-Friday):

> (609) 921-9000 (questions regarding registration or test administration procedures)

> (609) 734-5350 (questions regarding general policy)

Source: College Board. (1985). *Services for Handicapped Students*. New York: Author. Used by permission.

### 1985–86 ATP Services for Handicapped Students
### special test arrangements

| | Current services | | New services |
|---|---|---|---|
| | *Scholastic aptitude test* | *Achievement tests* | *Scholastic aptitude test* |
| Documentation of eligibility | Individual Educational Plan or 2 written statements from specialists | Individual Educational Plan or 2 written statements from specialists | Learning-disabled students with Individual Educational Plans or 2 written statements from specialists |
| Registration | ATP Services for Handicapped Students | Same | Same |
| Test dates | September 1 through June 30 | September 1 through June 30 English Comp. (Essay): only on December date Latin: special arrangements | November 2, 1985 and/or May 3, 1986 |
| Fees/fee waivers | $11.50 ($12.00 in New York State) | $18.50 ($19.00 in New York State) | $11.50 ($12.00 in New York State) |
| Test editions | | | |
|   Regular | Yes | Yes | Yes |
|   Braille | Yes | No | No |
|   Cassette | With book of supplementary figures embossed or with regular or large type for math SAT | No | No |
|   Large type | Yes | No | No |
| Test content | 2 SAT-Verbal sections, 2 SAT-Math sections, and 1 TSWE section | Not applicable | Same, plus standard equating section used in national administrations |
| Testing time | Up to 6 hours per day on 2 consecutive days | Same | Standard time plus $1\frac{1}{2}$ hours extra, for maximum of $4\frac{1}{2}$ hours |
| Answer sheet | MRC scannable or large block | Same | MRC scannable |
| Practice materials, *Bulletin*, and sample test | Regular, plus cassette | Regular type only | Regular, plus cassette |
|   Braille | No | | No |
|   Cassette | Yes | Not applicable | Yes |
|   Large type | No | | No |
| Testing room | Separate at own high school | Same | Separate at National ATP Test Center |

| | Current services | | New services |
|---|---|---|---|
| | *Scholastic aptitude test* | *Achievement tests* | *Scholastic aptitude test* |
| Aids | Reader, amanuensis, manual translator, magnifying glass, abacus typewriter, *not* calculator | Overhead projector or device allowing tactile reading (if visually handicapped) | None permitted |
| Score report designation | Nonstandard Administration | Same | Same |
| SAT Question-and-Answer Service | No | Not Applicable | Yes |

# Services for Handicapped Students GRE General

**Information bulletin, p. 8.**

## Test takers with handicaps

Special testing arrangements and test materials can be made available for persons with visual, physical, hearing, or learning disabilities provided these services are requested in writing sufficiently in advance of the test date.

The General Test is available in braille (1972 Nemeth code), in large type, and on cassettes, and a large-type answer sheet is available for all these editions. The cassette edition is accompanied by a set of illustrative materials—diagrams, charts, drawings, and the like—in either large type or braille, depending on the choice of the person taking the test. The illustrations are also described on the tape by the reader. Large-type answer sheets are available for the Subject Tests, but the test books are available only in regular type.

The test center will provide a test reader, a recorder of answers, a separate testing room, or extra time to complete the tests (up to six hours testing time per test), as appropriate. If requested in advance, an interpreter selected by the registrant will be permitted to sign the oral instructions given by the test supervisor before the test begins. Examinees who customarily employ a certain reader may request in advance that this reader be used. Specific requests must also be made for the use of any other aids customarily used by the examinee.

You may require only minor adjustments of the testing environment to take the tests under standard conditions. For example, you may need only wheelchair accommodations to be tested in the regular testing room or, if your hearing is impaired, to be seated where you can lip-read the supervisor's oral instructions or be given written instructions to follow.

If your condition is more disabling, you may want to find out before you register whether the graduate schools or fellowship sponsors to which you are applying will waive their GRE requirement for you.

In either case, whether you can test under standard conditions with minor environmental adjustments or whether you need special test conditions with minor environmental adjustments or whether you need special test conditions and special test materials, be sure to include a letter with your registration form. The letter should contain a description of the nature of your disability and should specify all the special testing arrangements you will need and whether or not you will require extra time. Select the test center you prefer from the list on pages 73–76, and indicate your choice of test center and scheduled test date in the letter. (Do not enter the code number of the test center on the registration form; instead, enter the code "11000-9.") Be sure to include your telephone number on your registration form so we can call you, if necessary, about your special requirements. Some registrants may be asked to further document their disability to help ETS determine whether testing under special conditions is appropriate.

Your letter, registration form, and test fee must be mailed in the same envelope in time to meet the special request deadline date. (See calendar on back cover.) Approximately two weeks before the test date, ETS will send you a letter confirming the arrangements made for you and identifying the testing location and testing supervisor.

There is no extra charge for the special testing materials or special-testing arrangements for handicapped test takers.

Please remember that standby registration is possible *only* if you can take the tests under standard conditions. If you require special conditions, you must register in advance, as indicated above, so that the test center supervisor will be prepared to meet your special requirements on the day of the test.

If you register and request special testing arrangements and later find you cannot attend the testing session, please contact ETS promptly and before the test date.

Educational Testing Service recognizes that when standardized tests such as the GRE are taken under nonstandard conditions, the scores may not accurately reflect the examinee's educational achievement. Therefore, a statement is included with reports of scores that were earned under nonstandard conditions pointing out the special nature of the score results and the importance of considering other indicators of academic achievement in the admission process.

Because of the small number of tests administered under nonstandard conditions each year, no separate percentile rank tables are available for interpreting the scores of test takers with handicaps.

Source: Graduate Record Examinations. (1986). *GRE Information Bulletin: 1986–87*. Princeton, NJ: Educational Testing Service.

# Appendix B

# Illustrative Test Items

## GRE Analytical Item Types

### Logical reasoning

47. If Ramón was born in New York State, then he is a citizen of the United States.

The statement above can be deduced logically from which of the following statements?

(X) Everyone born in New York State is a citizen of the United States.
(B) Every citizen of the United States is a resident either of one of the states or of one of the territories.
(C) Some people born in New York State are citizens of the United States.
(D) Ramón was born either in New York or in Florida.
(E) Ramón is a citizen either of the United States or of the Dominican Republic.

### Analytical reasoning

To apply to college a student must see the school counselor, obtain a transcript at the transcript office, and obtain a recommendation from Teacher A or Teacher B.

A student must see the counselor before obtaining a transcript.
The counselor is available only Friday mornings and Tuesday, Wednesday, and Thursday afternoons.
The transcript office is open only Tuesday and Wednesday mornings, Thursday afternoons, and Friday mornings.
Teacher A is available only Monday and Wednesday mornings.
Teacher B is available only Monday afternoons and Friday mornings.

40. A student has already seen the counselor and does not care from which teacher she obtains her recommendation. Which of the following is a complete and accurate list of those days when she could possibly complete the application process in one day?

(A) Friday
(B) Monday, Wednesday
(C) Monday, Friday
(X) Wednesday, Friday
(E) Monday, Wednesday, Friday

Source: Educational Testing Service. (1984). *GRE 1984–85 Information Bulletin.* Princeton, NJ: Author. Used by permission.

# GRE Quantitative Item Types

## Quantitative comparison

*Directions:* Each of the following questions consists of two quantities, one in Column A and one in Column B. You are to compare the two quantities and choose

(A) if the quantity in Column A is greater;
(X) if the quantity in Column B is greater;
(C) if the two quantities are equal;
(D) if the relationship cannot be determined from the information given.

*Note:* Since there are only four choices, NEVER MARK (E).

*Common Information:* In a question, information concerning one or both of the quantities to be compared is centered above the two columns. A symbol that appears in both columns represents the same thing in Column A as it does in Column B.

|  | Column A | Column B |
|---|---|---|
| 15. (B) | 9.8 | $\sqrt{100}$ |

## Data interpretation

*Questions 28–30 refer to the following table:*

**Percentage change in dollar amount of sales in certain retail stores from 1977 to 1979**

| Store | Percentage change | |
|---|---|---|
|  | From 1977 to 1978 | From 1978 to 1979 |
| P | +10 | −10 |
| Q | −20 | +9 |
| R | +5 | +12 |
| S | −7 | −15 |
| T | +17 | −8 |

28. In 1979 which of the stores had greater sales than any of the others shown?

(A) P  (B) Q  (C) R  (D) S
(X) It cannot be determined from the information given.

## Discrete quantitative

*Directions:* Each of the following questions has five answer choices. For each of these questions, select the best of the answer choices given.

22. The average of $x$ and $y$ is 20. If $z = 5$, what is the average of $x$, $y$, and $z$?

(A) $8\frac{1}{3}$  (B) 10  (C) $12\frac{1}{2}$  (X) 15  (E) $17\frac{1}{2}$

Source: Educational Testing Service. (1984). *GRE 1984–85 Information Bulletin.* Princeton, NJ: Author. Used by permission.

# GRE Verbal item Types

## Reading comprehension

*Directions:* The passage is followed by questions based on its content. After reading the passage, choose the best answer to each question. Answer all questions following the passage on the basis of what is *stated* or *implied* in the passage.

In the years following the Civil War, economic exploitation for the first time was provided with adequate resources and a competent technique, and busy prospectors were daily uncovering new sources of wealth. The coal and oil of Pennsylvania and Ohio, the copper and iron ore of Upper Michigan, the gold and silver, and the lumber and fisheries of the Pacific Coast provided limitless raw materials for the rising industrialism. The Bessemer process quickly turned an age of iron into an age of steel and created the great mills of Pittsburgh from which issued the rails for expanding railways. The reaper and binder, the sulky plow, and the threshing machine created a large-scale agriculture on the fertile prairies. Wild grasslands provided grazing for immense herds of cattle and sheep; the development of the corn belt enormously increased the supply of hogs; and with railways at hand, the Middle Border poured into Omaha and Kansas City and Chicago an endless stream of produce.

As the line of the frontier pushed westward, new towns were built, thousands of claims to homesteads were filed, and speculator and promoter hovered over the prairies like buzzards seeking their carrion. With rising land values, money was to be made out of unearned increment, and the creation of booms was a profitable industry. The times were stirring and it was a shiftless fellow who did not make his pile. If he had been too late to file on desirable acres, he had only to find a careless homesteader who had failed in some legal technicality and "jump his claim." Good bottom land could be had even by late-comers if they were sharp at the game.

This bustling America of 1870 accounted itself a democratic world. A free people had put away all aristocratic privileges and, conscious of power, had gone forth to possess the last frontier. But America's essential social philosophy, which it found adequate to its needs, was summed up in three words—preemption, exploitation, progress. Its immediate and pressing business was to dispossess the government of its rich holdings. Lands in the possession of the government were so much idle waste, untaxed and profitless; in private hands they would be developed. They would provide work, pay taxes, support schools, enrich the community. Preemption meant exploitation, and exploitation meant progress.

It was a simple philosophy, and it suited the simple individualism of the times. The Gilded Age knew nothing of enlightenment; it recognized only the acquisitive instinct. That much at least the frontier had taught the great American democracy; and in applying to the resources of a continent the lesson it had been so well taught, the Gilded Age wrote a profoundly characteristic chapter of American history.

12. According to the passage, increased corn production was mainly responsible for an increase in the

    (A) number of sheep (B) output of farm implements (X) supply of hogs (D) amount of pasture land (E) number of cattle

Source: Educational Testing Service. (1984). *GRE 1984–85 Information Bulletin.* Princeton, NJ: Author. Used by permission.

# SAT Verbal Item Types

## Reading comprehension

Each passage below is followed by questions based on its content. Answer all questions following a passage on the basis of what is *stated* or *implied* in that passage.

Mars revolves around the Sun in 687 Earth days, which is equivalent to 23 Earth months. The axis of Mars's rotation is tipped at a 25° angle from the plane of its orbit, nearly the same as the Earth's tilt of about 23°. Because the tilt causes the seasons, we know that Mars goes through a year with four seasons just as the Earth does.

From the Earth, we have long watched the effect of the seasons on Mars. In the Martian winter, is a given hemisphere, there is a polar ice cap. As the Martian spring comes to the Northern Hemisphere, for example, the north polar cap shrinks and material in the planet's more temperate zones darkens. The surface of Mars is always mainly reddish, with darker gray areas that, from the Earth, appear blue green. In the spring, the darker regions spread. Half a Martian year later, the same process happens in the Southern Hemisphere.

One possible explanation for these changes is biological: Martian vegetation could be blooming or spreading in the spring. There are other explanations, however. The theory that presently seems most reasonable is that each year during the Northern Hemisphere springtime, a dust storm starts, with winds that reach velocities as high as hundreds of kilometers per hour. Fine, light-colored dust is blown from slopes, exposing dark areas underneath. If the dust were composed of certain kinds of materials, such as limonite, the reddish color would be explained.

29. It can be inferred that one characteristic of limonite is its
    (X) reddish color
    (B) blue green color
    (C) ability to change colors
    (D) ability to support rich vegetation
    (E) tendency to concentrate into a hard surface

30. According to the author, seasonal variations on Mars are a direct result of the
    (A) proximity of the planet to the Sun
    (B) proximity of the planet to the Earth
    (C) presence of ice caps at the poles of the planet
    (X) tilt of the planet's rotational axis
    (E) length of time required by the planet to revolve around the Sun

31. It can be inferred that, as spring arrives in the Southern Hemisphere of Mars, which of the following is also occurring?
    (X) The northern polar cap is increasing in size.
    (B) The axis of rotation is tipping at a greater angle.
    (C) A dust storm is ending in the Southern Hemisphere.
    (D) The material in the northern temperate zones is darkening
    (E) Vegetation in the southern temperate zones is decaying.

## Analogies

Each question below consists of a related pair of words or phrases, followed by five lettered pairs of words or phrases. Select the lettered pair that *best* expresses a relationship similar to that expressed in the original pair.

Example:

YAWN : BOREDOM : :  (A) dream : sleep
(B) anger : madness  (C) smile : amusement
(D) face : expression  (E) impatience : rebellion

36. COW:BARN:: (A) pig:mud
    (X) chicken:coop  (C) camel:water
    (D) cat:tree  (E) horse:racetrack

## Antonyms

Each question below consists of a word in capital letters, followed by five lettered words or phrases. Choose the word or phrase that is most nearly *opposite* in meaning to the word in capital letters. Since some of the questions require you to distinguish fine shades of meaning, consider all the choices before deciding which is best.

Example:

> GOOD: (A) sour (B) bad (C) red (D) hot
> (E) ugly
>
> Ⓐ ● Ⓒ Ⓓ Ⓔ

1. VERSATILE: (X) unadaptable
   (B) mediocre (C) impatient (D) egocentric
   (E) vicious

2. FRAUDULENT: (A) rather pleasing
   (B) extremely beneficial (C) courteous
   (X) authentic (E) simplified

## Sentence completion

Each sentence below has one or two blanks, each blank indicating that something has been omitted. Beneath the sentence are five lettered words or sets of words. Choose the word or set of words that *best* fits the meaning of the sentence as a whole.

Example:

> Although its publicity has been ___, the film itself is intelligent, well-acted, handsomely produced, and altogether ___.
> (A) tasteless. .respectable
> (B) extensive. .moderate
> (C) sophisticated. .amateur
> (D) risqué. .crude
> (E) perfect. .spectacular
>
> ●ⒷⒸⒹⒺ

16. He claimed that the document was — because it merely listed endangered species and did not specify penalities for harming them.
    (A) indispensable    (X) inadequate
    (C) punitive    (D) aggressive
    (E) essential

Source: Educational Testing Service. (1984). *GRE 1984–85 Information Bulletin*. Princeton, NJ: Author. Used by permission.

# SAT Mathematical Item Types

## Multiple choice

In this section solve each problem, using any available space on the page for scratchwork. Then decide which is the best of the choices given and blacken the corresponding space on the answer sheet.

The following information is for your reference in solving some of the problems.

Circle of radius $r$: Area = $\pi r^2$; Circumference = $2\pi r$
The number of degrees of arc in a circle is 360.

The measure in degrees of a straight angle is 180.

*Definitions of symbols:*
= is equal to
≠ is unequal to
< is less than
> is greater than
≤ is less than or equal to
≥ is greater than or equal to
∥ is parallel to
⊥ is perpendicular to

*Triangle:* The sum of the measures in degrees of the angles of a triangle is 180.

If $\angle CDA$ is a right angle, then

(1) area of $\triangle ABC = \dfrac{AB \times CD}{2}$

(2) $AC^2 = AD^2 + DC^2$

*Note:* Figures that accompany problems in this test are intended to provide information useful in solving the problems. They are drawn as accurately as possible EXCEPT when it is stated in a specific problem that its figure is not drawn to scale. All figures lie in a plane unless otherwise indicated. All numbers used are real numbers.

1. If $\frac{9}{5} + \frac{x}{5} = 2$, then $x =$
   (A) 0   (B) 1   (C) 2   (D) 3   (E) 4

2. A triangle with sides of lengths 4, 8, and 9 has the same perimeter as an equilateral triangle with side of length

   (A) $5\frac{1}{2}$   (B) 6   (C) $6\frac{1}{2}$   (D) 7   (E) $7\frac{1}{2}$

## Quantitative comparison

*Questions 8–27* each consist of two quantities, one in Column A and one in Column B. You are to compare the two quantities and on the answer sheet blacken space

   A if the quantity in Column A is greater;

   B if the quantity in Column B is greater;
   C if the two quantities are equal;
   D if the relationship cannot be determined from the information given.

*Notes:*
1. In certain questions, information concerning one or both of the quantities to be compared is centered above the two columns.
2. In a given question, a symbol that appears in both columns represents the same thing in Column A as it does in Column B.
3. Letters such as $x$, $n$, and $k$ stand for real numbers.

| EXAMPLES | | | |
|---|---|---|---|
| | Column A | Column B | Answers |
| E1. | $2 \times 6$ | $2 + 6$ | ● Ⓑ Ⓒ Ⓓ |
| | | $x° \quad y°$ | |
| E2. | $180 - x$ | $y$ | Ⓐ Ⓑ ● Ⓓ |
| E3. | $p - q$ | $q - p$ | Ⓐ Ⓑ Ⓒ ● |

| | Column A | Column B |
|---|---|---|
| 8. (C) | 0 | $0 \times 2$ |
| 9. (A) | $a + 25$ | $a - 5$ |

Source: College Board. (1983). *Taking the SAT.* New York: Author.

# GRE Verbal Item Types

## Analogies

*Directions:* In each of the following questions, a related pair of words or phrases is followed by five lettered pairs of words or phrases. Select the lettered pair that best expresses a relationship similar to that expressed in the original pair.

1. COLOR : SPECTRUM : : (X) tone : scale
(B) sound : waves   (C) verse : poem
(D) dimension : space   (E) cell : organism

## Antonyms

*Directions:* Each question below consists of a word printed in capital letters followed by five lettered words or phrases. Choose the lettered word or phrase that is most nearly *opposite* in meaning to the word in capital letters. Since some of the questions require you to distinguish fine shades of meaning, be sure to consider all the choices before deciding which one is best.

5. DIFFUSE: (X) concentrate (B) contend
(C) imply (D) pretend (E) rebel

## Sentence completion

*Directions:* Each sentence below has one or two blanks, each blank indicating that something has been omitted. Beneath the sentence are five lettered words or sets of words. Choose the word or set of words for each blank that *best* fits the meaning of the sentence as a whole.

9. Early ____ of hearing loss is ____ by the fact that the other senses are able to compensate for moderate amounts of loss, so that people frequently do not know that their hearing is imperfect.

   (A) discovery . . indicated
   (B) development . . prevented
   (X) detection . . complicated
   (D) treatment . . facilitated
   (E) incidence . . corrected

# Appendix C

# Reports of ETS Research on Issues in Testing Handicapped People, 1982–86

## Joint CB/ETS/GRE Project— Technical Reports and Derived Journal Articles

Bennett, R. E., and Ragosta, M. (1984). *A research context for studying admissions tests and handicapped populations* (ETS Research Rep. No. 84–31, Studies of Admissions Testing and Handicapped People, Rep. No. 1). Princeton, NJ: Educational Testing Service.
See also: *Special Services in the Schools*, 1084, *1*(2), 21–29.

Bennett, R. E., Ragosta, M., and Stricker, L. (1984). *The test performance of handicapped people* (ETS Research Rep. No. 84–32, Studies of Admissions Testing and Handicapped People, Rep. No. 2). Princeton, NJ: Educational Testing Service.
See also: *Journal of Special Education*, 1985, *19*, 255–267.

Bennett, R. E., Rock, D., and Kaplan, B. (1985). *The psychometric characteristics of the SAT for nine handicapped groups* (ETS Research Rep. No. 85–49, Studies of Admissions Testing and Handicapped People, Rep. No. 3). Princeton, NJ: Educational Testing Service.
See also: Level, reliability, and speededness of SAT scores for nine handicapped groups. *Special Services in the Schools* (in press).

See also: SAT differential item performance for nine handicapped groups. *Journal of Educational Measurement*, 1987, *24*, 41–55.
See also: SAT verbal-math discrepancies: Accurate indicators of college learning disabilities? *Journal of Learning Disabilities*, 1987, *20*, 189–192.

Bennett, R. E., Rock, D., and Jirele, T. (1986). *The psychometric characteristics of the GRE General Test for three handicapped groups* (ETS Research Rep. No. 86–6, Studies of Admissions Testing and Handicapped People, Rep. No. 6). Princeton, NJ: Educational Testing Service.

Bennett, R. E., Rock, D. A., and Jirele, T. (1987). GRE score level, test completion, and reliability of visually impaired, physically handicapped, and nonhandicapped groups. *Journal of Special Education*, *21*.

Braun, H., Ragosta, M., and Kaplan, B. (1986a). *The predictive validity of the Scholastic Aptitude Test for disabled students* (ETS Research Rep. No. 86–38, Studies of Admissions Testing and Handicapped People, Rep. No. 8). Princeton, NJ: Educational Testing Service.

Braun, H., Ragosta, M., and Kaplan, B. (1986b). *The predictive validity of the GRE General Test for disabled students* (Studies of Admissions Testing and Handicapped People Rep. No. 10).

Princeton, NJ: Educational Testing Service.

Powers, D., and Willingham, W. (1986). *The feasibility of rescaling test scores of handicapped examinees* (ETS Research Rep. No. 86–39 and Studies of Admissions Testing and Handicapped People, Rep. No. 9). Princeton, NJ: Educational Testing Service.

Ragosta, M., and Kaplan, B. (1986). *A survey of handicapped students taking special test administrations of the SAT and GRE* (ETS Research Rep. No. 86–5, Studies of Admissions Testing and Handicapped People, Rep. No. 5). Princeton, NJ: Educational Testing Service.

Rock, D., Bennett, R. E., and Jirele, T. (1986). *The internal construct validity of the GRE General Test across handicapped and nonhandicapped populations* (ETS Research Rep. No. 86–7, Studies of Admissions Testing and Handicapped People, Rep. No. 7). Princeton, NJ: Educational Testing Service.

Rock, D., Bennett, R. E., and Kaplan, B. (1985). *The internal construct validity of the SAT across handicapped and nonhandicapped populations* (ETS Research Rep. No. 85–50, Studies of Admissions Testing and Handicapped People, Rep. No. 4). Princeton, NJ: Educational Testing Service.
See also: Internal construct validity of a college admissions test across handicapped and nonhandicapped groups. *Educational and Psychological Measurement*, 1987, *47*, 193–205.

## Other reports

Bennett, R. E. (1982a). Assessment: Eleven questions parents should ask. *Academic Therapy*, *17*, 589–594.

Bennett, R. E. (1982b). Cautions in the use of informal measures in the educational assessment of exceptional children. *Journal of Learning Disabilities*, *15*, 337–339.

Bennett, R. E. (1983a). A multi-method approach to assessment in special education. *Diagnostique*, *8*, 88–97.

Bennett, R. E. (1983b). Research and evaluation priorities for special education assessment. *Exceptional Children, 50*, 110–117.

Bennett, R. E., & Lennon, M. (1987). Referral. In C. R. Reynolds & L. Mann (Eds.), *The encyclopedia of special education: A reference for the education of the handicapped and other exceptional children and youth.* New York: Wiley.

Bennett, R. E., & Maher, C. A. (Eds.) (1986). *Emerging perspectives in the assessment of exceptional children.* New York: Haworth Press. Also as *Special Services in the Schools*, 1986, *2*(2/3).

Bennett, R. E., Rock, D. A., & Chan, K. L. (1987). *SAT Verbal-Math discrepancies: An accurate indicator of college learning disability? Journal of Learning Disabilities, 20*, 189–192.

Centra, J. (1986). Handicapped student performance on the Scholastic Aptitude Test. *Journal of Learning Disabilities, 19*, 324–327.

Harrison, R., and Ragosta, M. (1985). *Identifying factors that predict deaf students' academic success in college.* Unpublished report, Educational Testing Service.

Jones, D., and Ragosta, M. (1982). *Predictive validity of the SAT on two handicapped groups: The deaf and the learning disabled* (ETS Research Rep. No. 82–9). Princeton, NJ: Educational Testing Service.

Messick, S. (1984, March). Assessment in context: Appraising student performance in relation to instructional quality. *Educational Researcher*, pp. 3–8.

Packer, J. K. (1987). *SAT testing time for students with disabilities.* (ETS Research Rep. No. 87–37). Princeton, NJ: Educational Testing Service.

Ragosta, M. (1987). *Students with disabilities: Four years of data from special test administrations of the Scholastic Aptitude Test 1980–83* (College Board Rep. No. 87–2 and ETS Research Rep. No. 87–2). New York: College Entrance Examination Board.

Ragosta, M., and Nemceff, W. (1982). *A research and development program on testing handicapped people* (ETS

Research Memorandum 82–2). Princeton, NJ: Educational Testing Service.

Willingham, W. (1986). *Testing handicapped people: The validity issue* (ETS Research Rep. No. 86–26). Princeton, NJ: Educational Testing Service.

Willingham, W. (1987). *Handicapped applicants to college: An analysis of admissions decisions* (College Board Rep. No. 87–1 and ETS Research Rep. No. 87–1). New York: College Entrance Examination Board.

# References

Ackerman, P. T., Dykman, R. A., & Peters, J. B. (1977). Learning-disabled boys as adolescents—Cognitive factors and achievement. *Journal of the American Academy of Child Psychiatry, 16,* 296–313.

Ahn, H., Prichep, L., John, E., Baird, H., Trepetin, M., & Kaye, H. (1980). Developmental equations reflect brain dysfunctions. *Science, 210,* 1259–262.

Algozzine, B., & Ysseldyke, J. (1981). Special education services for normal children: Better safe than sorry? *Exceptional Children, 48,* 238–243.

American Association of Collegiate Registrars and Admissions Officers and the College Board (1980). *Undergraduate admissions: The realities of institutional policies, practices, and procedures.* New York: College Entrance Examination Board.

American Educational Research Association, American Psychological Association, and National Council on Measurement in Education. (1985). *Standards for educational and psychological testing.* Washington, DC: American Psychological Association.

Anderson, P. (1982). A preliminary study of syntax in the written expression of learning disabled children. *Journal of Learning Disabilities, 15,* 359–362.

Anderson, R. J., & Sisco, F. Y. (1977). *Standardization of the WISC–R performance scale for deaf children* (Series T, Number 1). Washington, DC: Gallaudet College, Office of Demographic Studies.

Andolina, C. (1980). Syntactic maturity and vocabulary richness of learning disabled children at four age levels. *Journal of Learning Disabilities, 13,* 372–377.

Angoff, W., & Anderson, S. (1963). The standardization of educational and psychological tests. *Illinois Journal of Education,* Vol. *54,* No. (1) 19–23.

Applebee, A. (1971). Research in reading retardation: Two critical problems. *Journal of Child Psychology and Psychiatry, 12,* 91–113.

Armstrong, D., Schneidmiller, K., White, C., & Karchmer, M. (1983, July). *Gallaudet College survey on postsecondary programs for hearing-impaired students: Preliminary results.* Paper presented at the meeting of the Association of Handicapped Student Services Providers in Postsecondary Education, Oakland, CA.

Astin, A. W., Green, K. C., Korn, W. S., & Schalit, M. (1985). *The American freshman: National norms for fall 1985.* Los Angeles: Higher Education Research Institute, Cooperative Institutional Research Program, University of California.

Astin, A. W., Hermond, M. K., & Richardson, G. T. (1982). *The American freshman: National norms for fall 1982.* Los Angeles: Higher Education Research Institute, Graduate School of Education, University of California.

Bauer, R. (1977). Memory processes in children with learning disabilities. *Journal of Experimental Child Psychology, 24,* 415–430.

Bauman, M. K., & Hayes, S. P. (1951). *A manual for the psychological evaluation of the adult blind.* New York: Psychological Corporation.

Bennett, R. E. (1981a). Elusive causes of poor schoolwork. In L. Gross (Ed.), *The parents' guide to teenagers* (pp. 293–294). New York: Collier Macmillan.

Bennett, R. E. (1981b). Professional com-.

**207**

petence and the assessment of exceptional children. *Journal of Special Education, 15,* 437–446.

Bennett, R. E., & Ragosta, M. (1984). *A research context for studying admissions tests and handicapped populations* (Research Rep. No. 84–31). Princeton, NJ: Educational Testing Service.

Bennett, R. E., Ragosta, M., & Stricker, L. (1984). *The test performance of handicapped people* (Research Rep. No. 84–32). Princeton, NJ: Educational Testing Service.

Bennett, R. E., Rock, D. A., & Chan, K. L. (1987). SAT Verbal-Math discrepancies: An accurate indicator of college learning disability? *Journal of Learning Disabilities, 20,* 189–192.

Bennett, R. E., Rock, D. A., & Jirele, T. (1986). *The psychometric characteristics of the GRE for three handicapped groups* (Research Rep. No. 86–6). Princeton, NJ: Educational Testing Service.

Bennett, R. E., Rock, D. A., & Kaplan, B. A. (1985). *The psychometric characteristics of the SAT for nine handicapped groups* (Research Rep. No. 85–49). Princeton, NJ: Educational Testing Service.

Bennett, R. E., Rock, D. A., & Kaplan, B. A. (1987). SAT differential item performance for nine handicapped groups. *Journal of Educational Measurement, 24,* 41–55.

Bennett, R. E., & Shepherd, M. (1982). Basic measurement proficiency of learning disability specialists. *Learning Disability Quarterly, 5,* 177–184.

Berk, R. A. (1982). Introduction. In R. A. Berk (Ed.), *Handbook of methods for detecting test bias* (pp. 1–8). Baltimore: Johns Hopkins University Press.

Blaha, J., & Vance, H. (1979). The hierarchical factor structure of the WISC–R for learning disabled children. *Learning Disability Quarterly, 2,* 71–75.

*Board of Education of Northport–East Northport School District v. Ambach,* 436 N.Y.S. 2d 564 (1981); aff'd in part and modified in part, 458 N.Y.S. 2d 680 (App. Div. 1982); cert denied, 104 S. Ct. 1598 (52 U.S.L.W. 3683, 1984).

Boder, E. (1971). Developmental dyslexia: Prevailing diagnostic concepts in a new diagnostic approach. In H. R. Myklebust (Ed.), *Progress in learning disabilities* (Vol. 2), pp. 21–44. New York: Grune & Stratton.

Bornstein, H. (1979). Systems of sign. In L. J. Bradford & W. G. Hardy (Eds.), *Hearing and hearing impairment* (pp. 155–172). New York: Grune & Stratton.

Braun, H., & Jones, D. (1980). *Graduate Management Admissions Test prediction bias study.* Princeton, NJ: Graduate Management Admissions Council and Educational Testing Service.

Braun, H., & Jones, D. (1985). *Use of empirical Bayes methods in the study of the validity of academic predictors of graduate school performance* (GREB No. 79–13P & ETS Research Rep. No. 84–34). Princeton, NJ: Educational Testing Service.

Braun, H., Jones, D. H., Rubin, D. B., & Thayer, D. T. (1983). Empirical bayes estimation of coefficients in the general linear model from data of deficient rank. *Psychometrika, 48*(2), 171–181.

Braun, H., Ragosta, M., & Kaplan, B. (1986a). *The predictive validity of the Scholastic Aptitude Test for disabled students* (Research Rep. No. 86–38). Princeton, NJ: Educational Testing Service.

Braun, H. I., Ragosta, M., & Kaplan, B. (1986b). *The predictive validity of the GRE General Test for disabled students* (Research Rep. No. 86–42). Princeton, NJ: Educational Testing Service.

Breland, H. M. (1978). *Population validity and college entrance measures* (Research Bull. No. 78–19). Princeton, NJ: Educational Testing Service.

Breland, H. M. (1979). *Population validity* (Research Monograph No. 8). New York: College Entrance Examination Board.

Breland, H. M., Wilder, G., & Robertson, N. (1986). *Demographics, standards, and equity: Challenges in college admissions.* Iowa City: American College Testing Program.

*Brookhart* v. *Illinois State Board of Education*, 534 F. Supp. 725 (C.D. Ill. 1982), rev'd, 697 F.2d 179 (7th Cir. 1983).

Bryan, T., & Bryan, J. (1975). *Understanding learning disabilities*. Port Washington, NY: Alfred.

Carpenter, D., & Miller, L. Spelling ability of reading disabled LD students and able readers. *Learning Disabled Quarterly*, 1982, *5*(1), 65–70.

Centra, J. (1986). Handicapped student performance on the Scholastic Aptitude Test. *Journal of Learning Disabilities*, *19*, 324–327.

Chalfant, J. (1984). *Identifying learning disabled students: Guidelines for decision making*. Burlington, VT: Northeast Regional Resource Center.

Civil Service Commission. (1956). *Tests for blind competitors for trades and industrial jobs in the federal civil service*. Washington, DC: Author.

Clark, M., & Grandy, J. (1984). *Sex differences in the academic performance of Scholastic Aptitude Test takers* (College Board Rep. No. 84–8). New York: College Entrance Examination Board.

Clements, S. D. (1966a). Learning disabilities—Who? [Abstract]. *Special Education: Strategies for Educational Progress*. (Selected papers, 44th Annual CEC Convention), 188. Washington, DC: The Council for Exceptional Children.

Clements, S. D. (1966b). *Minimal Brain Dysfunction in Children*. (NINDB Monograph No. 3, Public Health Service Bull. No. 1415). Washington, DC: U.S. Dept. of Health, Education, and Welfare.

Cohen, J. (1969). *Statistical powers analysis for the behavioral sciences*. New York: Academic Press.

Cohen, J. E. (1986). An uncertainty principle in demography and the unisex issue. *American Statistician*, *40*, 32–39.

Cohen, S. (1976). The fuzziness and the flab: Some solutions to research problems in learning disabilities. *Journal of Special Education*, *10*, 129–139.

Coles, G. (1978). The learning disability test battery: Empirical and social issues. *Harvard Educational Review*, *48*, 313–340.

College Entrance Examination Board. (1982). *Guide to the College Board Validity Study Service*. New York: Author.

College Entrance Examination Board. (1983). *10 SATs: Scholastic Aptitude Tests of the College Board*. New York: Author.

College Entrance Examination Board. (1984). *College-bound seniors: Eleven years of national data from the College Board's Admissions Testing Program 1973–83*. New York: Author.

College Entrance Examination Board. (1985). *ATP Services for Handicapped Students: 1985–86 information for counselors and admissions officers*. New York: Author.

College Entrance Examination Board. (1985). *Student bulletin for the SAT and achievement tests*. New York: Author.

Connolly, A. J., Nachtman, W., & Pritchett, E. M. (1971). *KeyMath Diagnostic Arithmetic Test manual*. Circle Pines, MN: American Guidance Service.

Corcoran, P. J. (1981). Neuromuscular diseases. In W. C. Stolov & M. R. Clowers (Eds.), *Handbook of severe disability* (pp. 83–100). Washington, DC: U.S. Government Printing Office.

Cordoni, B. K., O'Donnell, J. P., Ramaniah, N. V., Kurtz, J., & Rosenshein, K. (1981). Wechsler Adult Intelligence score patterns for learning disabled young adults. *Journal of Learning Disabilities*, *14*, 404–407.

Coveny, T. E. (1972). A new test for the visually handicapped: Preliminary analysis of the reliability and validity of the Perkins-Binet. *Education of the Visually Handicapped*, *4*, 97–101.

Craig, P., Myers, E., & Wujek, M. (1982). *Independent evaluation of the California Master Plan for Special Education: Final report*. Menlo Park, CA: SRI International.

Cronbach, L. (1971). Test validation. In R. L. Thorndike (Ed.), *Educational measurement* (2nd ed.) (pp. 443–507). Washington, DC: American Council on Education.

Cruickshank, W. M. (1976). *Cerebral palsy: A developmental disability*. Syracuse, NY: Syracuse University Press.

Cruickshank, W. M., Hallahan, D. P., & Bice,

H. V. (1976). The evaluation of intelligence. In W. M. Cruickshank (Ed.), *Cerebral palsy: A developmental disability* (3rd ed.) (pp. 95–122). Syracuse, NY: Syracuse University Press.

Cutsforth, T. D. (1951). *The blind in school and society: A psychological study.* New York: American Foundation for the Blind.

Darnell, W. (1980). Testimony presented to the National Academy of Sciences: National Research Council Panel on Testing Handicapped People.

Davis, C. J. (1970). New developments in the intelligence testing of blind children. In *Proceedings of the Conference on New Approaches to the Education of Blind Persons* (pp. 83–92). New York: American Foundation for the Blind.

Davis, W., & Shepard, L. (in press). The use of tests and clinical judgment by specialist in the diagnosis of learning disabilities. *Learning Disability Quarterly.*

Department of Education. (1982). *Programs for the handicapped: Clearinghouse on the handicapped.* July/August, No. 4.

Department of Education. (1985). *Seventh annual report to Congress on the implementation of the Education of the Handicapped Act.* Washington, DC: Author.

Department of Health, Education, and Welfare. (1977a). Nondiscrimination on the basis of handicap. *Federal Register, 42,* 22676–702.

Department of Health, Education, and Welfare. (1977b). Education of handicapped children. *Federal Register, 42,* 42474–518.

Department of Health, Education, and Welfare. (1977c). Assistance to states for education of handicapped children: Procedures for evaluating specific learning disabilities. *Federal Register, 42,* 65082–085.

Di Donato, P. A. (1986). The impact of the Grove City College decision on Section 504 of the Rehabilitation Act and other civil rights laws. *AHSSPPE Bulletin, 4*(2), 52–62.

Dikmen, S., Matthews, C. G., & Harley, J. P. (1975). The effect of early versus late onset of major motor epilepsy upon cognitive-intellectual performance. *Epilepsia, 16,* 73–81.

Donovan, W. H. (1981). Spinal cord injury. In W. C. Stolov & M. R. Clowers (Eds.), *Handbook of severe disability* (pp. 65–82). Washington, DC: U.S. Government Printing Office.

Driscoll, N. B. (1985). Minimum competency testing of the handicapped: A review of legal challenges. *Special Services in the Schools, 2*(1), 95–101.

Duran, R. (1983). *Hispanics' education and background: Predictors of college achievement.* New York: College Entrance Examination Board.

Easton, J., & Halpern, D. (1981). Cerebral palsy. In W. C. Stolov & M. R. Clowers (Eds.), *Handbook of severe disability* (pp. 137–154). Washington, DC: U.S. Government Printing Office.

*Education of the Handicapped.* (1986, January 8). P. 7.

*Education of the Handicapped.* (1983, June 29). Pp. 1–3.

Educational Testing Service. (1980). *Test use and validity.* Princeton, NJ: Author.

Educational Testing Service. (1984a). *Guide to administering ETS tests: 1984–85.* Princeton, NJ: Educational Testing Service.

Educational Testing Service. (1984b). *Practicing to take the GRE General Test* (2nd ed.). Princeton, NJ: ETS for the Graduate Records Examinations Board.

Epps, S., McGue, M., & Ysseldyke, J. E. (1982). Interjudge agreement in classifying students as learning disabled. *Psychology in the Schools, 19,* 209–220.

Evans, F. R. (1980). *A study of the relationships among speed and power aptitude test scores, and ethnic identity* (College Board Report RDR 80–81, No. 2, and ETS RR 80–22). Princeton, NJ: Educational Testing Service.

Farina, A., & Felner, R. D. (1973). Employment interviewer reactions to former mental patients. *Journal of Abnormal Psychology, 82,* 268–272.

Florida Department of Education, Division of Public Schools. (1981). *Florida Statewide Assessment Program: Visually impaired students special assessment.* Tallahassee: State of Florida, Department of Education.

Frauenheim, J. (1978). Academic achievement characteristics of adult males who were diagnosed as dyslexic in childhood. *Journal of Learning Disabilities, 11,* 470–483.

Freston, C., & Drew, C. (1974). Verbal performance of learning disabled children as a function of input organization. *Journal of Learning Disabilities, 7,* 424–428.

Friedman, J., & Pasnak, R. (1973). Accelerated acquisition of classification skills by blind children. *Developmental Psychology, 9,* 333–337.

Frostig, M. (1972). Visual perception, integrative function and academic learning. *Journal of Learning Disabilities, 5,* 1–15.

Galaburda, A., & Geschwind, N. (1982). Dyslexia update. *Neurology and Neurosurgery, 33,* 3–7.

Gardner, E. F., Rudman, H. C., Karlsen, B., & Merwin, J. C. (1982). *Stanford Achievement Test Intermediate 1 Form E: Norms booklet for fall.* New York: Psychological Corporation.

Goldman, R. D., & Slaughter, R. E. (1976). Why college grade point average is difficult to predict. *Journal of Educational Psychology, 68*(1), 9–14.

Graduate Record Examinations Board. (1986). *GRE information bulletin: 1986–87.* Princeton, NJ: Educational Testing Service.

Greenberg, B. L., & Greenberg, S. H. (1971). The measurement of college potential in the hearing handicapped. *American Annals of the Deaf, 116*(3), 372–381.

*Grove City College* v. *Bell, 465* U.S. 555, 104 S.Ct. 1211 (1984).

Gulliksen, H. (1950). *Theory of Mental Tests.* New York: Wiley.

Guskin, S. L. (1982). The effects of knowing someone is handicapped on decision making: A review of the literature. In S. Sherman & N. Robinson (Eds.), *Ability testing of handicapped people: Dilemma for government, science, and the public* (pp. 169–185). Washington, DC: National Academy Press.

Gutkin, T. B., & Reynolds, C. R. (1981). Factorial stability of the WISC–R for white and black children from the standardization sample. *Journal of Educational Psychology, 71,* 227–231.

Hallahan, D., & Kauffman, J. (1978). *Exceptional children: Introduction to special education.* Englewood Cliffs, NJ: Prentice-Hall.

Harris, Lou and Associates. (1986). *The ICD survey of disabled Americans: Bringing disabled Americans into the mainstream.* New York: Author.

Harrison, R. H., & Ragosta, M. (1985). *Identifying factors that predict deaf students' academic success in college.* Unpublished report, Educational Testing Service, Princeton, NJ.

Hayes, S. P. (1941). *Contributions to a psychology of blindness.* New York: American Foundation for the Blind.

Hayes, S. P. (1950). Measuring the intelligence of the blind. In W. Donahue & D. Dabelstein (Eds.), *Psychological diagnosis and counseling of the adult blind* (pp. 77–96). New York: American Foundation for the Blind.

Horn, W., O'Donnell, J., & Vitulano, L. (1983). Long-term follow-up studies of learning disabled persons. *Journal of Learning Disabilities, 16,* 542–555.

Jastak, J. F., & Jastak, S. R. (1965). *The Wide Range Achievement Test manual of instructions.* Wilmington: Guidance Associates of Delaware.

Jensema, C. (1978). A comment on measurement error in achievement tests for the hearing impaired. *American Annals of the Deaf, 123*(6), 496–499.

Jensen, A. R. (1980). *Bias in mental testing.* New York: Free Press.

Johanson, P. L. (1986). *A summary of major developments in testing of hearing-impaired persons.* Washington, DC: U.S. Office of Personnel Management, Office of Staffing Policy.

Johnson, R., & Heal, L. W. (1976). Private employment agency responses to the physically handicapped applicant in a wheelchair. *Journal of Applied Rehabilitation Counseling, 7,* 12–21.

Johnson, D., & Myklebust, H. (1967). *Learning disabilities: Educational principles and procedures.* New York: Grune & Stratton.

Jones, D. H., & Ragosta, M. (1982). *Predictive validity of the SAT on two handicapped groups: The deaf and the learning disabled* (Research Rep. No. 82–9). Princeton, NJ: Educational Testing Service.

Jordan, J. E., & Felty, J. (1968). Factors associated with intellectual variation among visually impaired children. *American Foundation for the Blind Research Bulletin, 15,* 61–70.

Joreskog, K., & Sorbom, D. (1984). *LISREL 6: An analysis of linear structural relationships by the method of maximum likelihood.* Mooresville, IN: Scientific Software.

Karchmer, M. A., Milone, M. N., & Wolk, S. (1979). Educational significance of hearing loss at three levels of severity. *American Annals of the Deaf, 124,* 97–109.

Kaufman, A. S. (1975). Factor analysis of the WISC–R at 11 age levels between $6\frac{1}{2}$ and $16\frac{1}{2}$ years. *Journal of Consulting and Clinical Psychology, 43,* 135–147.

Kaufman, A. S. (1976a). Verbal-performance IQ discrepancies on the WISC–R. *Journal of Consulting and Clinical Psychology, 44,* 739–744.

Kaufman, A. S. (1976b). A new approach to the interpretation of test scatter on the WISC–R. *Journal of Learning Disabilities, 9,* 160–168.

Kaufman, A. S. (1981). The WISC–R and learning disabilities assessment: State of the art. *Journal of Learning Disabilities, 14,* 520–526.

Kavale, K. (1981). The relationship between auditory perceptual skills and reading ability: A meta-analysis. *Journal of Learning Disabilities, 14,* 539–546.

Kavale, K. (1982). Meta-analysis of the relationship between visual perceptual skills and reading achievement. *Journal of Learning Disabilities, 15,* 42–51.

Keogh, B. (1983). Classification, compliance, and confusion. *Journal of Learning Disabilities, 16,* 25.

Keogh, B., Kukic, S., Becker, L., McLoughlin, R., & Kukic, M. (1975). School psychologists' services in special education programs. *Journal of School Psychology, 13,* 142–148.

Kirk, S., & Elkins, J. (1975). Characteristics of children enrolled in the Child Service Demonstration Centers. *Journal of Learning Disabilities, 8,* 630–637.

Kirsh, B. (1986). *Availability of services for handicapped examinees: 1985 survey results.* Internal Educational Testing Service draft paper, Educational Testing Service, Princeton, NJ.

Kraft, G. H. (1981). Multiple sclerosis. In W. C. Stolov & M. R. Clowers (Eds.), *Handbook of severe disability* (pp. 111–118). Washington, DC: U.S. Government Printing Office.

Krefting, L. A., & Brief, A. P. (1977). The impact of applicant disability on evaluative judgments in the selection process. *Academy of Management Journal, 19,* 675–680.

Laing, J., & Farmer, M. (1984). *Use of the ACT assessment by examinees with disabilities* (Report No. 84). Iowa City: American College Testing Program.

Landers, S. (1986, August). Task force collecting LD data. *APA Monitor,* p. 42.

Lawrence, J., Kent, L., & Henson, J. (1981). *The handicapped student in America's colleges: A longitudinal analysis. Part I: Disabled 1978 college freshmen* (ERIC Document Reproduction Service No. ED 215 625). Los Angeles, CA: Higher Education Research Institute, Inc.

Lawrence, J., Kent, L., & Henson, J. (1982). *The handicapped student in America's colleges: A longitudinal analysis. Part 3: Disabled 1978 college freshmen three years later.* (ERIC Document Reproduction Service No. ED 226 694). Los Angeles, CA: Higher Education Research Institute, Inc.

Lewis, L. L. (1957). Relation of measured mental ability to school marks and academic survival in the Texas School for the Blind. *The International Journal for the Education of the Blind, 6,* 56–60.

Linn, R. L. (1978). Single-group validity, differential validity, and differential prediction. *Journal of Applied Psychology, 63,* 507–512.

Liscio, M. A. (Ed.). (1986a). *A guide to colleges for mobility impaired students.* Orlando, FL: Academic Press.

Liscio, M. A. (Ed.). (1986b). *A guide to colleges for visually impaired students.* Orlando, FL: Academic Press.

Lord, F. M. (1980). *Applications of item response theory to practical testing problems.* Hillsdale, NJ: Lawrence Erlbaum.

Lowenfeld, B. (1971). Psychological problems of children with impaired vision. In W. M. Cruickshank (Ed.), *Psychology of exceptional children and youth* (3rd ed) (pp. 211–307). Englewood Cliffs, NJ: Prentice-Hall.

Mangrum, C. T., & Strichart, S. S. (Eds.). (1985). *Peterson's guide to colleges with programs for learning-disabled students.* Princeton, NJ: Peterson's Guides.

Mattis, S., French, J., & Rapin, I. (1975). Dyslexia in children and young adults: Three independent neuropsychological syndromes. *Developmental Medicine and Child Neurology, 17,* 150–163.

Maxey, J., & Levitz, R. S. (1980, April). *ACT services for the handicapped.* Paper presented at the meetings of the American Association of Collegiate Registrars and Admissions Officers, New Orleans.

McCarthy, J., & McCarthy, J. (1969). *Learning disabilities.* Boston: Allyn & Bacon.

McCullough, B. C., & Zaremba, B. A. (1979). Standardized achievement tests used with learning disabled and non-learning disabled adolescent boys. *Learning Disability Quarterly, 2,* 65–70.

McKinney, J. (1984). The search for subtypes of specific learning disability. *Journal of Learning Disabilities, 17,* 43–50.

McLoughlin, J., & Netick, A. (1983). Defining learning disabilities: A new and cooperative direction. *Journal of Learning Disabilities, 16,* 21–23.

Meadow, K. P. (1980). *Deafness and child development.* Berkeley: University of California Press.

Menyuk, P., & Flood, J. (1981). Linguistic competence, reading, writing problems and remediation. *Bulletin of the Orton Society, 31,* 13–28.

Mercer, J. (1973). *Labeling the mentally retarded child.* Berkeley: University of California Press.

Messick, S. (1975). The standard problem: Meaning and values in measurement and evaluation. *American Psychologist, 30*(10), 955–966.

Messick, S. (1984). Assessment in context: Appraising student performance in relation to instructional quality. *Educational Researcher,* Vol. *13,* No. 3, 3–8.

Miller, C., & Chansky, N. (1972). Psychologists' scoring of WISC protocols. *Psychology in the Schools, 9,* 144–152.

Miller, C., Chansky, N., & Gredler, G. (1970). Rater agreement on WISC protocols. *Psychology in the Schools, 7,* 190–193.

Mindel, E. D., & Vernon, M. (1971). *They grow in silence.* Silver Spring, MD: National Association of the Deaf.

Myklebust, H. (1964). *The psychology of deafness.* New York: Grune & Stratton.

Naglieri, J. A. (1981). Factor structure of the WISC-R for children identified as learning disabled. *Psychological Reports, 49,* 891–895.

Nester, M. A. (1984). Employment testing for handicapped persons. *Public Personnel Management Journal, 13,* 417–434.

Nester, M. A., & Sapinkopf, R. C. (1982). *A federal employment test modified for deaf applicants* (OPRD–82–7). Washington, DC: U.S. Office of Personnel Management, Office of Personnel Research and Development.

Nickoloff, O. M., II. (1962). Attitudes of public school principals toward employment of teachers with certain physical disabilities. *Rehabilitation Literature, 23*(11), 344–345.

Nolan, C. Y., & Ashcroft, S. C. (1969). The visually handicapped. *Review of Educational Research, 39,* 52–70.

Norman, C., & Zigmond, N. (1980). Characteristics of children labelled and served as learning disabled in school systems affiliated with Child Service Demonstration Centers. *Journal of Learning Disabilities, 13,* 542–547.

O'Donnell, L. (1980). Intra-individual discrepancy in diagnosing specific learning disabilities. *Learning Disability Quarterly, 3*(1), 10–18.

Ozias, D. K. (1975). Achievement assessment of the visually handicapped. *Education of the Visually Handicapped,* Vol. *7,* 76–84.

Packer, J. (1987). *SAT testing time for students with disabilities.* (ETS Research Rep. No. 87–37). Princeton, NJ: Educational Testing Service.

Parker, T., Freston, C., & Drew, C. (1975). Comparison of verbal performance of normal and learning disabled children as a function of input organization. *Journal of Learning Disabilities, 8,* 386–393.

Petersen, C. R., & Hart, D. H. (1979). Factor structure of the WISC–R for a clinic-referred population and specific subgroups. *Journal of Consulting and Clinical Psychology, 47,* 643–645.

Poplin, M., Gray, R., Larsen, S., Banikowski, A., & Mehring, T. (1980). A comparison of components of written expression abilities in learning disabled and non–learning disabled students at three grade levels. *Learning Disability Quarterly, 3*(4), 46–53.

President's Committee on Employment of the Handicapped. (Undated). *The disabled college freshman.* Washington, DC: Author.

Quigley, S. P. (1979). Environment and communication in the language development of deaf children. In L. J. Bradford & W. G. Hardy (Eds.), *Hearing and hearing impairment* (pp. 287–298). New York: Grune & Stratton.

Ragosta, M. (1980). *Handicapped students and the SAT* (Research Rep. No. 80–12). Princeton, NJ: Educational Testing Service.

Ragosta, M. (1986). *Students with disabilities: Four years of data from special test administrations of the SAT 1980–83.* New York: College Entrance Examination Board.

Ragosta, M., & Kaplan, B. A. (1986). *A survey of handicapped students taking special test administrations of the SAT and GRE* (Research Rep. No. 86–5). Princeton, NJ: Educational Testing Service.

Ragosta, M., & Nemceff, W. (1982). *A research and development program on testing handicapped people* (RM–82–2). Princeton, NJ: Educational Testing Service.

Raminiah, N. V., O'Donnell, J. P., & Ribich, R. (1976). Multiple-group factor analysis of the Wechsler Intelligence Scale for Children. *Journal of Clinical Psychology, 32,* 829–83.

Raudenbush, S. W., & Bryk, A. S. (1985). Empirical Bayes meta-analysis. *Journal of Educational Statistics, 10,* 75–98.

Rawlings, B. W., Karchmer, M. A., & De Caro, J. J. (Eds.). (1983). *College and career programs for deaf students.* Washington, DC: Gallaudet College; and Rochester, NY: National Technical Institute for the Deaf at Rochester Institute of Technology.

Redden, M., Levering, C., DiQuinzio, D., & the Task Force on a Model Admissions Policy. (1978). *Recruitment, admissions, and handicapped students: A guide for compliance with Section 504 of the Rehabilitation Act of 1973.* Washington, DC: American Association of Collegiate Registrars and Admissions Officers and the American Council on Education.

Rehabilitation Act of 1973. PL 93–112; 87 Stat. 355. (September 26, 1973.)

Reid, D., & Hresko, W. (1981). *A cognitive approach to learning disabilities.* New York: McGraw-Hill.

Report to the Ad Hoc Committee to Define Deaf and Hard of Hearing. *American Annals of the Deaf,* 1975, *120,* 509–512.

Reynolds, C. (1985). Critical measurement issues in learning disabilities. *Journal of Special Education, 18*(4), pp. 451–475.

Reynolds, C. R., & Gutkin, T. B. (1980). Stability of the WISC–R factor structure across sex at two age levels. *Journal of Clinical Psychology, 36,* 775–777.

Reynolds, M. C., & Birch, J. W. (1977). *Teaching exceptional children in all America's schools.* Reston, VA: Council for Exceptional Children.

Rickard, T. E., Triandis, H. C., & Patterson, C. H. (1963). Indices of employer prejudice toward disabled applicants. *Journal of Applied Psychology, 47,* 52–55.

Rock, D., Bennett, R. E., & Jirele, T. (1986). *The internal construct validity of the GRE General Test across handicapped and nonhandicapped populations*

(Research Rep. No. 86–7). Princeton, NJ: Educational Testing Service.

Rock, D. A., Bennett, R. E., & Kaplan, B. A. (1985). *The internal construct validity of the SAT across handicapped and non-handicapped populations* (Research Rep. No. 85–50). Princeton, NJ: Educational Testing Service.

Rock, D. A., Werts, C., & Grandy, J. (1982). *Construct validity of the GRE Aptitude Test across populations: An empirical confirmatory study* (Research Rep. No. 81–57). Princeton, NJ: Educational Testing Service.

Rose, G. L., & Brief, A. P. (1979). Effects of handicap and job characteristics on selection evaluations. *Personnel Psychology, 32,* 385–392.

Ross, D. R. (1970). A technique of verbal ability assessment of deaf students. *Journal of Rehabilitation of the Deaf, 3*(3), 7–15.

Ross, M. B., & Salvia, J. (1975). Attractiveness as a biasing factor in teacher judgments. *American Journal of Mental Deficiency, 80*(1), 96–98.

Rubin, D. B. (1980). Using empirical Bayes techniques in the law school validity studies. *Journal of the American Statistical Association, 75,* 801–816.

Rudner, L. Using standard tests with the hearing impaired: The problem of item bias. *Volta Review,* 1978, *80,* 31–40.

Rugel, R. P. (1974). WISC subtest scores of disabled readers: A review with respect to Bannatyne's recategorization. *Journal of Learning Disabilities, 7,* 48–55.

Sattler, J. M. (1982). *Assessment of children's intelligence and special abilities* (2nd ed.). Boston: Allyn & Bacon.

Scales, W. (1983). *Disabled student services annual data bank.* College Park: University of Maryland.

Schein, J., & Delk, M. (1974). *The deaf population of the United States.* Silver Spring, MD: National Association of the Deaf.

Schildroth, A. (1976, January). *The relationship of nonverbal intelligence test scores to selected characteristics of hearing impaired students.* Paper presented at the Third Gallaudet Symposium on Research in Deafness, Gallaudet College, Washington, DC.

Schlesinger, H. S., & Lee, M. (1980). Sensory disabilities. In E. L. Pan, T. E. Backer, & C. L. Vash (Eds.), *Annual Review of Rehabilitation* (Vol. 1, pp. 356–381). New York: Springer.

Schmeiser, C., Kane, M., & Brennan, R. (1983). Testing the handicapped: An issue of comparability. *Bar Examiner, 52*(2), 16–23.

Schooler, D. L., Beebe, M. C., & Koepke, T. (1978). Factor analysis of the WISC–R scores for children identified as learning disabled, educable mentally impaired, and emotionally impaired. *Psychology in the Schools, 15,* 478–485.

Semel, E., & Wiig, E. (1975). Comprehension of syntactic structures and critical verbal elements by children with learning disabilities. *Journal of Learning Disabilities, 8,* 53–58.

Shepard, L. A. (1982a). *Assessment of learning disabilities* (ERIC/TM Rep. No. 84). Princeton, NJ: Educational Testing Service.

Shepard, L. A. (1982b). Definitions of bias. In R. A. Berk (Ed.), *Handbook of methods for detecting test bias* (pp. 9–30). Baltimore: Johns Hopkins University Press.

Shepard, L. A. (1983). The role of measurement in educational policy: Lessons from the identification of learning disabilities. *Educational Measurement: Issues and Practices, 2*(3), 4–8.

Shepard, L. A., Smith, M., & Vojir, C. (1983). Characteristics of pupils identified as learning disabled. *American Educational Research Journal, 20,* 309–331.

Sherman, S., & Robinson, N. (Eds.). (1982). *Ability testing of handicapped people: Dilemma for government, science, and the public.* Washington, DC: National Academy Press.

Silverstein, A. B. (1977). Alternative factor analytic solutions for the Wechsler Intelligence Scale for Children—Revised. *Educational and Psychological Measurement, 37,* 121–124.

Smith, L. M. (1982). *The college student with*

*a disability: A faculty handbook.* Washington, DC: U.S. Government Printing Office.

Smits, B. W., & Mommers, M. J. (1976). Differences between blind and sighted children in WISC verbal subtests. *New Outlook for the Blind, 70*(6), 240–240.

*Southeastern Community College v. Davis,* 574 F.2d 1158 (4th Cir. 1978), rev'd, 442 U.S. 397, 99 S.Ct. 2361 (1979).

Spear, L. C., & Sternberg, R. J. (1986). Cognitive assessment with disabled readers. *Special Services in the Schools, 2*(2/3), 71–84.

Spungin, S. J. (1980). *Testing in the visually handicapped: Problems and issues.* National Academy of Sciences testimony.

Stanovich, K. E. (1986). Cognitive processes and the reading problems of learning disabled children: Evaluating the assumption of specificity. In J. K. Torgesen & B. Y. L. Wong (Eds.), *Psychological and educational perspectives on learning disabilities* (pp. 87–131). Orlando, FL: Academic Press.

Stark, R. E. (1979). Speech of the hearing-impaired child. In L. J. Bradford & W. G. Hardy (Eds.), *Hearing and hearing impairment* (pp. 229–248). New York: Grune & Stratton.

Stevens, G. (1981). Bias in the attribution of hyperkinetic behavior as a function of ethnic identification and socioeconomic status. *Psychology in the Schools, 18,* 99–106.

Stokoe, W. C. (1980). Language and deaf experience [excerpt]. In C. Baker & R. Battison (Eds.), *Sign language and the deaf community* (pp. 265–267). Silver Spring, MD: National Association of the Deaf.

Stolov, W. C., & Clowers, M. R. (Eds.). (1981). *Handbook of severe disability.* Washington, DC: U.S. Government Printing Office.

Sullivan, P. M. (1982). Administration modification on the WISC–R performance scale with different categories of deaf children. *American Annals of the Deaf, 127,* 780–788.

Suppes, P. (1974). A survey of cognition in handicapped children. *Review of Educational Research, 44,* 145–175.

Susser, M. (1973). *Causal thinking in the health sciences concepts and strategies of epidemiology.* New York: Oxford University Press.

Swineford, F. (1974, March). *An assessment of the Kuder–Richardson Formula (20) reliability estimate for moderately speeded tests.* Paper presented at the meeting of the National Council for Measurement in Education, New Orleans.

Tarver, S., Hallahan, D., Kauffman, J., & Ball, D. (1976). Verbal rehearsal and selective attention in children with learning disabilities: A developmental lag. *Journal of Experimental Child Psychology, 22,* 375–385.

Terman, L. M., & Merrill, M. A. (1973). *Stanford-Binet Intelligence Scale: 1973 norms edition.* Boston: Houghton Mifflin.

Thorndike, R. (1963). *The concepts of over- and under-achievement.* New York: Teachers College Press.

Thurlow, M., & Ysseldyke, J. (1979). Current assessment and decision-making practices in model LD programs. *Learning Disability Quarterly, 2*(4), 15–24.

Tillman, M. H. (1967). The performance of blind and sighted children on the Wechsler Intelligence Scale for Children: Study I. *International Journal for the Education of the Blind, 16*(3), 65–74.

Tillman, M. H. (1973). Intelligence scales for the blind: A review with implications for research. *Journal of School Psychology, 11*(1), 80–87.

Tobias, S., Cole, C., Zibrin, M., & Bodlakova, V. (1982). Teacher-student ethnicity and recommendations for special education referrals. *Journal of Educational Psychology, 74,* 72–76.

Torgesen, J. (1977). The role of nonspecific factors in the task performance of learning disabled children: A theoretical assessment. *Journal of Learning Disabilities, 10,* 27–34.

Torgesen, J. (1985). Memory processes in reading disabled children. *Journal of Learning Disabilities, 18*(6), 350–357.

Torgesen, J., & Dice, C. (1980). Characteristics of research on learning disabilities. *Journal of Learning Disabilities, 13,* 531–535.

Trismen, D. A. (1967). Equating braille forms of the Sequential Tests of Educational Progress. *Exceptional Children,* 419–424. Volume *33.*

Trybus, R. J., & Karchmer, M. A. (1977). School achievement scores of hearing impaired children: National data on achievement status and growth patterns. *American Annals of the Deaf, 122*(4), 62–69.

van Rijn, P. (1976). *Testing the handicapped for employment purposes: Adaptations for persons with dyslexia* (Technical Memorandum 76–4). Washington, DC: Personnel Research and Development Center.

Vander Kolk, C. J. (1977). Intelligence testing for visually impaired persons. *Visual Impairment and Blindness,* Vol. *71,* 158–163.

Vander Kolk, C. J. (1981). *Assessment and planning with the visually impaired.* Baltimore, MD: University Park Press.

Vellutino, F. R. (in press). Recent advances in the study of developmental dyslexia. *Scientific American.*

Vellutino, F., Steger, B., Moyer, S., Harding, C., & Niles, J. (1977). Has the perceptual-deficit hypothesis led us astray? *Journal of Learning Disabilities, 10,* 375–385.

Vinsonhaler, J., Weinshank, A., Wagner, C., & Polin, R. (1983). Diagnosing children with educational problems: Characteristics of reading and learning disability specialists, and classroom teachers. *Reading Research Quarterly, 18*(2), 134–164.

Vogel, S. (1974). Syntactic abilities in normal and dyslexic children. *Journal of Learning Disabilities, 7,* 103–109.

Wagner, R. K. (1986). Phonological processing abilities and reading: Implications for disabled readers. *Journal of Learning Disabilities, 19*(10), 623–630.

Wallbrown, F. H., & Blaha, J. (1979). The hierarchical factor structure of the WISC–R for reading disabled children. *Multivariate Experimental Clinical Research, 4,* 73–80.

Wallbrown, F. H., Blaha, J., Wallbrown, J. D., & Engin, A. W. (1975). The hierarchical factor structure of the Wechsler Intelligence Scale for Children—Revised. *Journal of Psychology, 89,* 223–235.

Ward, A. A., Fraser, R. T., & Troupin, A. S. (1981). Epilepsy. In W. C. Stolov & M. R. Clowers (Eds.), *Handbook of severe disability* (pp. 155–167). Washington, DC: U.S. Government Printing Office.

Warren, S., & Brown, W. (1973). Examiner scoring errors on individual intelligence tests. *Psychology in the Schools, 10,* 118–122.

Wechsler, D. (1949). *Wechsler Intelligence Scale for Children manual.* New York: Psychological Corporation.

Wechsler, D. (1955). *Manual for the Wechsler Adult Intelligence Scale.* New York: Psychological Corporation.

Wechsler, D. (1974). *Manual for the Wechsler Intelligence Scale for Children–Revised.* New York: Psychological Corporation.

White, K. O. (1978). *Testing the handicapped for employment purposes: Adaptations for persons with motor handicaps* (Professional Series 78–4). Washington, DC: U.S. Government Printing Office.

Wiig, E., & Fleischmann, N. (1980). Prepositional phrases, pronominalization, reflexivization, and relativization in the language of learning disabled college students. *Journal of Learning Disabilities, 13,* 571–576.

Willingham, W. (1976). *Validity and the Graduate Record Examinations Program.* Princeton, NJ: Educational Testing Service.

Willingham, W. (1985). *Success in college.* New York: College Entrance Examination Board.

Willingham, W. (1986). *Testing handicapped people: The validity issue* (Research Rep. No. 86–26). Princeton, NJ: Educational Testing Service.

Willingham, W. (1987). *Handicapped applicants to college: An analysis of ad-*

*missions decisions* (College Board Rep. No. 87–1 & ETS Research Rep. No. 87–1). New York: College Entrance Examination Board.

Willingham, W., & Breland, H. (1982). *Personal qualities and college admissions.* New York: College Entrance Examination Board.

Witkin, H. A., Birnbaum, J., Lomonaco, S., Lehr, S., & Herman, J. L. (1968). Cognitive patterning in congenitally totally blind children. *Child Development, 39,* 767–786.

Wong, B. (1982). Strategic behaviors in selecting retrieval cues in gifted, normal-achieving, and learning disabled children. *Journal of Learning Disabilities, 15,* 33–37.

Woodcock, R. W. (1973). *Woodcock Reading Mastery Tests manual.* Circle Pines, MN: American Guidance Service.

Ysseldyke, J. (1983). Current practices in making psychoeducational decisions about learning disabled students. *Journal of Learning Disabilities, 16,* 226–233.

Ysseldyke, J., Algozzine, B., & Epps, S. (1983). A logical and empirical analysis of current practices in classifying students as handicapped. *Exceptional Children, 50,* 160–166.

Ysseldyke, J., Algozzine, B., Regan, R., & Potter, M. (1980). Technical adequacy of tests used by professionals in simulated decision making. *Psychology in the Schools, 17,* 202–209.

Ysseldyke, J., Algozzine, B., Richey, L., & Graden, J. (1982). Declaring students eligible for learning disability services: Why bother with the data? *Learning Disability Quarterly, 5,* 37–44.

Ysseldyke, J., Algozzine, B., & Thurlow, M. (Eds.). (1980). *A naturalistic investigation of special education team meetings* (Research Rep.). No. 35. Minneapolis, MN: University of Minnesota, Institute for Research on Learning Disabilities.

# Index